CHELSEA: Football Under the Blue Flag

CHELSEA
Football Under the Blue Flag

Brian Mears
with Ian Macleay

MAINSTREAM
PUBLISHING

EDINBURGH AND LONDON

First published in Great Britain in 2001 by
MAINSTREAM PUBLISHING COMPANY (EDINBURGH) LTD
7 Albany Street
Edinburgh EH1 3UG

ISBN 1 84018 432 9

A catalogue record for this book is available from the British Library

Typeset in Berkeley Book and Helvetica
Printed and bound in Great Britain
by Butler and Tanner Ltd.

Contents

Let no man be judged entirely by his past.
Oscar Wilde, An Ideal Husband

Acknowledgements

This book would not have been written without the help I received from a great many people. My gratitude to Terry Venables, who provided help and encouragement despite his huge workload. Flaubert said you should not meet your idols, but Terry was the exception. A special mention to Alan Collis who introduced Brian to me. As Bogart said, it was the start of a beautiful friendship. Alan has campaigned for Chelsea all his life and is a very talented writer. Matt Allen of 442 helped with the information on Jimmy Greaves. I am indebted to my lawyers, Peter Harris and Alex Chapman, for life-saving guidance.

For behind-the-scenes roles, I thank John Linney and Donna Carrina of the Object group.

I also want to thank some of the Chelsea boys who stood in the rain with me over the years: Mickey Milsom, David Whyte, Barry Yates, David Ayling, Billy Meyers, Nicky Blicky and Maltese Jim. Specialist Chelsea knowledge came from Paul and Kevin.

Finally, thanks to my family.

Foreword: Cool and the Gang

When Brian Mears asked me to write the introduction of his book I was pleased to do it because nobody has really covered the most exciting period in the club's tumultuous past.

I was lucky enough to captain Chelsea in the '60s. I played alongside the men who became some of the most important names in its star-studded history. Nobody had ever seen a team like the young boy Blues of that era. They wrote the book on style and invented a spontaniety and swagger that is reflected in their present-day counterparts. They were entertainers as well as footballers. It was the beginning of an exhilarating revolution of enormous social and economic changes. It was also the era when football made the quantum leap from back-page to front-page news.

No team mirrored those changes more than Chelsea Football Club. I think the area of London in which the club is situated had a lot to do with it, no other club in the capital could boast of being the centre of the universe of a generation. They were the point where the worlds of showbiz and sport collided head on. This is the story of a group of young men who came together for a short time and paid a high price for the creativity and glamour. A story of games won and lost, careers that soared and crashed, of derring-do and euphoria.

Brian is a lifelong Chelsea fan. His family founded the West London Club, now one of the most powerful in Europe. His father Joe was my chairman. The Mears empire loved their teams like a child, like a brother, like a father. Joe watched over me and the chaps with commitment and utter faith. We were a family, that is why it was such a wrench to leave Stamford Bridge. The reason I joined Chelsea, along with a clutch of brilliant young talent, was that I thought I had a better chance of breaking through there than I would have at 'big' clubs like Tottenham. In those days the top clubs bought domestically whereas today they ransack Europe for talent. Chelsea are among the biggest exponents of this.

I made my first-team début at sixteen and a half. The team was packed with superb youngsters like Eddie McCreadie, Barry Bridges, Bert Murray and Bobby Tambling. Chelsea were the *Young Guns* times eleven. A tube ride away, Bobby

Moore and Martin Peters were breaking through into the West Ham side at similar ages. We were all victims of our own early success, something had to give. The 'Diamonds' were perceived as casualties but from the dissolved glory George Graham and I went on to other things and Chelsea fans saw another influx of juicy talent as Charlie Cook, Alan Hudson, Ian Hutchinson *et al* surfed the crest of the blue wave.

When Joe Mears presided over Chelsea he was detached by his position, whereas Brian was likeable, humorous and down to earth. In this manner he tells comprehensively a remarkable story of saints and sinners, superstar hellraisers, geniuses and mavericks.

With Brian as chairman, Chelsea produced a winning team from the nucleus of my side that played football at the highest level of sophistication this country has ever seen. For a long time he negotiated the agenda of a group of characters that Charles Dickens could not have created. For *Eastenders* read *Westenders*. Chelsea and glamour had a symbiotic relationship but tragedy, martyrdom and controversy have always haunted them. It was his decision to attempt a compelling history of those events. A question I am still asked to this day is which was the greater team? The self-styled young Venables' lions of the stunning Osgood/Hudson side were technically superior. I talked to the combative midfielder John Hollins, who played in both sides and can claim a certain gravitas on the subject. We were both of the view that had Tommy Docherty kept the 'Diamonds' together they may well have been the first Chelsea team to win the Championship since Ted Drake's in 1955. After all, Don Revie persevered with his industrial strength Leeds side after some sparse years. The Chelsea class of '65 would have been better equipped to deal with the marathon slog of winning the title because of their more direct style.

The task of extracting points from difficult away fixtures and avoiding upsets at the hands of extremely average opponents were both pitfalls the great cup-winning side of the '70s and the modern Chelsea teams have encountered.

Football represents hope to many people, something that makes them feel special, a certain thing. Chelsea fans always expected something back for their uncompromising commitment. Football is bigger today than ever: this morning's news bulletins talk of a 'government obsessed with football'. Despite it being high summer the top clubs are already making stupendous purchases in a frenzy of activity. Chelsea, run by the Mears family, are architects of the current situation.

Terry Venables
Summer 2001

Prologue

Two things only the people anxiously desire, bread and the circus games.
Juvenal (AD 60–130), Roman statesman and writer.

It was 20 May 2000. That spring, the wettest and greyest spring in living memory, bled into the wettest, greyest early summer in living memory. On the morning of the twentieth, the Prime Minister's wife, Cherie Blair, presented him with a son called Leo. Later in the day Chelsea met Aston Villa in the first FA Cup final of the new millennium, the last ever to be played out in the crumbling mausoleum of the old twin-towered Wembley Stadium. The match was deadly dull and Villa were subsequently blamed by Chelsea for not making a game of it. They were accused of trying to win the Cup on penalties. These days the game is plagued by that kind of paranoia because the stakes are so much higher; everyone is a lot more edgy because it's such a long way down. The camera panned in on the celebs still using Chelsea as their own little vanity vehicle. In a sea of Armani I spotted the former Sports Minister Tony Banks, David Mellor and Lord Richard Attenborough. Why is it that whenever I see Dickie I am reminded of the American poet Walt Whitman's quip about deserving his enemies but not believing that he deserved his friends?

Chelsea won the competition by a solitary goal, thanks to an appalling error by the Aston Villa goalkeeper, David James. In the one demonstration of skill in the game Gianfranco Zola bulleted over a pukka free kick, James made a woefully inept attempt at catching the ball and Roberto Di Matteo became a Chelsea legend by slamming home the winner. Of the current squad Di Matteo is a favourite of mine, talented and innately hip. He is also the only player to have scored in two FA Cup finals for Chelsea Football Club. But if anybody should have joined the pantheon of greatness it is Zola, an Italian in the tradition of Michelangelo – pure genius.

An alien looking down on the event, 11 earthlings chasing a ball and another 11 earthlings around a field watched by 79,000 other earthlings paying through the nose for the privilege, could be forgiven for thinking it was all a bit bizarre. I must admit that even after all this time, I still sometimes find it a mite surreal.

I watched the game on television, one of the much reduced audience of just over seven million viewers who snoozed through perhaps the poorest match ever played at Wembley, certainly in recent times.

I should have smelt a rat long before. The most expensive player in the history of the club at that time at £10 million, Chris Sutton, a player deserving of veneration and patience, was not even included on the subs bench. Shortly afterwards the club shelled out another £15 million for another striker, Jimmy Floyd Hasselbaink. Hasselbaink's side, Atletico Madrid, had just been relegated and he was not considered good enough to play in Euro 2000. For strikers it always was a sellers' market, even before the game went into orbit. Clubs could name their price and get it, though only a handful of the big transfer forwards ever turned out to be successful.

My former captain, Terry Venables, putting a spin on things as only he could as a pundit, predicted a close game. Terry wore a shirt (possibly cut by Thomas Pink of Sloane Square) the colour of the jersey once emblazoned with the lion crest of CFC, worn by players a lifetime ago, only yesterday, when we were young.

Before the game we were treated to the sight of opera singer Lesley Garrett, in a sickly green outfit, singing 'Abide with Me'. For a moment I thought we were going to have to listen to Sir Cliff Richard, who had entertained the troops when Chelsea last pitched their caravan at Wembley. Given the symbiotic relationship between television and the top football clubs, I wondered how much longer they could peddle this stuff. On the other channels more rousing entertainment was to be found in Rex Harrison's performance in *My Fair Lady* or Channel Four's racing coverage. The event was further devalued by the sight of Chelsea captain Dennis Wise apparently conducting some sort of Crazy Gang ritual by bringing his infant son to the ceremony of collecting the cup; another mind-bogglingly tacky gimmick scooped from the bucket of swill that passes for modern football. I could not somehow see Ron Harris, a previous cup-winning captain of Chelsea, including his offspring in the festivities.

Wise was lauded as Chelsea's most successful player, but whatever his technical and leadership qualities he seems incapable of beating a man with the ball. But then I was used to the awesome Charlie Cooke, the best flank player of all time to wear the Pepsi blue of Chelsea. Comparisons between today's players and former heroes are hard to calibrate. Perhaps the athletic level of earlier generations was not as high as in the contemporary game, but the tackling was unquestionably harder. You have to be careful not to be left behind in the age of the dinosaurs, but if Dennis Wise was the club's best player (as he undeniably was) than there is a problem. Wise was voted man of the match. I would have given it to Rex Harrison. Mind you, Wise had a better Cockney accent than Audrey Hepburn.

By this time I was becoming physically nauseated by the extended celebrations. My mind cast back 30 years to the gladiatorial battle that was the Chelsea v Leeds United Cup final of 1970. That match was the first-ever replayed final when no quarter was asked for or given, perhaps the most epic final of the twentieth century – certainly the hardest and most brutal. Every one of the players could look after themselves. They gave as good as they got and they stuck together. Leeds, managed by the late Don Revie, were the losers, but I would back Revie's team to give either of the modern-day sides a two-goal start and a thrashing. The personal duels roll off my tongue: Osgood against Charlton, Baldwin v Bremner, Hutchinson and Hunter, Webb and McCreadie, Madely and Cooper. Now, three decades later I give you Boateng and Wise (and his son), bit players in a game which has been reinvented so that families can spend their cash in peace in the soccer supermarket, reinvented so that the nouveau riche can sip Chardonnay at the latest corporate junket.

In the post-game interviews Paul Merson, the only Villa star to play anywhere near his true potential, said that his only plan was to make it through the evening. As a recovering alcoholic whose career was almost crippled by drink and drugs, the pressures off the field must have been nearly as intolerable as those on it. The temptation was still there – there was always an excuse for fluiding it – as were the hangers-on. When a star burns out, the entourage moves on to the new kid in town – a town I would never eat lunch in again. Chelsea had the blueprint on such events. I saw plenty of it, fracture and failure, and enough careers drowned in a sea of booze to build sides that would have dominated the game.

Four nights after furling an eyebrow at the disgraceful events at Wembley I watched Real Madrid crush Valencia to lift the European Cup for the eighth time. The football played was from a different planet than that inhabited by the apathetic Cup finalists. Valencia had rumped Barcelona in the semi-finals and the Catalan side had put Chelsea to the sword in the previous round. The gulf between Chelsea and the cream of Europe still seemed yawning. Now Chelsea have the money they lacked then, but not the class or the style.

After the cup win over Leeds in the '70s, Chelsea had swept into Europe to win the now defunct European Cup Winners' Cup with a victory over Real Madrid. But something was rotten in the state of Denmark. It all seemed shallow and superficial, a house of cards. Although Chelsea had won the cup, in the eyes of many they'd had a poor season. They had failed to win the Premier League by a distance and had not even qualified for the cash-heavy Champions League by finishing in the top three places. The season before, despite amazingly losing only three league games, they had also missed out on the title. That elusive championship was still just out of their grasp. Like the green light at the end of the dock in F. Scott Fitzgerald's classic novel *The Great Gatsby*, the prize seemed always to be tantalisingly near but somehow just out of reach. Chelsea did win it once though, back in 1955, when the Mears family were in charge. It was the finest moment of a footballing dynasty that should have ruled for a century.

The enduring legacy of Chelsea Football Club, some will tell you, started with monomania, a cheque book and some foreign mercenaries, but really it began a long, long time before, with a man called Mears who had a dream . . .

Brian Mears
August 2001

Chapter One: Champions

If this thing was just about the music it would have died a long time ago.
Malcolm Maclaren, the inventor of punk rock.

Good old Mal. I used to drive past his shop every morning. You could say that if this thing were just about football Chelsea would have died a long time ago. Most first novels are disguised autobiographies; this autobiography is a disguised novel.

Cynics will tell you that Chelsea had won the Champions League twice in 1955 – the first and the last time. At 4.40 p.m. on 23 April 1955 they became champions after beating Sheffield Wednesday 3–0. It was in their Golden Jubilee year, and in typical Chelsea fashion it went to the last match of the season. The 52 points collected by them was the lowest recorded championship-winning total by any team, a record that will never be beaten. (For the benefit of younger readers, if this sounds an incredibly low figure, only two points were awarded for a win in those days.)

Wednesday were a poor side (not much changes in 50 years) and were stone bottom of the league with exactly half Chelsea's number of points. The only player they had of note was Albert Quixall. In Beckham fashion he was tipped as the future 'golden boy' of English soccer. Albert was later to join Manchester United for a fee that smashed the British transfer record. Like I said, not much changes.

Quixall missed a good chance when we were nervously clinging to a 1–0 lead given to us when Eric 'Rabbit' Parsons (a player about as tall as Wise) headed home. Parsons was the crowd's favourite, or the nearest thing to it at the time. He was famous for his 'rabbit' dashes down the wing and so earned the nickname. The winger was signed from West Ham and he was an ever-present in the title-winning side. Eric was an early version of Clive Walker; he would just put his head down and run. Boy, he was fast! In 177 first-team games he scored 42 goals.

'Give me lucky generals,' Napoleon famously said. Ted Drake, our manager at the time, might have asked for lucky players. Drake was Chelsea manager from 1952–61. I had followed his career as a top-class striker long before then, and knew of his exploits at Arsenal, scoring seven goals from eight shots in one match. Our luck held when the Wednesday keeper was injured when he clashed with our star striker Roy Bentley and was carried off on a stretcher. Subs were as unheard of as Nokias in those times and a defender went into goal.

Bentley was always a big name in the game. Chelsea bought him from Newcastle (as they did Hughie Gallacher) for £11,000 in 1948. He repaid them by being top scorer in eight straight seasons. England gave him 12 caps and in 367 Chelsea games he blasted in 150 goals. Roy was exceptionally fast. Only Barry Bridges, centre-forward in the Docherty era, was quicker off the mark. In the air he was simply magnificent; he could soar like a stunt pilot. In those times players' roles were highly stereotyped, but Roy bucked the system by playing his own roving role. His running across the forward line was effortless and elegant, and his devastating close control lured defenders in to be destroyed by a sudden explosion of pace. Bentley captained the Chelsea side and is still the only man to have led them to the title. He was the original 'Super Trouper'.

Wednesday fought hard but two late goals, one of them a penalty by Peter Sillett and the other a joke effort by 'Rabbit' Parsons, clinched the game. With Portsmouth, Chelsea's only rivals, being held down at Cardiff the title was theirs. The good old boys were drinking whisky and rye.

In November Chelsea were lying at twelfth but a remarkable run up the table clinched the title. If ever they achieve this again (I should live so long), that is how they will do it. I can never see a Chelsea side leading from the front.

I saw some amazing games over the years, but the fixtures against Manchester United and Wolves always stick in my memory. We lost 6–5 at home to United in front of 55,966 with a hat-trick from debutante Seamus O'Connell. United legend Dennis Viollet scored three goals, and the others were scored by Tommy Taylor (2) and Jackie Blanchflower. Taylor was killed in the Munich disaster a few years later along with the man of the match, Duncan Edwards. Edwards was simply the greatest player I ever saw. His loss to United and England was incalculable.

What was amazing about the match was that the eleven goals scored were compressed into just over an hour's play. Chelsea manager Ted Drake said it was 'a match of a lifetime, and nothing quite as remarkable has ever been seen here at Stamford Bridge'.

Chelsea's double over Wolverhampton Wanderers effectively won them the title. The four points gleaned from both of these victories represented exactly the difference between them and second-placed Wolves. At Molineux the pitch was ankle deep in mud and with three minutes left the score was locked at 2–2 when Wolves scored from a disputed penalty. Chelsea somehow came back from 3–2 down to grab a 4–3 win with two breakaway goals. The season before we had finished on the wrong side of an 8–1 tonking, which is still the heaviest defeat in Chelsea history. That defeat actually was the springboard for the title bid. A new training schedule was introduced and changes were made in the management team.

A penalty featured in the return fixture with the Wolves. Seventy-five thousand sardined into the Bridge for it. The gates were shut at 2.15 with an estimated 25,000 on the street outside. Wolves, in the best traditions of the modern game, stifled Chelsea's attacks and with 15 minutes left the match remained scoreless. Then our chum O'Connell, who was an England amateur, cracked in a terrific shot and Billy Wright, the most famous defender in the game (until the emergence of one Robert Chelsea Moore), punched it over the bar. There was no dispute about this, even the people in the nosebleed seats saw it. Today he would have seen red cardboard, but it took a lengthy dispute between the ref and most of the Chelsea team before a free kick was awarded. Sillett, signed from Southampton the year before, stepped up to smash it home and take his place in the Chelsea Hall of Fame.

Frank Blunstone was another player who made sure that the trophy came to Stamford Bridge that year. Blunstone was a class act; like Miles Davis, he had a timeless talent. Frank was signed from Crewe for £7,000 in 1953 and proved to be one of the greatest Chelsea signings ever. He was an outside-left, or left-winger. A quaint, old-fashioned concept I agree, but one you will hear a great deal about in the coming pages. Blunstone at his peak was a souped-up version of Gronkjaer or Zender. He overcame a broken leg to win five England caps and play nearly 350 games for the club, scoring 54 goals. Frank was one of John Major's all-time Chelsea greats. Major would always speak of Frank with a wistful tone in his voice. Frank was at his zenith when the former Prime Minister first started taking the 49 bus over Battersea Bridge to watch the Blues. The complete unpredictability of Chelsea amazed him and he would remember how they have outclassed top sides one week, winning at a canter, and the following lost a cup game to a side from a lower league. Once a fan always a fan, if the talent is durable. That is why respectable middle-aged women camp out on the freezing pavements for a week and a half to buy tickets for Cliff Richard concerts.

It was a clean sweep for Chelsea that year. They won everything going in the way of leagues; the Football Combination, Metropolitan League and SE Counties League. Another winner was a Mr G. Burgin of Notting Hill, who registered the millionth click of the Stamford Bridge turnstiles and was presented with a season ticket for the following season. It was an abattoir of Chelsea's hopes. G. Burgin saw Chelsea finish sixteenth, which I think was some sort of record for the lowest spot recorded by the champs the following season. In league terms it was downhill all the way after that.

WHERE DO I BEGIN?

It all started two centuries ago in the last years of the nineteenth century. My grandfather, Joseph Theophilos Mears, and his brother, Henry Augustus (Gus) Mears, tried to buy the leasehold of Stamford Bridge. At that time it was the HQ of an organisation called the London Athletic Club. Before then it had been a market garden, which seemed somehow appropriate. JT and Gus were visionaries. Their father was Joseph Mears, one of London's major contractors. They had their fingers in more pies than a blind Highbury caterer. If they had been around today they would doubtless be dot com millionaires, downloading life, fluttering paper around the city, driving around in black Porsches and wearing Prada and nouveau Cerrutti, living in a world of laptops and limos where the only ordinary people they met served them at Starbucks.

You see, they had a dream, their agenda was already set and that was to build the best football stadium in London, one that did not include hotels, conference centres or shopping malls. London only had one stadium of note, Crystal Palace. Palace was the number one stadium. It got all the big dates but when the First World War started the Army requisitioned it as an arms dump. Dump being a key word here. If one of the German airships had got lucky and dropped a bomb on the pitch it would have blown a hole in South London that would have swallowed Croydon. Crystal Palace never reopened.

The Mears boys raised the stakes. Both were sporting chaps who had played football all their lives. They hatched the audacious plan of building a stadium after spending a lot of time thinking about it. Who was that guy in the Remington adverts; Victor Kiam? He liked the product so much he bought the company. Well, the Mears brothers loved football so much they *formed* the company. The club would work depending on how much money was spent. A monster was created, packed full of so many characters that it was big even when it was a blatant waste of resources. That is what this book is about; the characters of Chelsea and how it grew to be a billion-pound industry.

The whole deal took years to go through and it was not till 1904 that the Mears actually took control of the site. It cost less than £5,000. They had no game plan as such. They just wanted to build a stadium from ground zero. At the time it was uncertain as to whether or not it would be used solely for Cup finals and internationals or by a club side, existing or new. Eventually a new club was formed in 1905, born out of the Mears's overbrimming enthusiasm and phenomenally accurate business instinct. 1905 was also the year of my father's birth. First they went to the Fulham chairman Sir Henry Norris and asked him if Fulham wanted to make the Bridge their home for £1,500 a year. Gus talked the talk but Fulham declined, preferring to develop their own site at Craven Cottage. I wonder what Mr Fayed would have said of such an interactive venture. Jimmy Hill, then a young shaver, to my knowledge was not part of the deal.

I've heard of a pub without beer but this must have been the first time there was a ground without a team. Gus had been keen to sell the site to Great Western Railway, who wanted to turn it into every Arsenal fan's dream of what Chelsea should be; a slag heap. My father always told an amusing story about this. Gus and JT had a financial adviser and factotum in Fred Parker, who was quick to see the money to be made from developing and renting the ground. Parker was always a beacon of objectivity. He had this great saying: 'Today's headlines are tomorrow's chip wrappers.' But the pair needed convincing. It was a time of enormous uncertainty. One day Fred the futurist turned up for a crunch meeting. He had to explain his dream. Gus had a rather fierce dog and the canine bit a lump out of Parker's leg. This was long before all that fuss about Norman 'Bite Your Legs' Hunter, the Leeds defender and long-term vigilante of Chelsea strikers. Rather than make a fuss, Parker was nonchalant about the matter and this incident persuaded Gus that as Fred was such a cool guy he must also be correct in his judgement about the future of Stamford Bridge. Gus decided he could earn a crust in the football world. It was a serendipitous meeting. So, thanks to a dog bite Chelsea was formed. There's a moral there somewhere, I'm sure.

So a club was born instantly, but it would take them 50 years to become an overnight success and win the Championship. Almost another 50 years has rattled by while we wait for another. At one time the favourite name for the club was London FC. Now there's an idea – maybe one day there will be a London team. Terry Venables, a visionary, was predicting this 20 years ago. Terry could always hear the sound of distant thunder before anyone else. As football becomes more like *Rollerball* each year, I do see the time when you will have cities playing one another and there will be games like Liverpool v Milan, London v Rome, Glasgow v New York. It will happen. We already have the Champions League, which to my mind is the Euro League that was mooted in the ideology of the '70s.

Nicknames suggested for the new club included 'The Little Strangers' (which would have been useful around 1976), 'The Chelsea Chinamen' (?), 'The Buns' (very droll) and, perplexingly, 'The Cherubs' (think Zola). They eventually agreed on 'The Pensioners' and the stigma backlash started then. It was interesting to note that even back then it was a name suggestive of 'the lights of other days'. In 1905, though, the name of Chelsea FC was chosen despite the proximity of Fulham Town Hall and the Tube station now called Fulham Broadway, then called Walham Green. The ground soon came together, designed by Archibald Leitch who had created the grandiose stadiums, Hampden and Ibrox. At that time all the decent football grounds were either in Scotland or, perish the thought, up north in England. Stamford Bridge was the second largest stadium in the country after Crystal Palace, which was as horrific as Wembley in the closing years of the twentieth century. Then there were some more problems about the rebuilding of Wembley if the papers are to be believed. To this day Chelsea should be indebted to the genius of Leitch.

Based on Archie's Scottish designs, Stamford Bridge was built like a bowl, with one main stand, the East one, the symbol of a new dawn, of the future to come. The stand was built to hold 5,000 with a paddock in front. The remaining sides were open, built up with thousands of tons of soil and clay excavated from the nearby District Line. The original plans indicated a capacity of 95,000. That was their master plan to storm the battlements of an unwelcoming football industry.

The first attempt by the entrepreneurs to join a league came when they approached the Southern League, but they were turned down, as their application was blocked by Fulham and Tottenham Hotspur. They had better luck with the football league and were admitted to the Second Divison. The first league match was against Hull, and the day of the locust was 11 September 1905. Chelsea won 5–1.The first match actually played at Stamford Bridge was a friendly against Liverpool. Not many people know that.

It cost sixpence (2p) to be admitted to the ground, one shilling (5p) to go into the enclosure and 7p for the old grandstand, subsequently replaced by the East Stand. A season ticket cost a guinea (£1.05), but if you were a lady it was half price. Seemed reasonable value.

Chelsea's original colours were light-blue shirts with white shorts. The away strip was maroon. The design of the shirt was the old granddad vest later popularised by Don Johnson in *Miami Vice*.

FAT BOY SLIM

The most famous member of the new team was the goalkeeper, Willie 'Fatty' Foulkes. He was Chelsea's first captain. Willie was 6 ft 3 in, just a little shorter than the Dutchman De Goey but there the resemblance ends, because Willie weighed in at over 22 stone. Stamford Bridge was the first ground to use ball boys. They were mainly employed to help out Willie. The first Chelsea manager, John Tait Robertson (who also happened to play for Chelsea), always maintained that a couple of skinny, under-nourished ball boys would make Willie look even more gargantuan. To emphasise his bulk even more, the club's smallest player, a tiny winger called Moran, would trot out behind the great man. Chelsea were showbiz right from day one.

Willie was born in Shropshire and was nearly 30 when he joined Chelsea from Sheffield United, where he had won two Cup medals. He had played for England against Wales and had also played cricket for Derbyshire. He could certainly have also played for England if they had fielded an eating team. One of the many stories told about him concerned an early away trip to Burton. At the team's hotel, Willie decided to go down for dinner early. The away crowds that bait any plump Chelsea fan with the now legendary 'Who ate all the pies?' chant would have been in hooligan heaven, because that is literally what the goalkeeper did. When the rest of the team came down they found that all eleven plates had been cleared. It's just as well that there were no subs then. Mr Foulkes redeemed himself the next day, though, by stopping two penalties. That begat another apocryphal story. The Burton manager raged at the poor forward who had missed two penalties, screaming that both kicks were straight at Foulkes. 'Yeah, but where else could I place the kicks? There was nowhere else to aim,' replied the forward.

Willie had actually scored a goal for Sheffield United in a vital Cup match; it was the first time such a thing had happened in the Cup. An extract from an early programme of that maiden season informed us that: 'With not many minutes to go they were a goal to the bad and could not penetrate the home defence. Then Foulkes took matters into his own hands . . . leaving his goal absolutely undefended, [he] actually went right up the field and took his place as a sixth forward and, what was more, scoring a goal.'

In training Willie had a habit of hitting the punch balls so hard that he broke the rope that strung them. The club tried everything, even wire, but the ball took more punishment than Lennox's sparring partners.

Football had never seen a goalkeeper like Foulkes, before or after. When he came for the ball with his arms out, distracted opposing forwards said it was like the sun going out.

I would like to say that Foulkes' story ended happily. But like so many involving our heroes in Blue, it was tinged with sadness and ended in tears. Willie was essentially a vaudeville act; he only stayed a season and ended up at Bradford City, where he wound down his incredible career. When he left football he fell on hard times and was reduced to working a sideshow near the donkey rides on Blackpool beach. It was the old 'beat the goalie routine' and the Big Man ended up diving on the sands, shot-stopping to keep him in burgers. (As chairman I saw a few donkeys in my time at Chelsea that could easily have ended up in similar circumstances.)

In 1916 Willie Foulkes, Chelsea's first superstar and greatest (at least in terms of physique) player, died at the age of 40 after catching a cold that turned into pneumonia.

Chelsea finished third that first-ever season, just missing out on promotion. They scored plenty of goals and attracted big crowds (60,000 for a Good Friday visit from Manchester United; some things never change). The message was clear even then. Chelsea are more than a football club – they are a way of life.

Chapter Two: Genie in a Bottle

Jimmy Greaves scoring was like someone shutting the door of a Rolls-Royce.
Geoffrey Green

In the dismal flood-ravaged autumn of 2000, Jimmy Hasselbaink plundered four goals in Chelsea's 6–1 thrashing of a hapless Coventry City. Jimmy scored his goals in less than an hour on that filthy Saturday afternoon. The £15 million striker then proceeded to miss enough chances to have put the Blues' score into double figures as the amateur-looking City defence crumbled in the incessant rain. The high-tech logging of match stats indicated that Hasselbaink had a total of seven shots on goal and scored from four of them. Two efforts were blocked, with only one actually off target. Chelsea fans started to reach for their record books, wondering when was the last time a Blues striker had hit the net four times at Stamford Bridge. Gianluca Vialli, the previous manager who had signed Jimmy from Atletico Madrid, had scored four times at Barnsley two seasons before, and Kerry Dixon had been the last player to score four goals at Stamford Bridge, against Gillingham in a League Cup match.

'The past is a foreign country,' the novelist L.P. Hartley noted hauntingly. 'They do things differently there.' This thought surfaced in my mind when I recalled a player who had scored three or more goals for Chelsea in 13 League matches, a Chelsea player who reached the stellar heights of goalscoring celebrity – Jimmy Greaves, perhaps the greatest goal-scorer of all time. Certainly he has every right to be nominated as the finest striker to play in the Pepsi Blue of Chelsea.

Greaves was born in East Ham in February 1940, when Hitler's bombs were falling like autumn rain on the East End. It always amused me that Chelsea stole Greaves from under the very noses of West Ham. Towards the end of his golden career he turned out for the Hammers, but it was Chelsea fans who saw the genius emerge from his chrysalis. David Beckham, England's best footballer, also hails from that part of the world.

Jimmy's father was a London tube driver who lived to the ripe old age of 80. Greaves had a stable childhood, and was the head boy at his school, Kingswood

Secondary School in Hainault, Essex. Young Greaves was sports mad and it was only when he found out that he was too old to gain Essex schools representative honours at cricket he decided to leave school. James was 15 at the time and decided to join Chelsea Football Club, on the other side of town, after being discovered by the greatest scout since Baden-Powell, a chap called Jimmy Thompson.

Thompson was a little fellow who always wore a bowler hat. Despite looking more like a City clerk than a talent scout, he brought a procession of top names to the club including Barry Bridges, Bobby Tambling and Terry Venables. Greaves was the jewel in his star-studded crown. What would the conveyor belt of talent he brought be worth on the open market today? It is incalculable. With the jury still out on Chelsea's present-day youth system, I wonder how much they could do with a Jimmy Thompson in their set-up. The line-up that commenced the match in the 2–0 defeat at the Valley to Charlton in November 2000 included only one player that could be remotely regarded as a Youth product. His name is Dalla Bona and he was recruited from Italy. It is a global game now, but Chelsea's success was built on the recruitment and development of London boys.

Greaves had more records than Sinatra; the most prolific goalscoring season of his career was in 1956–57 while still an apprentice professional. He smashed in an unbelievable 114 goals in Chelsea youth team matches. Yes, that's right – 114 goals. The club presented him with plaque to commemorate the achievement. I don't know if he still has it. Today he would be rewarded with a huge house and a fleet of Mercedes, Porsches and Bentleys.

Jimmy played with some superb youngsters in that Chelsea youth side. One in particular stands out. His name was David Cliss, and he was seen as the brightest of the bunch. He had everything – pace, power and tremendous skill – and he scored almost as many goals as Greaves. Cliss loved to wave his foot over the ball like a wand, mesmerising defenders. It is hard to overstate just how good the Chelsea youth team was. If they were playing today they would be acclaimed as world-beaters. Joe Cole is the contemporary equivalent. Chelsea had a handful of them, all discovered by Thompson. It is my regret that I cannot name a Chelsea home-grown player of the last decade as notable as any of those lads. The young players are out there, but the game now seems so compartmentalised and bereft of ideas.

Cliss, for some mindbogglingly mysterious reason, never made it. He had a handful of league matches then drifted out of the game.

Jimmy was to make it, though, and he made it bigger than any Chelsea player, past or present. He was unstoppably brilliant. His game plan was simple; just score, then score again and again and . . .

On the first day of the following season the 17 year old made his league début against Tottenham at White Hart Lane. He was marked by the legendary Danny Blanchflower, captain of Spurs and future manager of Chelsea. I did not think any player could have out-thought Blanchflower strategically, but at some point in the second half Jimmy lost him and scored an equaliser to thrillingly open his account. Before the game the Spurs crowd taunted the slim youngster in the baggy shorts. Greaves was quiet, unflappable, living for the moment when he could really put the ball into the net. In the years to come they were to deify him.

Scoring on his début was an incredible record that he maintained throughout his career. He scored on his début at every level he played, for clubs and country. In his four-year spell at Chelsea he scored 124 goals in 157 league games. Four seasons was a blink of an eye in which to get his shots in (literally). In two of them he was the division's top scorer with 33 goals in 1958–59 and 41 in 1960–61.

Those are the stats, but they are only black and white. In those early years the hungry young East Ender went in merciless pursuit of the ageing, slowing giants of the game. I recall him scoring five times against England captain Billy Wright as Chelsea slaughtered Wolves 6–2. The genius of Greaves could only be fully appreciated by those who had the pleasure of seeing him clinically score goals. The first time I ever saw him play was when he was in the South East Counties League team. I forget how many he scored that day. It was a few – sometimes he would score ten or more in a game. I thought he looked like an iceberg, immovable and three-fourths beneath the surface. As he left the field he looked as if he was at his happiest, like *Just William* in the Richmal Compton books circulated among members of his gang. The stocky striker was like a Swiss Army knife, providing different tools for different needs. A deft flick with his right foot, a hammer blow with his left. The ability to dribble round defenders almost at will, coupled with the close control that enabled him to take the ball up to the goalkeeper, forcing him to commit himself then executing almost a little pas de deux before rolling the ball into the net. Like all great champions, from Ali to Garry Kasparov, he did not just beat his opponents, he destroyed them. He was like a cobra leading the attack; compact, autonomous, the cool detachment of his temperament standing him in good stead throughout his career.

It was often said that great strikers hunted in pairs, Keegan–Toshack, Dixon–Speedie, Osgood–Hutchinson, Fowler–Owen and Yorke–Cole. In the Premier League they appear an interchangeable troupe to me. Greaves was a predator, though, a lone gun and like the very greatest of strikers he operated on his own, in a hermetic world where the true genius was making things happen in the inferno of a packed penalty area when the boots were flying and the elbows were swinging. Jimmy was 'the Outlaw Josie Wales', the light cavalry. His tactics were hit and run, stealth and guile were the tools of his trade. Greaves was deadly. He had an indefinable energy. He was such a unique and exciting player; Greaves' speed of thought meant that he could read the game better than most. He would seem to disappear from a game, only to dramatically re-emerge to score a vital goal time after time. Greaves typified what I saw football as – something exciting.

Jimmy joined the pantheon of great Chelsea stars at a very young age and must rank as the most feared striker of all time; it was just impossible to counter him. Greaves had the X-factor that elevated him to icon status. Only Gianfranco Zola of the present Chelsea squad could be compared to him. Like Greaves, Zola is predominantly left footed; he has an awesome appreciation of the game's angles; and he cannot head a ball. Zola was a treat to watch as he rounded off his long and distinguished career. He is almost a Chelsea immortal.

Bill Shankly insisted football was a simple game, as did Brian Clough. Greaves was of the same opinion. He played in a deceptively simple way, with a deft touch. This was especially noticeable in his first few seasons in top-class football. He called Chelsea the 'All the Best Club', because Ted Drake's team talks were very short and before the team left the dressing-room to go out on the field Ted would say 'All the best'. The jinking Greaves would then go out and score as many goals as he could whilst the pitiful Chelsea defence would do their best to make a game of it by giving away as many goals as they could.

Perhaps that is where Jimmy gained his abhorrence of tactics. His laid back, casual attitude used to annoy theorists like the late Sir Alf Ramsey and was in my view the reason for his omission from the line-up for the 1966 World Cup final. Greaves failed to win the trust of Alf, and from that you may draw your own conclusions.

Greaves played in England's first three games in the 1966 World Cup. An attack of hepatitis had caused him to miss five months of the preceding season and had robbed him of that vital half-yard of pace that was such an integral part of his game. Greaves was injured against France in the group match. He was unfit for the quarter-final against Argentina and Geoff Hurst took his no. 10 shirt and scored the winner. Hurst, who also managed Chelsea till I sacked him, kept his place in the semi-final against Portugal and in the final against West Germany. Anybody who has ever watched a ball being kicked can tell you what happened next. Hurst scored the first World Cup final hat-trick in history. The fans thought it was all over for Greaves, but Jimmy carried on doing what he did best, putting the ball into the net. In an alternative universe, perhaps Greaves would have found even more space and time against the German defence that wet summer's afternoon so long ago. But then I am just a Chelsea fundamentalist.

It was said that in the early days of Greaves' highly successful television career he struggled when discussing tactics, and that it was only when his simplistic views and natural Cockney humour were allowed to shine through that the real Greaves emerged. Much of his comedy was incongruously great. He was a real one-off.

Our paths were to meet again over the years, even after he retired at a preposterously young age, nine goals short of a staggering 500 in top-class games. We played together in the 'Goal diggers' side which included other famous footballers like Rod Stewart and Elton John. Greaves' England career merits attention, in 57 games he scored 44 times to finish as their third-highest scorer. Only Bobby Charlton and Gary Lineker scored more, and that was in a lot more games. He scored six hat-tricks in his England career. Hughie Gallacher, the other Chelsea grandmaster striker, scored five trebles for Scotland.

The Chelsea years enjoyed by Greaves were, to borrow from Edith Wharton, the age of innocence. Goals were easier to score then because it was a far more open game. Football was changing rapidly, though, and the start of the '60s saw the first rumblings of the massive upheaval in the game. Greaves' overall strike rate was to slow significantly with the advent of the 4–2–4 system. Teams became more negative and packed their midfield and defences out. Now football has passed way beyond being the Saturday recreation it was when Greaves played, to become a ruthless billion-pound business. The way I see it is that we are moving from co-modifying goods and services to co-modifying culture; football, and Chelsea in particular, being a culture which is now a brand name.

Jimmy was the Ronan Keating of his day, the perfect gentleman with no vices. The media (though such a thing did not really exist in its present form then) left him well alone because he seemed so uninterestingly normal. The era was pre-Beatles, and the country was still very middle class. Football was untainted by sensationalism.

At 21 Greaves became the youngest player to score 100 league goals, and in less than three years he had doubled that figure. His average score per game was .691. Chris Sutton, who cost Chelsea £10 million, scored one league goal in his single traumatic season at the club.

It was common knowledge that Tottenham were keen to add Greaves to what was then called the 'Bank of England team'. They had just become the first team that century to win the double and the future looked golden. At that point they were poised to dominate football in the way Liverpool did in the '80s and

Manchester United did in the last decade. In recent years Spurs have fallen away badly in the race to be London's top club; in the year 2000 Tottenham were the epitome of workaday anonymity. A week after his four-goal burst, Hasselbaink scored two more goals as Chelsea romped to an effortless 3–0 win over Greaves' old team. Tottenham were then managed by George Graham, who was to follow in Greaves' footsteps as a Chelsea striker only a few seasons after Jimmy's departure to Milan. Pictures of Greaves and the 1960–61 double team adorned the walls of the Tottenham training complex, a sepia-tinged reminder of a past that continues to haunt them as, like Chelsea, they strive for a championship last won in a bygone era.

Graham admitted shortly before the Chelsea game that: 'We are like Newcastle and Everton, big clubs who have lost their way. But the great thing about football is that you must never lose the dream that if you get things right and build properly, you can recover and go on to great things again.' George was later sacked.

Jimmy Greaves could be said to be the personification of that dream. Chelsea and Arsenal are the dominant forces in the capital, with Spurs a very poor third. Their financial clout at the start of the '60s was immense and they were literally a chequebook side. They were managed by a dour Yorkshire man called Billy Nicholson, whose blade-sharp deals had brought a cluster of great names to White Hart Lane: Danny Blanchflower, Dave Mackay (a midfield dynamo who if he were playing today would make Roy Keane look like a shrinking violet) and the tragic John White were all purchased at great expense for the time. Today their transfer fees would not cover Keane's weekly pay cheque and their wages hardly run to those prawn sandwiches Keane was on about.

Chelsea had the chance to sign the phenomenal Dave Mackay from Hearts in a cut-price deal but Ted Drake amazingly turned down the business. I travelled with Jimmy Thompson up to Scotland to watch Mackay dominate the game. Jimmy came back raving about his performance but Drake informed us he had a better player in Sylvan Anderton. 'Who?' I hear you say. Exactly.

Greaves was discontented with his role at Chelsea; he was tired of carrying the whole team on his young shoulders. He was caught up in a treadmill and it was squeezing him dry emotionally. If Chelsea had bought a player like Mackay perhaps things would have turned out differently. Though Greaves' goalscoring never suffered, he hit five against West Brom as well as a hat-trick of hat-tricks in his last season at the Bridge. However, the rest of the team had stagnated. Often in a match I would see Jimmy cradle his head in his hands as the defence made another howler. His wife Irene was agitating for a move. Greaves was at the top of a decidedly shaky tree, but he wanted to win honours and be festooned with more medals and gongs than Marshal Zhukov.

One day my father summoned me to his home to attend a meeting Greaves had convened. He had requested a move and preliminary talks were going on. I was surprised to see his wife there. Despite lengthy talks, the Greaves could not be dissuaded from thinking that their future lay beyond Stamford Bridge. My father was desperate that Greaves did not go to Tottenham. It would have caused an outrage amongst the Chelsea fans. They were not so volatile as they were to become in the next decade, but nevertheless the implications would have been immense. There always seemed to be a certain friction with Tottenham fans amongst the Chelsea supporters. Even before the birth of the Shed, the Chelsea fans were endlessly inventive in their humour and unrepentantly scathing in their dissection of certain players' careers. Tottenham were always seen as the enemy. This was to manifest itself after the 1967 'Cockney' Cup final and led to the bad blood that spilled over into subsequent league clashes and is still felt even today.

Miles Ticher's excellent '*Guardian* Football Diary' contained a piece about an incident in the autumn 2000 clash: 'Though booing of black players is more common these days in Serie A than SW6, a poisonous strain of anti-Semitism lives on amid the glitzy facilities at Stamford Bridge.' A fan reported on a visit to the Shed Bar (touted by the club as a traditional sports bar) to watch Chelsea v Tottenham on the big screen with other ticketless fans. 'The singing and chanting were all too authentic. I thought "Spurs are on their way to Auschwitz" had gone the way of club lotto,' he writes after realising he had 'paid a tenner to stand in an '80s racist theme park for two hours'.

Greaves always looked smart. He favoured the city look in an era when most players wore blazers, club ties and flannels. He used to wear knotted, sober ties. His shoes looked like they had just come out of the box and his hair was always short and razor cut, though perhaps it was not as luxuriantly coiffed as the man from L'Oréal, Ginola, or as closely shaven as Beckham's. Greaves had simple tastes, he loved gardening and watching *Coronation Street*. At pre-match meals he would stick to salads and cups of tea. He was always smiling and cracking jokes about his team-mates.

After the defection of Keegan, Peter Taylor has been propelled into the England set-up. Apart from his coaching prowess and impressive playing accomplishments he is famous for his Norman Wisdom impersonation. Taylor broke my heart on Valentine's Day '76 with two superb goals for Crystal Palace that dumped Chelsea out of the FA Cup. I can upstage him now, though, by stating that Greaves was doing a wonderful recreation of scenes from Wisdom's movie *Trouble in Store* long, long before Taylor. Jimmy actually bore a striking resemblance to the young Wisdom.

That night, though, Greaves was telling my father that he wanted to be anything but a Chelsea player. Joe Mears still had a few cards left to play. He decided to sell Greaves to AC Milan. A ban on foreign players had been lifted and the big Italian clubs were soon scouring Europe for the cream of the crop. In the last five years the trend was reversed, but prior to that it was all one-way traffic, with players going from England to Italy.

The agent acting for Milan was an amazing character called Gigi Peronace. Today the sale of crowd favourites is usually spun by the football club's publicity machines as the players' own fault. Sinister figures from abroad are usually mentioned. Peronace was a character straight out of a Mario Puzo novel, and indeed Mario wrote *The Godfather* around the time Jimmy was at his peak. Peronace had a rich and motley life. At first I did not take to him; I did not want Greaves to leave Chelsea especially to go to North London or even Milan. My initial assessment of Peronace was that he was the catalyst for Jimmy's desire to leave. Everyone who met him agreed that he could charm the birds out of the trees.

We eventually became friends and he invited me to his lavish apartment in Knightsbridge, adjacent to Harrods – a Hasselbaink free kick away from Mohammed Al Fayed's office. Peronace was the man who made the deals, the chosen mediator. I can see him now in the treasure-filled flat, carpets everywhere and two enormous wolfhounds. Gigi was always exceptionally well groomed and most evenings he would greet me beautifully dressed in either a Cerrutti suit or a bold tweed jacket. He perpetually had a cigar of Babylonian dimensions in his mouth and he was forever sipping some Italian beer (which looked and tasted like urine) from a green bottle. We would talk football for hours. Gigi inhabited a world of immense privilege, and was as much at home in the coffee shops of Milan or the beach clubs of Forte Dei Marmi as he was in the drawing rooms of London SW1. Erudite, educated and more cosmopolitan than a Benetton Christmas card, he cut a dashing figure and everyone who came in contact with him at Stamford Bridge was impressed by his ingenuity. Greaves and co. were seduced by the charm of this really smooth operator. Not only did he have the depth of football knowledge, he had the financial brains. Peronace is what the French call *interess* – if he met you and decided that you were useful to him, he would charm you; if he decided that you were not he would not even remember your name. Behind his affable manner was a cold, calculating mind.

The field he was in was highly lucrative, but it could also be murky. One evening in Knightsbridge he seemed a little subdued and preoccupied. I was always willing to lend a sympathetic ear to my new friend's problems. After a pre-prandial Martini he explained that he thought there may be the possibility of money-laundering going on in Italy, with some world-famous names involved. He explained to me how it worked in outline. I found it staggering and frankly unbelievable. At that time I could never see it happening here. The risks appeared too great, as did the consequences. Decades later his conversation was to come back to haunt me.

A fee of £80,000 was agreed for the goal ace, Greaves. Jimmy started to have second thoughts about the move to the kaleidoscopic whirl of Italian football. Although Peronace had certainly glamorised the Italian set-up, I was convinced that in his heart Greaves did not really want to leave.

A player called George Eastham (who was to prove a nemesis to Chelsea by scoring a cup final winner against them as a swansong to his career) was involved in a history-making case around that time. The case was the Bosman ruling of its era. Eastham was fighting his then club, Newcastle, against the contract ruling which prevented him from joining a club of his choice when it ran out. After a bitter legal wrangle, Eastham won the case and joined Arsenal. The maximum wage was abolished and player power was born. The stage was set for the free-for-all which eventually led to the situation we have in football today. The FA commented that the wages-to-turnover ratio was absurd. The early '60s were the time that free agency militated against untrammelled greed.

Jimmy's last few months at Chelsea were a strain on us all, and difficult for everybody concerned. At the transfer talks he appeared sheepish and for the first time I saw doubt in his character. His wife Irene dominated the negotiations – it seemed to me that it was her decision that Jimmy should leave Stamford Bridge.

Tragedy hit the Greaves family in the last few weeks of his time at Chelsea. His son James Jr died in his cot. Milan insisted that Greaves was to fulfil his contract with them, threatening him with expulsion from the world game. Perhaps that was when something tipped over for him. It is a cliché now – football hero succumbs to drink – but nobody ever thought that it would happen to Jimmy Greaves. The compulsive drinking which was to blight his life in later years was in my view triggered by the dislocation caused by the tragedy at the time of his transfer. The alcohol addiction which destroyed the careers and lives of so many great Chelsea stars was a substitute for a real sense of identity, in my opinion. The players formed a sort of romantic attachment to the person that drink made them. Greaves has admitted that he liked to do his drinking in private so he did not waste time talking. This was unlike many of his predecessors, who could be classed as social drinkers and did most of their boozing in public. The tougher a man is, the longer he can hold out under the immense pressure he is under.

Greaves' last game at Stamford Bridge was perhaps his greatest. A huge crowd gathered at the ground for Jimmy's farewell to Chelsea. If his début was exciting, then his departure was sensational. Jimmy hit all four goals as Chelsea came from 3–1 down to beat Nottingham Forest by the odd goal in seven. Two of them were vintage, Greaves perfectly retaining his balance as he clipped the ball home using the inside of his foot rather than blasting with his instep.

Poor old Forest, the perennial fall guys for the Greaves goal machine. Greaves scored in all 24 league games against them in his goal-drenched career. The next team on his hit list were Burnley with 19. Strangely enough Chelsea were very low in his tally. After he left he only scored four times against us. I think that was something to do with the marking of one Ron Harris. Harris policed Greaves as closely as he did George Best. As a man marker he was the most underrated defender of his generation.

The Forest game was poignant because not only was it a formidable expression of Greaves' genius at its greatest, but it was effectively the end of the 'All the best' culture. Greaves became less relaxed as an individual; maybe the struggle to survive became more acute inside him. In his Chelsea days I always thought he was seeing how high he could fly before, like Icarus, the gods clipped his wings. Far too many players today profit from our failure to make a distinction between fame and talent, but Greaves truly was supremely talented.

The pitch was engulfed with fans as Greaves was chaired from the pitch after the Forest game. The script was pure 'Roy of the Rovers'. Today I would fear he would be torn to pieces like Orpheus. There was one more twist, though – one that left a bitter taste. Chelsea needed Greaves to travel with them to Israel to appear in a lucrative friendly. Jimmy opted out and was banned for a fortnight by the club. He missed an England match as a result.

THE ITALIAN JOB

For a while it looked as though Greaves would never get to Milan. His wife Irene was heavily pregnant and, mindful of the loss of their first son, Greaves was anxious to look after her. He stayed on in London to see the birth of his son Danny. Danny was to later play league football for Southend. It was strange that years later the late Matthew Harding was to nickname one of his sons 'Greavesy' after his all-time Chelsea boyhood hero. Harding's son Luke was heavily influenced by the culture of Chelsea. The first time I met Harding he asked me all about Greaves.

Eventually Greaves arrived in Italy a month behind schedule, having clocked up a large fine for his lateness. Waiting for him was one Nero Rocco. Brash and egocentric, a chap who could have been a warder at Wormwood Scrubs, he could teach Brian Clough a thing or two about tyranny. Rocco's brief was simply to crush the spirit of the little Englishman and protect the Rossoneris' investment.

Greaves lasted less than four months but in that time he managed to score 9 goals in 14 games, an amazing return. Once again he maintained his record of scoring on his début. He netted in a 2–2 draw with Botafogo at the San Siro. Years later Chelsea fans eulogised Wise in song – 'Scoring a f*****g good goal in the San Siro' – but Jimmy beat him by about 28 years. Greaves was a total outcast in Milan. Just as Ranieri struggled to speak English, Greaves did not speak a word of Italian. Chelsea received flak in the press at their inability to find an interpreter who could do their new manager linguistic justice, but Jimmy had precious little help to lift him above the corporate mediocrity of Milan.

There will always be people who can't take the easy way out. We all know them; the suffering superstars who cannot fail to see the darkness all around when the rest of us would look the other way. Greaves, like Osgood, was his own worst enemy. He hated hypocrisy and falsity and instantly felt trapped by the Milanese system, and Rocco, who stubbornly ruled over him. In a short space of time he was completely fed up, frustrated and tired of pouring his soul into the sterile matches that stereotyped the Italian game. The Milan striker was singled out for harsh punishment by the opposing sides and received no support from his team-mates.

The single-mindedness and self-confidence started to drain away from the exiled Londoner, to be replaced by neurosis. I was determined to bring him back to Chelsea but his mind was set on a move to Spurs. Perhaps the whole thing was a set-up. Chelsea offered him far more to return to West London than the salary paid by Spurs. I knew that a player like Greaves came along only once in a lifetime and that long term we would struggle without him. How can you replace Greaves?

Eventually he signed for Spurs for exactly a pound less than £100,000. Billy Nicholson did not want him burdened under the £100k price tag. It seems a laughable amount now, but in those days it was almost unthinkable.

Greaves' 'Roy of the Rovers'-style career continued. He made his début for Spurs against Blackpool and scored three times in a 5–2 win. One of the goals scored is to this day his personal favourite, an acrobatic left-footed scissors kick that threatened to remove the netting, not to say the goalkeeper's fingers. It was a startlingly great goal, my favourite of his, even if it was not scored for Chelsea. Jimmy had picked up the trick in the Milan training camp, where he had spent the mind-numbingly long afternoons watching the Italians improvise and polish up on their dazzling techniques. So not all of his time had been wasted in Italy.

The rest, as they say, is history. Greaves went on to top the goalscoring charts four more times with Tottenham. His goals helped them win two FA Cup finals (one of them against Chelsea) and the European trophy eight years before Chelsea repeated the trick. Chelsea were relegated the following season.

Chapter Three: Eldorado

The first time I ever laid eyes on Terry Lennox he was drunk in the back of a Rolls-Royce.
Raymond Chandler, The Long Goodbye

So began Chandler's classic detective novel. The first time I ever saw Terry Venables he was sober and he was yet to own a Rolls-Royce. He was like a character from a pulp fiction novel, though.

A glance at the Chelsea professional staff of the early '60s reveals some household names: Peter Bonetti, two international full-backs in Eddie McCreadie and Ken Shellito, a baby-faced John Hollins, and two names that dominate the headlines still today, Venables and Graham, arguably the greatest managers of their generation. Only Sir Alex Ferguson's track record stands up to greater scrutiny. It was a constant puzzle to Chelsea fans over the wilderness years that the man at the helm was a self-confessed Liverpool fan in Bobby Campbell, or an Ian Porterfield rather than El Tel or George.

THE MAN WHO SOLD THE WORLD

Venables was the personification of the early-'60s mod culture. All the 'faces', the main Chelsea fans, were mods. Terry would have been equally at home in the Scene club as he was on the training ground. To me Venables will always be the quintessential 'Chelsea Boy'. This was before the long-haired Alan Hudson strutted his stuff down the Kings Road, even before one Michael Greenaway became number one all-time fan and leader of the Shed Boys. From which grew the feared 'Headhunter' gangs. Terence Frederick Venables was ducking and diving before Dennis Wise was even thought of. He was as London as Ray Davies singing 'Waterloo Sunset', as tough as Ray Winstone in *Scum*, as cool as Paul Weller singing about the 'Burning Sky' and as fly as Arthur in *Minder*. The lead singer of the pop group Blur, Damon Albarn, would die to have been Terry Venables circa 1965, leading out the boys in blue in their whippet prime, a gold lion on his chest, twirling the ball on his little finger. It could be said that for a while he appeared to hold the whole world in his hands. Perhaps he did; perhaps he still does.

Whilst some of the taut-bodied Chelsea players would spend their time hanging round the billiard halls or coffee houses in the Kings Road, others would be chasing the heartbreakingly beautiful girls that worked in the boutiques there. A few were cultivating drink habits, but Venables was grafting. There were several clues to his future career. 'He was into more businesses than ICI,' Malcolm Allison, his lifelong pal and mentor, once told me. Terry always had great career aspirations. He seemed to exude a sense of restlessness; there was a vague dissatisfaction behind the easy line of chat and half smile. I wonder sometimes when I see him have his little early evening chats with Des on TV what he really thinks of the offensively large wads of cash now offered to lesser talents than his and the rest of the class of '65.

That Chelsea period must have been the most satisfying period of Terry's life. Captain of Chelsea at such an exciting time in the club's history, Venables must have felt as though he were king of the world. It was an intoxicating brew of power, talent, gall and glamour. It was fish and chips, lager and lime, midnight-blue mohair suits, tonik jackets and button-down, pin-through, powder-blue tab collars. Momentarily London was the hip capital of the Western world and the Kings Road was the crux of it. To me it was like a gyroscope spinning fast, so very fast.

The band that epitomised that era more than any other, the Rolling Stones, lived in Edith Grove when they first came up to London. Edith Grove was a Marcel Dessaily clearance away from Stamford Bridge. The elegant Frenchman never hacks the ball away, unlike some of the defenders I employed at Chelsea. However, if he were to slice a clearance over the Shed End and the wind were strong enough, it would have landed in the Stones' back garden. I used to see Jagger in the Kings Road frequently. By this time he had made the jump from the condemned flat in Edith Grove to the millionaires' row of Cheyne Walk. Jagger was always in a place called the Drug Store, later made famous in his hit album *Let it Bleed*. 'Album' – forgive me, what an old-fashioned term; rather like the position of wing-half, which was the one Venables played in. Jagger was my guest at Chelsea years later, when he came to one of our floodlit cricket nights. Jagger is a huge cricket fan and very knowledgeable, though I never knew what team he supported.

Venables was the Mick Jagger of football, in that after nearly 40 years in the business he is still top of the heap. Born in the East End on 6 January 1943, the only child of Frederick Charles Venables and his Welsh-born wife Myrtle Ellen, daughter of a coal miner, he was brought up in Dagenham, a few miles from the birthplace of Jimmy Greaves. Dagenham was known as 'Corned Beef City'. It was a tough upbringing; the war had not long ended and times were hard, with food rationing still in force. Everybody ate corned beef, despite its bilious smell. Of course, there were no BSE scares in those days.

It is said that Terry started playing football at about three years old. One of his uncles was in the navy and brought him back a bright red water-polo ball. Terry would kick it from the family's terraced council house in Bonham Road to the nearby park. A star was born. He was soon in trouble with the authorities at his junior school for smashing the staff-room window with a crisp half-volley. He was hauled up before the headmaster accused of throwing the ball through the window, the teachers refusing to believe that anybody could kick it that hard.

Terry grew up obsessed with soccer. You may not like this, but he was a devout Spurs fan. At the age of 11 he was signing in his autograph book as manager of Spurs. Diamond sharp at grammar school, he rejected overtures to go to college, choosing instead the academy of Stamford Bridge, whose headmaster was Ted Drake. Discovered by Jimmy Thompson, he was coached by Dick Foss and Dickie Spence, who nurtured the cream of London's youngsters. Spence had been a skilful winger pre-war and had played for England. His record of 19 goals in season 1934–35 still stands and, in the age of wing-backs and flank players, always will. Pat Nevin came closest in modern times, as did Venables' team-mate Bert Murray (nicknamed 'Ruby' after the Atomic Kitten of the time).

Venables soon blossomed and came under the wing of Drake. Memory is a movable feast, we rewrite the past as we go along, but he always told the story of how the ex-England centre-forward gave him and full-back Peter Sillett a lift to Sloane Square, Terry sitting in the back and the massive Sillet ensconced in the passenger seat. As the car nosed to a gentle halt at the lights at the end of Fulham Road, Drake, beautifully dressed in his blue chalk-stripe Jermyn Street suit, was giving a long and harrowing rap about the pressures of running a big club like Chelsea. The car remained stationary at the traffic lights for five minutes. An exasperated policeman on foot patrol came over and recognising the Chelsea boss, asked him if anything was wrong as the lights had changed at least four times.

Ted Drake turned to Peter and said, 'My God, Peter, I thought you were doing the driving.' That made a big impression on Venables; he saw then the enormous pressure on a man chosen to run a big team.

I watched Venables work his way up rapidly. He reminded me of a young Ray Liotta, fresh out of the *Goodfellas* movie in his stylish Italian suits. He even had a partnership in a bespoke tailoring business with George Graham and Ron Harris. The business had its premises at 40 Old Compton Street, just off Shaftesbury Avenue and near the heart of clubland. The Mods' nirvana of the Scene club was very close. As I recall, though, the business did not really challenge the great fashion houses of Europe. Giorgio Armani was given a pretty clear shot at the title. It was said that the patronage of our friend Norman Wisdom did not help the venture. Norman was infamous for his appalling check suits. I recall he tried to get me to buy a particularly nasty pinstripe effort. Perhaps Ted Drake bought it.

Terry's pal Hollins managed the Chelsea team that was relegated at the end of the '80s. At one time he had on his books the Dixon–Speedie–Nevin combination which was the brightest collection of players down at the Bridge since the glory period of the great cup-winning days. Still it went wrong, and a potential title-winning side became another legion of the damned. As players, however, there was nothing to separate them. In my view, Hollins was the equal of Terry, both men having a very high workrate and the energy of the Beatles in their Hamburg period, and both possessed a tremendous shot. Venables at the very highest level did not have the great talent of Hudson, or even Hoddle, gifts more explicable than those of a Monet or a Lennon. They had God-given talents; Venables' talent was more self-made. He was a Bonaparte of the training ground. It was like the difference between the Beatles and Oasis; Venables lacked the invention of Hudson and the vision of Hoddle. Even former players like the two Mickeys, Hazard and Fillery, who are now largely forgotten outside a relatively small circle of diehard Chelsea fans, had talent at least comparable to Terry's. But what all of them lacked was his aching ambition.

The club that both Venables and Hollins found themselves a part of had the camaraderie of a Spitfire squadron in the Battle of Britain summer of 1940. Chelsea had entered the '60s under a cloud with the departure of Greaves and the sacking of Ted Drake. Without Greaves, Chelsea struggled for goals. In January 1961 Chelsea were knocked out of the cup at home by little Crewe Alexandra. It was terrible humiliation and signalled the downfall of Drake. Crewe had been thrashed 13–2 by Spurs in the Cup the year before, so it could not have been worse. Well, thinking about it, had *we* lost 13–2 to Spurs it would have been worse. The loss of Greaves was devastating. I have never seen a talent like his; he was irreplaceable. Sometimes I thought he must have entered into some Faustian pact whereby he sold his soul to become the greatest goal-scorer ever.

DOCTOR'S ORDERS

Ted Drake was sacked as Chelsea slid into the Second Division and was replaced by Tommy Docherty, perhaps the most outrageous manager of all time. He was the Malcolm McLaren of football. Tommy had joined the club from Arsenal and became Drake's number two. Born in the Gorbals, a tough part of Glasgow, he fought his way up to the very top. Docherty was the Zelig of Chelsea; he became anyone you wanted him to be. In his first full season in charge, 1962–63, Chelsea won promotion. Venables played in every game and soon made a name for himself as the rising star in London. The season was incredible. Hitchcock could not have dreamed up a better end to it. Typical CFC, doing it the hard way, the only way they know. Always did, always will.

Chelsea started the season like greyhounds and throughout the autumn played brilliantly. Cardiff City were put to the sword by six goals, with Venables scoring the goal of the season with a savage half-volley that simply whistled into the net. I recall a particularly exciting seesaw 4–2 home win over Newcastle. Chelsea, with Venables in peak form, raced to a 3–0 lead early in the first half, but Newcastle hit back with two fine goals to set up a tremendous finale. A late goal by crowd favourite Barry Bridges sealed it. It was an unforgettable match and it made an indelible impression on a young man taken to the Bridge for the first time by his father. That young man was Matthew Harding and years later I was to sit in a luxury hotel with him and reminisce about our earliest Chelsea memories. Cat Stevens once sang about the first cut being the deepest. The first cut was for Matthew the start of a lifelong love affair which, like all great love affairs, ended in tragedy.

By Christmas Chelsea were six points clear (don't forget this was the Jurassic period when only two points were awarded for a win). The age of the dinosaurs was followed by the ice age, because at the start of 1963 a huge freeze hit the country. This was long before global warming was even heard of and for months we were inactive. Docherty took the team away to Malta to try to get the players fit by playing a local side. The trip was a disaster, with one of the first recorded incidents of crowd trouble marring the match and a bitter dispute over the gate receipts breaking out with the reptilian owners of the ground.

We returned to worse trouble. The momentum of our long run had gone. We lost nine matches out of an unlucky run of 13. At Easter we appeared to lose our last chance of promotion when we were defeated 1–0 at home by eventual champions Stoke. It was chaos. The late Stanley Matthews still played at the age of 48, an amazing talent but almost unbelievable to modern students of the game. He was basically a one-trick pony, but what a trick it was. The stripy-shirted maestro would shuffle up to the full-back, rolling the ball from boot to boot before cradling it in his right. Everybody in the ground knew he was going on the outside, but when Stan worked the 'Ali shuffle' the defender was drawn in momentarily, just long enough for the Prince of the Potteries to be away. I recall a young bullet-headed defender crash tackling 'Stan the man' after the old boy had left Eddie McCreadie on his backside. A collective wince went up from the crowd. Matthews was still held in reverence and such harsh treatment was frowned upon in the game and by the older supporters. You cannot imagine anyone pushing 50 playing at that level today. That was the first time I ever recall seeing Ron Harris. The shaven-headed young man was to upset a few more people over the years with his tackling.

The Stoke débâcle meant that we had to win our last two games to have the remotest chance of going up. The first game was up at Sunderland, our main rivals for promotion and formidable opponents. Docherty gambled big time; the Scot packed the team with defenders. Docherty, Venables and myself went to Luton the previous Monday to spy on Sunderland. Tommy must have spotted some inherent weakness there because he hatched a bold tactical plan. Tommy Harmer, a tiny ball-player bought from Tottenham for £5,000 to coach the youngsters, was pitched into combat. Harmer scored an early goal that stunned Sunderland. It was to prove to be one of the most vital in the club's history, and merited an 'X-file' of its own, so bizarre were the circumstances. The little forward won a corner on the right and Bobby Tambling, the club's highest-ever scorer, crossed a dipping inswinger. Harmer was on the goal-line just hoping for a knock down. Them's the breaks. The ball flew in off his groin and was scrambled home. Venables, up on a raid and hoping for a rebound, could not believe it. The late Victor Meldrew would not have believed it either. Sunderland thought it was a load of bollocks!

Chelsea hung on grimly to win despite massive pressure from Sunderland. The home side only needed to equalise to win promotion but a heroic performance by the Chelsea defence denied them. Docherty admitted to me that the team he had picked to play at Sunderland was not the best Chelsea team, but believed it to be the best for that particular job. I was the only director to make the trip, as my father had already sustained two heart attacks and it was thought that the strain would be too much for him to bear. Too right; it nearly did for me. In the last minute the Sunderland winger George Mulhall finally shook off the attentions of his man-marker Ron Harris, cut inside, accelerated past a blue shirt and blasted in a tremendous shot. It looked a certain goal and the Sunderland crowd, by now almost breathless, let out one last mighty roar as the ball hurtled through the late afternoon air on its way to a date with the back of the net. Peter Bonetti, aka 'The Cat', had other ideas though and threw himself at the swerving ball to make an incredible save. It literally was a heart-stopping moment. That was the difference between gaining promotion and staying put for a further season. Later I found out that the local sports paper had even gone so far as to print up before the match headlines emblazoning 'Promotion'. It would not be the first time that the papers got it wrong about Chelsea.

Chelsea had to win the next game at home to Portsmouth by a big score to clinch promotion on goal average, not difference like today. They did it in style, winning 7–0. Tambling went goal mad and hit four. Venables was on target also that amazing night. The first goal was headed in by a chap called Derek Kevan; comparisons with Sutton could be made, because for the time the fee paid to West Brom was big money. Like Chris, he scored just one goal. He was a panic buy to clinch promotion. Kevan was a strange chap and once asked me if he could take his pet dog on the coach to an away game.

At half-time the Blues were 3–0 up and cruising towards the big time. I went down into the dressing-room and recall Docherty demanding more goals. 'Chelsea have lost games before after being three ahead, go for more quick goals and sew it up.' They certainly did.

Back in the top flight I sensed for the first time that the club could be serious contenders for major honours. In season 1962–63 the club consolidated. Venables, showing remarkable maturity, quickly made his mark in the big time. He was rewarded with two England caps in 1964 and seemed destined for a stack of caps but he never added any more to his collection. Hudson won only two; I think Sammy Lee of Liverpool won a lot more, but who do the fans remember?

Nobody paid their dues more than Terry. He won caps at every level where it was possible to win honours, including an amateur cap. He should have won a lot more caps, but with England manager Alf Ramsey building for the impending World Cup he seemed to overlook the young Chelsea captain. Perhaps, like Greaves, there was something a bit too flash about him for Ramsey to be comfortable with. I recall talking to Ramsey once after he had visited the Bridge and him remarking that certain players in the game behaved like 'spivs', a curious term with its echoes of garish Teddy-boy clothes and black market goods. I found it a curiously old-fashioned term even for a quarter of a century ago. It told me that Ramsey was out of touch with the modern world. Spiv? How profound. Venables' modern-day public persona would have cut no ice with him either.

Was Venables a spiv? Would Alf have bought a used car from him? Around that time Venables switched from the orthodox wing-half number 4 shirt to the attacking midfield role and the famous number 10 shirt. The high spot of the season was Chelsea's first-ever FA Cup win over Spurs in the Third Round. We forced a draw at Tottenham thanks to a header from our winger Bert Murray and four nights later over 70,000 packed into the Bridge to watch us put them out 2–0. Bobby Tambling from a Murray cross fired us ahead, then Murray headed in from a Tambling cross. It was Venables, captaining the side, who now ran the game from midfield. Chelsea were like flies buzzing all over the Spurs aristocrats, pressing, insinuating. I recall an audacious Venables sidefoot in the opening moments of the match that switched the direction of play and caught out the Spurs defence. It was a risky rather than a complicated technique, but it boosted the ego of the young Blues team. Against the ageing Spurs defence Chelsea looked fit, fluent and formidable. After the match I saw Spurs boss Bill Nicholson chewing the fat with the earnest-looking press boys; Venables was the buzzword and already Nicholson was ponying up the idea of a Venables–Greaves axis in the Tottenham line-up. Tottenham still had a war chest in those days, and with the average age of the Chelsea side being 21 Nicholson found it all a tad worrisome. They had taken Greaves from us but the balance of power was shifting to West London. Greaves had been shackled in both games by Harris making his cup début.

We looked set for a cup run with a home draw against Huddersfield, but they knocked us out in a drab match. That was when I met Harold Wilson, who always told me he knew more about football than politics. This is one of politics' enduring myths.

CATCH US IF YOU CAN

Season 1964–65 and 1965–66 were two of the most colourful, event-packed seasons in the club's spectacular history. Chelsea simply exploded across the headlines. Venables was the youngest of the young Turks. I was not immune to his flattery and attention, and we became good friends. He was always up to something; a crackpot scheme about wigs, then singing at the Hammersmith Palais till a horrified Tommy Docherty put the block on it. The music-loving Docherty had changed the strip to all blue: royal-blue shirts, royal-blue shorts (replacing the traditional white shorts) and white socks. Chelsea were also the first English club to have a number on their shorts. Celtic were the first British club to have this fashion, but they had no number on the back of their world-famous green-and-white hooped shirts.

Venables was the backbone of the team as Chelsea went through the first ten matches unbeaten. We seemed unstoppable but on the last night of September, we ran into a red machine called Manchester United with George Best at the controls. It was his first game in London, the town he now calls home. Best brought us down to earth with a sharp thud. That night he was unplayable, roasting our defence with his scintillating runs. Looking back with my watery eyes I can still see his bewildering changes of direction and his amazing control at high speed. Time after time Best pushed the ball past the blue-clad defenders with the outside of his foot. This was a skill he used in a tight spot with Eddie McCreadie, giving him barely enough space to explode home a shot for the Old Trafford side's opening goal. We had nobody to compare to him; it was a great psychological advantage to have George on your side. Perhaps that night I knew in my heart we still had a long way to go before we were true championship contenders, though in the early spring of 1965 Chelsea were top of the table and still in the hunt for the cup.

A game that people have forgotten in that era was our 1–0 victory over West Germany's prospective World Cup XI in Duisberg in February of that year. This was little over a year before the World Cup final and the West German XI included Beckenbauer, Tilkowski and Libuda. It was a wonderful Chelsea team performance and when Barry Bridges scooted through ten minutes from time to score with a well-executed strike from Venables' pass it rounded off a perfect night. I cannot recall a club side playing and beating foreign opponents of international calibre before or after. It could be said that Chelsea played their part in winning the World Cup for England.

A few weeks after that not-so-famous victory, Venables scored in the first leg of the Football League Cup final at Stamford Bridge against the holders, Leicester. The League Cup final in those days was played on a home and away basis and since then has had numerous sponsors and guises. Now they call it the Worthington Cup. The finals used to be played at Wembley. Chelsea have had a somewhat chequered history in the tournament but that season they were determined to win it. That was the fifth year of the League Cup and a London club was yet to triumph. It was another bizzare match, with Eddie McCreadie drafted to centre-forward because Barry Bridges was selected to play for the Football League against their Scottish equivalents in Glasgow. This was the prelude to Bridges winning his first full England Cup. In those days there were no massive squads maintained by the clubs and more often than not representative matches clashed with league and cup fixtures. Today it brings a smile to my face when I read of what a vortex twenty-first-century football is. I enjoy hearing of the ridiculously pressured lives of the top stars after achieving high levels of corporate responsibility and anxiety. The pressure was on Barry Bridges, though, because already the talk at Stamford Bridge was of a sensational young striker about to burst onto the scene by the name of Peter Osgood. Instant karma. The Windsor-born youngster had already made his début for the first team in an earlier round of the League Cup. Nine days before Christmas 1964 Peter Osgood had scored both Chelsea's goals in a 2–0 victory over Workington in a fifth-round replay. The world was soon to hear more of him, a great deal more.

McCreadie was the hero that night, though, with a goal that could have come out of the yet-to-be-written Peter Osgood Bumper Book of fantastic goals. The game was poised at 2–2, Leicester more than holding their own and looking forward to taking Chelsea back to Filbert Street. Tambling had opened the scoring and Venables had cracked home a penalty as easily as if he was booting the red polo ball in his local park all those years before. The rain was teeming down, as it does in the new millennium, when McCreadie picked the ball up well inside his own half and began dribbling upfield. At first the goal looked safe, with defenders shepherding him across the field towards the touchline. Suddenly he surged forward. The goal almost defied analysis, with determination, luck and judgement playing as big a part as ball control and precise technique. A sudden angled turn, and wrong-footed defenders left him with a chance of a shot. In goal that night for Leicester was Gordon Banks, perhaps the greatest goalkeeper this country has ever produced. (Though this book might make a convincing claim for Peter Bonetti as the greatest club keeper.) As Ron Harris rather wickedly put it once, Banks had both his eyes then (he was to lose one in a car smash a few years later, ending his career) and threw himself at the Scottish international as he shaped to shoot. Eddie tricked him though, as he let the ball roll a second longer before tapping it into an empty net. They both collapsed in a heap as the Bridge went mad at one of its greatest ever solo goals.

The only comparison is Spurs' Argentinian star Ricky Villa's winner in the 1981 FA Cup final. Ricky's solo goal was captured on film for posterity but unfortunately there is no record of McCreadie's marvel. Villa's goal was scored in a higher stakes game. You could add that he beat more players and an international goalkeeper in Joe Corrigan. But McCreadie's goal was carved out on the mudflats of Stamford Bridge and was against Banks, though the jury is still out on which was the better goal.

A few weeks later Venables took Chelsea back to Leicester to defend their narrow lead and defend it they did, with some ferocious tackling and hard running. Docherty was desperate to collect his first (and only) silverware for Chelsea and they played it like a Euro game, no risk, very tight. It ended 0–0 and Venables collected a tankard. Who said the Doc never won anything at Chelsea?

In the intervening weeks we experienced the bitter taste of defeat as we lost in the semi-finals of the FA Cup to Liverpool. Chelsea were now known as the 'Catch Us If You Can' team. A world-famous London pop group called The Dave Clark Five (now they would be called a 'boy band') brought out a record from the film of the same name. These lads hailed from Tottenham and even had a publishing company called Spurs Music (and you thought it started with Chas and Dave). Chelsea fans adopted the song and soon turned it into a homage to their favourites. It caught the mood of the team at that time. Young, vibrant, quick, no time to lose. Snappy like the slick passing game Chelsea employed under Venables, pass and move. 'Keep on Running' was another record from that era, by the Spencer Davis Group featuring the wonderful voice of Stevie Winwood. These songs could have been written with Terry in mind.

The hard-running, quick-fire passing was a style that was coalescing around a few teams but Chelsea had it as their business plan first. To Venables it was a kind of Holy Grail. Liverpool were to modify it and use it to trample on everybody else in the ensuing years. In the early '60s there was little to choose from between the two sides, both had hard-nosed Scots driving them on. They were ideological partners, geopolitical partners (Merseyside v London, Beatles v Stones). Both clubs had a growing army of fanatical fans creating an identity first. There was no spin then and no marketing machine to target the audience. Both the fans and the players were hungry for success. The first superstars were starting to emerge. Soon, though, the Docherty–Venables team was to implode under the weight of their own expectations, relationships going sour, becoming hopelessly routine, dazed, confused, blurred, almost bankrupt of ideas – but that was a little later, when the gyroscope stopped swirling.

On 27 March 1965, Chelsea lost 2–0 to Liverpool in the semi-final at Villa Park, Birmingham. As always with Chelsea it was a game that they were expected to win and consequently they found a way to blow it and collect the booby prize. A few nights before, Liverpool had played an important European match and were expected to be too fatigued to overcome the young lions from the Kings Road. Chelsea were perhaps a little over-confident but when centre-half John Mortimore headed in what appeared to be a perfectly valid goal in the first half the Blues looked set for Wembley. I was speculating as to where to buy the new suit I had promised myself if we reached Wembley when the ref disallowed it. Midway through the second half, with Liverpool showing no signs of running out of steam, fate intervened.

The Reds winger Peter Thompson, another player with a deceptive change of pace, beat Bonetti all ends up with a snap shot from 25 yards. To this day Chelsea fans claim that maybe Eddie McCreadie should have closed the England winger down with one of his sliding tackles rather then attempt to jockey him out of position. That's football – hero one day, scapegoat the next.

Near the end, with 'You'll Never Walk Alone' blaring out all around me, Ron Harris scythed down Liverpool hardman Ian St John and Billy Stevenson made it 2–0 from the spot. Game over.

The Harris tackle on St John has passed into the folklore of Chelsea Football Club and people who saw it (now well into their anecdotage) still shudder at the memory. The sight of Harris with his studs raised going in on the Liverpool number nine as the thin Blue line cracked is still a vivid image from that period. Ron has woven this into the after-dinner act he performs nowadays and finishes it off with the 'Late tackle? I got there as quick as I could ref' routine. St John was later to carve out a long career in television with Jimmy Greaves. The 'Saint' was the straightman in a show riddled with the unintentionally hilarious patois of the 'Cor strike a light' school, of the variety of Professional Cockney played by Greaves. On that cold spring day at Villa though, St John knew better than to exchange wise-cracks with a vengeful Harris.

St John was always quick to headbutt but when he saw Harris standing over him the idea was put out of his mind. The other memory of that day was the look on Venables' face as the beaten Blues trudged exhausted from the Villa Park pitch. They had given their all for Chelsea but had been outgunned on the day by a superior team. Perhaps something died a bit then in the club. It was the first inkling that the dream was outside our grasp.

Chelsea extracted a little revenge on Good Friday a few weeks later when they thrashed Liverpool 4–0 at Stamford Bridge in the league. Venables snatched the fourth goal with a crafty free kick that shredded their defensive wall like an old cabbage. Liverpool were the greatest at sucking up other people's ideas and plagiarised the move from the Venables' songbook. They scored from it to great acclaim in Europe but if they got the royalties it was Venables who wrote the song.

I would see him working hard at his game. He was always watching and learning, soaking up the knowledge of every talented person who crossed his path. He was always chatting to Harmer, hero of the Sunderland victory and the most experienced pro at the club. Like Zola, Venables was a great exponent of free kicks. He was always looking for the edge that would swing a contest his way. In the claustrophobic world of modern football, time and space were the most valuable of commodities. A dead ball specialist could unpick the most organised of walls. Terry was soon aware that if Chelsea put a player on each end of the wall and they 'peeled off' as soon as the kick was taken, the keeper would be unsighted as the ball flew through the resulting space. In his way he was as good as Beckham is today.

The victory gave Chelsea an outside chance of the league title but once again controversy was to wreck their title hopes and fan the flames. Docherty took the lads up north for the last vital matches but sent home eight of them for a breach of club discipline, including Venables, McCreadie, Graham and Bridges. I was away on business so to this day I still do not know the real story. Rumours reached me that things were not as reported. The volatile Docherty was always a short trip away from the self-destruct button. I saw the power struggle between Venables and Docherty reaching crisis point. The tension between the two of them was always there, and by a strange quirk of fate as I type these words Docherty is on *Talk Sport* questioning Venables' involvement at Middlesbrough. Nothing ever changes. In a strange way, this relationship was to mirror the conflict between Venables and Sugar and echo the problems

Matthew Harding experienced with the regime at Stamford Bridge. A parallel could even be drawn between Ruud Gullit, Gianluca Vialli and their problems. The crux of the argument was that Docherty felt his position was being undermined by his young captain. 'Venables was too damn cheeky for his own good,' was Docherty's famous quote.

Venables was too much for the Doc to handle. Sometimes I would drop in on the Doc's surgery as he gave his team talks. Chelsea's manager would turn to Venables and ask him for his comments. Terry always had an expressive face; for years on Brian Moore's *Big Match* opening credits they would show a clip of Terry waggling his eyebrows at a throw-in. Like his mentor Sgt Bilko or Chandler's detective hero, he could ad lib any situation. The term 'media savvy' must have been coined with him in mind.

Venables would infuriate Docherty by a shrug of his shoulders or a look of total bewilderment at the Doc's tactics. The look was a straight cop from Norman Wisdom's act. Perhaps he had seen it when Norman had a fitting for one of his suits.

The sending-home incident unleashed a media frenzy. I cannot imagine what it would be like if it had happened today. They would probably bring out special tabloid editions to cover it. My father flew home from holiday in France to be greeted by more cameras than there were at the *Big Brother* house. I went to pick him up at the airport and he cracked, 'Is there someone famous on the plane?' The Doc told us the players had broken a curfew, the players blamed the manager for setting them up. We lost our last three matches and finished third. The 'catch us if you can' days were over . . .

Chapter Four: The Whole of the Moon

I saw the crescent, you saw the whole of the moon.
The Waterboys, 'The Whole of the Moon'

GEORGE GRAHAM

If Terry Venables was the Paul Newman character in the classic western *Butch Cassidy and the Sundance Kid*, then George Graham was the gunfighter played by Robert Redford, Sundance. The Kid was quiet, tough, and even prettier than his handsome partner. He was deeper, highly intelligent, moody, the sort that looked like he could cause trouble if pushed.

George was born in Bargeddie in Scotland on 30 November 1945, the same birthday as Winston Churchill and Gary Winston Lineker. He grew up in the next village, a place called Baillieston. George was the youngest of five boys and two girls. His father died of tuberculosis when he was only a fortnight old and his mother had a hard time bringing up a large family on a pittance. That early setback was to define his character and give him the underlying strength that was his trademark. George, like Hughie Gallacher before him, was another 'tanna' ball player, honing his skills in the kickabouts on the roads of the council estate where he grew up. Sometimes he would practise against a wall with a small goal chalked on it. This gave him the mastery of angles that made him such a deadly striker.

George played his first organised football in the Ayrshire and Coatbridge district school team. In the same team was the legendary Willie Henderson, a superb winger who graced the Rangers and Scotland sides. Affectionately known as 'Wee Willie', he was in the class of Charlie Cooke who could compare with Giggs or Figo today. Henderson and Graham, an irresistible combination, helped their team win the Scottish Schoolboys Cup. Soon George went on to win five schoolboy caps for his country. That is when his path first crossed that of a young Ron Harris, then playing for England in a midfield role. Barry Fry (people forget what a brilliant youngster he was) and Tommy Smith of

Liverpool also lined up for England in what must have been a formidable defence. Those games attracted crowds of 70,000 and were played at Wembley. George left school at 15, chased by the top sides on both sides of the border.

The boy from Bargeddie had witnessed first hand on the terraces of Hampden the superb Real Madrid side winning the European Cup 7–3 against Eintracht. The final was played in Glasgow that year. George advocated that of all the thousands of matches he was involved in, that game was the greatest display of football he ever saw. Imagine the young chap marvelling predictably at the sight of Alfredo di Stefano breaking from deep to score. That beautiful image was to haunt the dreams of George Graham throughout his life.

Ted Drake, at the behest of the genius talent-spotter Jimmy Thompson, invited Graham down to London for a week's trial at Chelsea. It was around the time that Jimmy Greaves was concluding his transfer to AC Milan. George was having a nightmare start to his London visit. He felt miserable and alienated, and his first trial game was postponed because the training ground was flooded after a storm of biblical proportions. The young Scot hated the bright lights of the big city and quickly returned home, very much like Greaves' stint in Milan. Newcastle were close to signing Graham but he opted to join Villa in 1960. A large Scottish contingent at Villa Park was a decisive factor in his choice.

The future Arsenal and Spurs manager made a huge impact in the Youth World Cup of 1963, which was played in England. It was a who's who of soon-to-be stars. George scored a hat-trick in the memorable clash with Greece held at Tooting, not far from Chelsea's old training ground in Mitcham. A riot broke out amongst the Greek fans and the trouble spilled over into the dressing-room. Mythology has it that George was knocked out by a pin-eyed Greek who was certainly not bearing gifts.

Scotland were knocked out by England, the eventual winners. Their team featured Harris again, along with another future Chelsea star, John Sissons. George spent four mainly unhappy years at Villa. Scoring on his full début against Liverpool, his time there started brightly. Bill Shankly was so impressed that he tried to lure him to Liverpool, without any success. George became increasingly frustrated with life at Villa. He thought that they were a team of the past, most of them ready to be dragged kicking and screaming to the knackers yard. If they were around today they would be offered an EC redevelopment grant. The young players had to do all the running for the older established pros, who only seemed interested in playing for themselves.

Villa had signed a player called Tony Hateley from Notts County. Big Tony was renowned for his ability in the air although he was less gifted on the ground, clueless almost. George's first-team chances were limited and the club were also worried about his growing reputation as a young playboy. In June

1964, Docherty, who had been monitoring his lack of progress in the Midlands, moved quickly to sign him. The fee was beyond embarrassment, £6,000, which was low even for those far-off days. The wretched time was over and the good (well, almost good) times were about to roll.

The young striker was an instant hit with Chelsea, scoring on his début against Sunderland. Luck plays a large part in football; the Sunderland defence was lumpen that day and was not helped by the fact that they had a 15-year-old in goal. George never looked back and ended up the top scorer in his first season at Chelsea, scoring 23 goals in 1964–65.

Docherty used him as an orthodox striker in the mould of Ian Hutchinson or Mark Hughes, a role that Geoff Hurst was to play so well for England. The glancing header that looped past Argentina's Antonia Roma in the controversial 1966 World Cup quarter-final was typical of the goals Graham scored for Chelsea. George was not as courageous a striker as Hurst or Hutch, but then who was? Technically he was a more gifted player than both, as he was to prove in his midfield role at Arsenal in their glory days. In his Chelsea career, though, he was essentially a target man and their finest exponent of heading. George's soaring reputation at Chelsea was based on his aerial power, the majority of his goals being near-post headers coming from set pieces.

I think one of the main reasons for his managerial success was that he quickly won the respect of established internationals. This was because they knew of his proven track record, not only as a manager but as a player. Les Ferdinand made the point that George 'has played in cup finals'.

His spell at Chelsea was brief and at times stormy. I used to see him driving his battered old Hillman Minx into the Bridge from his digs in Stamford Hill. Dave Sexton, Docherty's assistant, was a huge influence on him at that stage. Sexton spotted that beneath the laid-back, playboy image lay a deep-rooted love of the game. Popular with both the crowd and his team-mates, he had a reputation as a hell raiser. This was at odds with the strict, patriarchal image he cultivated as a manager. At Arsenal he seemed to rule with a rod of iron. The lessons he learned at Chelsea stood him in great stead throughout his career, the Blackpool débâcle in particular. In his own words, 'Tommy at Chelsea used to stand on the bridge and walk on the deck at the same time, a mistake for any manager.'

It was said that the young fighter Cassius Clay, before he blurred into Mohammed Ali, based his early persona on a wrestler called 'Gorgeous George'. George was a superhero he used to watch on Saturday afternoon TV. The Chelsea fans in 1965 had their very own 'Gorgeous George', who was the epitome of style and class. In the opening weeks of his Chelsea career he was very withdrawn. I used to see him flicking up the collar of his jacket like a schoolboy behind the bike sheds. He struggled to adapt. The Chelsea team then were nearly all Londoners (yes, honestly) who had grown up together from the youth teams. I recall Greaves' favourite song was 'Maybe It's Because I'm a Londoner'. Not one you get a lot of requests for now down at the Bridge, I bet. The morale amongst the players in the early days was sky-high. Their humour was very barbed and intricate, but the the swathes of ego that were to become part of the club's mentality in later years were not yet there. Like all macho environments, camaraderie was everything and gaining acceptance and respect was not easy. What did George and Terry talk about? A mutual love of music was the link that welded their friendship of nearly 40 years. Both were huge Sinatra fans.

George's drinking and fondness for the ladies never quite made the same impact on the headlines as that of his contemporary Peter Osgood. His headstrong independence never severed him from the basis of his wealth, fame and popularity, as it did with Hudson. Both Venables and Graham were cult heroes to the Shed, merely by being themselves. To this day, neither has been fooled by their own press for one second.

Season 1965–66 was another marathon, madcap season for Chelsea. They played 59 games in all, including runs to the semi-finals of both FA Cup and the Inter-Cities Fairs Cup, but soon the thread was to unravel. The Fairs Cup was a forerunner of the UEFA Cup. It was particularly strong because you only had big city teams with vast resources participating in it. Micro teams like Valeranga of Oslo, who Chelsea beat a few years ago in their Cup Winners' Cup-winning season, would simply not have figured. Some of the wonderful outfits that played in the competition that season were Red Star Belgrade, Sporting Lisbon, Antwerp, Valencia and Munich.

The season started slowly, with Docherty meditating on last season's failure and already showing signs of discontent with how things were progressing. He started tinkering with the side in gathering confusion. Joe Fascione, an underrated talent, played a few games on the flank. Peter Osgood, at the height of his creative power, was Docherty's great white hope, though. In a blaze of publicity Docherty moved Bridges, then the current England centre-forward, to the wing to accommodate Osgood in the number nine berth. The Chelsea supremo announced to the world that he would play Osgood in ten consecutive games, irrespective of his performances. The 'Wizard of Os', as he was instantly dubbed, soon repaid his faith. After a wobbly patch, the glints of brilliance were there for all to see. Osgood became the dominant force that season, dovetailing perfectly with Graham in a short-lived but successful striking partnership. Osgood was in those early days a gangly youth with wild, bushy hair. In later years, his main partner in crime, Alan Hudson, would look at the pictures from those far-off days and comment on his striking resemblance to a young Michael Barrymore. I was amongst the 7,936 Chelsea fans who saw his début that freezing night against Workington. As I meandered down the Kings Road to the steaming mug of tea that awaited me after the game, I wondered just how good he was.

Players have truncated careers and are brushed aside like rotting leaves when they are over. They circle the bowl then get sucked down. Some things survive, fragments in crumbling scrapbooks, a beam from a distant lighthouse. Graham and Osgood fell into this category. Docherty felt uneasy around George; he was too well dressed and unnaturally handsome to be a footballer.

Graham scored in the first-round, first-leg win over the unexceptional Roma in September. Roma are now one of the top clubs in Italy thanks to the signing of Gabriel Basituta, that pyrotechnic one-man display of attacking fire. The hero of the night was Venables, though, as he scored his first senior hat-trick to rout the Italian side. The second goal was another free-kick gag only Terry would have the cheek to pull. At first he pretended to organise the kick, awarded about 12 yards outside the penalty area, and placed the ball firmly down. The Docherty diamond geezer then waved the wall back pacing out the ten yards in an operatic way. To add spice to the act he held up his fingers, miming a count. A gap appeared in the Roma wall as the Italians were fooled into thinking he was going to stride back to take the kick. Instead he shouted back to Hollins to pass the ball to him. John rolled it forward and Terry instantly sidefooted it into the Roma net to score easily. Always clowning in those days, on and off the field. Flying out to Rome for the return leg Venables pulled one of his most famous stunts.

Blazered and Brylcreemed, the chaps were killing time at Heathrow before the flight to the war zone in Rome. I think the fare for the Supporters Club trip was £20. That would not cover the cab fare from Stamford Bridge to the airport these days, Terry was sitting at an empty airline check-in counter chatting to his close friend George, no doubt planning how to get away from the Doc. Both were wearing dark blue cashmere blazers and club ties. A passenger confusing them with airline staff requested directions, Venables always a frequent flyer pointed them out. Soon a line had formed of passengers eager to book in. Venables played along with the gag, handing out boarding cards, checking in luggage and enlisting Graham's help in stamping documents. The joke backfired though because soon the thing got out of hand as the crowd swelled. Docherty spotted the commotion and came over to me snapping, 'What are they up to now?'

'Come Fly With Me', the Sinatra anthem, was always a favourite of Terry's. He would croon a version in his short season at the Palais but that day at

Heathrow Airport he took it literally. The fun at the airport was soon forgotten as we faced the riot that erupted in Rome.

The first leg had been a roughhouse with Eddie McCreadie sent off; even Harris admitted it had been lively. Today Eddie would have been banned automatically from the return game. The Italian press whipped up a hate campaign against Chelsea, accusing the Stamford Bridge crowd of spitting at their players as they walked off the pitch. This was years before punk rock, whose birthplace was in the Kings Road, made such behaviour fashionable. Rome was the scene of the gladiatorial battles thousands of years before, but when Chelsea stepped out onto the pitch that night we all felt like Russell Crowe. Some nights you can smell the fear, the hate and the craziness. In the late '70s, when the game was in the grip of hooliganism, I could predict the nights when trouble would break out. Without doubt this was one of them. There was a bad moon rising.

My father was hit by a tomato, which splattered over his Gieves and Hawkes suit. Perhaps it was chucked by a Cerrutti fan, it was certainly a throw of Olympic proportions. As he flicked the vegetable away with his finger he smiled over at me and George, who was walking along the touchline, saying 'The natives are restless tonight.' I know he liked tomato sauce with his pasta, but this was absurd.

That was just the start; throughout the match Chelsea were pelted with everything the Roma fans could lay their hands on, fruit, coins, stones and paper rained down, even bottles of urine. The old Millwall joke crossed my mind, something about if they did not like the ref they would throw a bottle at him and if they really took a dislike to him they would pee in it before chucking it. I do not know whether the bottles were the same brand as those drunk by Gigi Peronace in his Knightsbridge flat when he was negotiating the Jimmy Greaves transfer.

A railing was ripped out of the fence and chucked at George Graham. It was like an Apache war lance and lodged in the pitch, just missing Boyle. George had more balls than most and ignored it. The verbal assault was a torrent of abuse, Venables was the chief target, he just grinned that Terry grin and cupped his ear. I did not understand the words but the message was understandable. Fireworks and flares exploded on the terrace. Graham was the subject of deliberate attempts at provocation throughout the game. Elbowed in the face, his toes stomped on, the usual. Another of their specials was when a Roma defender stopped dead in front of a running Chelsea player, this always ended with a free kick awarded to the home side. It finished 0–0 but the nightmare was not over yet. After the game we were invited to a banquet but en route the coach was ambushed by hundreds of angry Roma fans. The engine stalled and the windows started to disintegrate as the coach was bricked. If only their strikers had the accuracy of their fans. Docherty was a tower of strength as the fans tried to tip the coach over onto its side. They would have succeeded but the driver somehow managed to restart and we managed to roar away. Tommy was hit by a coin just under the eye and to this day still carries the scar. The battle of Rome ended with Roma being banned for three years from European competition.

Eddie MCreadie could have been killed by a brick through the rear window – only the bag at the back of his head saved him.

CHELSEA SILENCE THE KOP

After that, Liverpool never seemed as intimidating. In January 1966 we were drawn away to Liverpool, the Cup holders who had gone on to beat Leeds at Wembley after dumping us out at Villa Park. Docherty was desperate for revenge, I never saw him take a game so seriously. He saw Liverpool as the yardstick by which we measured our progress. We got off to the worst possible start. The tie was played in freezing conditions and the pitch was like the ice rink at Somerset House. In the opening minute Harris slipped in the slush as he went to crash tackle that fellow Peter Thompson again, Thompson whipped over a perfect cross and Roger Hunt (only a few months away from a World Cup winners medal as Hurst's strike partner), nodded a simple goal. It was a gift and the Blues looked on their way out of the cup already. Peter Osgood had other ideas though. The 'Wizard' grabbed a shock equaliser minutes afterwards. It was vital to level before Liverpool could settle into their stride, Bobby Tambling took a quick corner, Graham rose to back head and Osgood threw himself forward to head the first of a clutch of brilliant Chelsea cup goals. Sensing blood, Chelsea tore Liverpool apart in a devastating display of counterpunching. Venables' side was never happier than when a team was coming at them. They could counterpunch better than Prince Naz. Docherty had instilled such consummate quality into them. Perhaps that is the main difference between the Chelsea of then and the twenty-first-century line-up. Also, the camaraderie of the players was quite different then than now – one for all and all for one! The modern side create from the back and take the game to their opponents. The Mark 1 superside Chelsea loved soaking up the punishment then striking out like Ali against George Foreman in Zaire. Three times Bridges broke through on the run to face the bulky Liverpool goalkeeper Tommy Lawrence. The Everton fans nicknamed him 'the flying pig' I seem to recall. Three times he flew through the air to foil Barry, twice the ball hit his stomach, the other time his feet. Greaves would have had a hat-trick in that position with those chances. No disrespect to Barry, he was an England class player but Docherty made his life a misery sometimes over missed chances. At half-time it was still level, Docherty had asked Harris to defend the Kop in the first half so the Liverpool side did not have the decided advantage of kicking into that end in the closing stages. Named after a famous battle of the Boer War, the Kop was born in 1906, and made of cinders and rubble that was subsequently concreted over. Little had changed since then. The Shankly period saw an unprecedented bond between players and fans. The mass swaying to and fro and the spontaneous humour gave a degree of intensity to the atmosphere that was impossible to match anywhere. So many late penalties were given in front of the Kop as they roared their favourites on. Opponents and referees were simply overwhelmed.

Venables was oblivious to it. The Kop had the world premiere of their new work, 'If You All Hate Terry Venables, Clap Yer Hands'. Before he took a corner in the first half he borrowed a photographer's long-lensed camera and pretended to be shooting at the Kop with a machine-gun.

Liverpool stepped up a gear and were like a pack of wolves coming at the Londoners. Chelsea denied them though and midway through the second period they created a stunning winner. The move started with a Bonetti throw to McCreadie and ended five flowing passes later with Tambling heading over a bewildered Lawrence from Graham's centre. The atmosphere was the most electric I had known at Anfield. Near the end, with the Liverpool attack blunted by the tiger tackling of Ron Harris, the Kop melted away. Nobody stayed to clap off the heroic Londoners, so much for the sporting scouses with the Corinthian spirit. They always used to give us a good hand when they beat us though. Over 4,000 Chelsea fans made the trip north and gave us fanatical support which more than matched the Liverpool fans. That was one of the first occasions that I heard the 'Zigger Zagger' chant from the Chelsea pen.

THE KANGAROO KID

The next round of the cup saw the other finalists from 1965, the emerging bad boys Leeds, visit the Bridge. Bobby Tambling put Chelsea ahead in the opening minutes and that is how it stayed, thanks to Bonetti. One point blank save in the dying minutes from Jack Charlton was just incredible. It robbed Leeds of a deserved draw. A camera crew followed Docherty around for a week in early *Big Brother* style. He watched the game from a little observation post on the roof of the old East Stand, the camera squeezed in there and recorded his reaction when Tambling smashed home the winner. When he uttered the immortal line 'Go on my little diamonds', a thousand banners were born. Chelsea became

'Docherty's Diamonds'. Sandwiched around the Leeds game were three epic games with AC Milan, Jimmy Greaves' old firm. The Italian giants had been busy since Jimmy had defected to London, winning the championship and then the European Cup. The previous season, though, they had thrown away a seven-point lead (shades of our promotion season) to lose the league to their bitter rivals, Inter. That is why they were consigned to the Fairs Cup, rather like top clubs appearing nowadays in the UEFA Cup when they are booted out of the Champions League. That Milan side was crammed with talent. It included Cesare Maldini, father of the legendary Paolo. Cesare also managed his country. Another superstar was the famous defender Karl Schnellinger, who played in three World Cups for Germany. Giovanni Rivera was the kingpin of the side, the 'golden boy' of Italian football, an extraordinary grandstanding talent who was the era's Italian equivalent of Beckham. Another thunderingly good player was the Brazilian Amarildo, who replaced the injured Pelé in the 1962 World Cup. Some team.

We played at the San Siro three times that season. The previous October we had been invited to play against a combined AC and Inter Milan XI. AC had their usual suspects on duty and Inter chipped in with men like Luis Suarez, Facchetti and Sandro Mazzola. What that little lot would fetch on today's market could have funded the Millennium Dome for another few months. Chelsea went down 2–1 in a superb match. We lost by the same score in the first-leg tie against AC. The San Siro stadium hit me between the eyes every time I went there. There was a blaring noise from the bugles and horns used by the Milanese fans. George Graham headed our solitary goal, stealing half a yard on Maldini to get a vital touch. Graham almost shot a real opportunist equaliser in the dying minutes. The next day the *Daily Express* dubbed him the 'Kangaroo Kid'. Docherty noticed the susceptibility of the Milan side to driven crosses. Graham powered in our first goal in the home leg. His massive leap enabled him to soar above the Milan defence to thump in Venables' corner early in the game to set Chelsea up for a great victory. Heading was as much about anticipation as technique. George just got there first. Osgood scored the second with an incredible shot on the turn after spinning Schnellinger like a top. The Bridge was on fire as he hit the ball 'off his laces' and high into the net. Os had always a greater preparedness to use a shot earlier than most. In his early career his mentality was to shoot on sight.

Just on half-time, with Milan wilting under the ceaseless running of the Chelsea side, their Brazilian winger Sormani clipped in a vital goal. Sormani, who had played in the same Santos team as Pelé, squared the tie at 3–3. At the end of the game Harris lost the toss for the right to stage the third match. Incredible to think that matches of that importance were decided on the spin of a coin.

There were 59,541 in the Bridge that night, the gates were closed an hour before the kick off. The receipts for that match were £21,813, a record for any Chelsea home match, 57,847 fans had witnessed the Leeds Cup match four days before. When Chelsea played Milan in the Champions League the media talked about how glittering it all was but Venables' Chelsea team drew massive gates to watch them take on and beat the best sides in Europe.

Chelsea went back to Milan in early March and forced a 1–1 draw with Barry Bridges scoring. Eventually they went through on the spin of a coin, Ron successfully calling. Milan were due to lose out having won the previous four spins, three of them giving the right to stage play-offs at the San Siro and one actually putting them through.

March '66 was a particularly hectic time. Early in that month Manchester United visited the Bridge. It was three days after their epic 5–1 European Cup victory in Benfica. At that time the most significant result in the history of the club. The night that Best made the quantum leap from the spindly Irish youth with the overblown talent to icon. Best was still sporting the sombrero that he had brought back from Portugal and was immortalised hammily by the paparazzi. The Doc correctly predicted that United would still be walking on cloud nine. The Chelsea manager instructed Tambling and Graham to attack them from the very start, before they had settled. It worked like a dream and they both scored in the opening four minutes. That was how it stayed; 2–0, a famous victory in front of another massive crowd. Phew! Chelsea had another round in the Fairs Cup to negotiate against TSV München plus two rounds of the FA Cup. Graham was persistently stealing the headlines and scored the winner against Shrewsbury Town in the fifth round. Again he was on target against Hull. The Tigers were knocked out on their own ground after scoring two late goals at the Bridge to force a draw. Fixture congestion meant that Chelsea had the home game against Hull on the Saturday, the second leg of the TSV München game on the Tuesday then on to the replay up at Hull on Thursday. Funnily enough that was election night and there was a fuss in the papers about it. The season like so many before perished on the vine. At the time critics said that Chelsea were not up to it, or to use that modern hateful expression 'up for it', whatever that is supposed to mean. When it came to the crunch they were found wanting. The inhuman demands made upon such a young team were too much for anybody. Examine the facts. In the space of a few months they had beaten the German World Cup side, AC Milan, Liverpool and Leeds, the previous year's cup finalists, a Manchester United team that included Best in the most dazzling form of his career (as well as Bobby Charlton and Dennis Law, both in their prime). The only thing that beat them was fatigue. The game is faster today, but an Owen or a Hasselbaink still receives more protection than George Graham or Osgood (who was soon to find this out in the most horrific manner) ever did. The Venables–Graham side could have been the greatest Chelsea side of all time in my view, and perhaps for a short while in that wet spring of 1966 it was.

Sheffield Wednesday beat Chelsea 2–0 in the FA Cup semi-final at Villa Park which for the second season running became a boneyard of Chelsea dreams. Chelsea were fancied to win even more heavily than they were against Liverpool. Sheffield Wednesday were just a workman-like side. When I saw the pitch, though, my heart sank. The surface was heavier than a Led Zeppelin concert. It had rained all week and was churned up. I would rather have played the game back in Rome with the spearchuckers and pee bottles. Wednesday started dishing out leather early, George Graham was singled out as being the main threat and took a buffeting in the first few moments that knocked the stuffing out of him. Bridges went down from a forearm smash that would have been banned in a WWF tag match. After a purple patch of magical goals Osgood was looking tired and run down. A new strip was devised by the Doc for the semi-final; heavily influenced by the Italian trips, he had decided to adopt the colours of Inter, navy with black stripes. He was keen to make this the permanent strip, the only proviso being that we won. The team looked to Venables. Docherty had stripped him of the captaincy around the time of the Blackpool Eight and given it to Ron Harris, phoning Terry in the middle of the night to inform him of this fact. Villa Park was a Rourke's Drift for Terry Venables though, the odds were so high. It was left to a former Chelsea youth player by the name of Jimmy McCalliog to run the game. The problem was that Docherty had sold him to Sheffield Wednesday the season before for a record fee for a teenager. McCalliog was very highly rated at the club, particularly by Tommy Harmer, now a youth team coach. Due to the form of Venables, young Jimmy was unable to break into the first team and Chelsea reluctantly sold him. Today, with the squad system, a player with the talent of Jimmy McCalliog would have been accommodated.

McCalliog scored the second goal for Wednesday with a diving header near the end. It signalled the end of Venables' career at the Bridge. The defeat at the hands of the artisans of Sheffield proved more than Docherty could bear. In a fit of pique he started to dismantle the Diamonds. Graham alleged that Docherty told him in the dressing-room that the players were still the future of the club. Outside, though, he was telling the tabloids that the team was not good enough.

Barcelona were next on our agenda, but the Doc was carrying out his own version of the movie *Brewster's Millions*, in which a football manager has to splurge as much money in as short a time as possible in the hope that he gets more money. The Doc went out and bought Charlie Cooke from Dundee as a replacement for Venables and Ron's brother Alan Harris returned to the club.

In the first game in the hilly coastal region of Catalonia the Blues lost 2–0. The Battersea-born winger Peter Houseman made a rare start in the first team. The Doc was concerned that Graham and Osgood were not getting the service to exploit their aerial superiority. Only Bonetti saved Chelsea that night as the classy Barca strikers bombarded them throughout the game. The return match was played out in bizarre circumstances. Docherty called the local fire brigade out to water the pitch, as he had an idea that a sodden pitch would suit Chelsea more than Barca. Docherty gave Cooke his Chelsea début; it was the only time that both he and Venables were to play at Stamford Bridge. Two own goals gave Chelsea a draw. Harris (R.) and his brother Alan also played that night, lost the toss and Chelsea went back to the towering Nou Camp stadium.

The '66 team were outclassed in the same manner as Barcelona crushed Vialli's team in the Champions League. The play-off semi-final was the first European football match that was transmitted back to England and shown live on closed circuit TV. The game in Barcelona was watched by over 40,000 fans whilst 9,000 filed into a rainy Stamford Bridge to watch on six screens. They had a grim evening as Barca cruised to a 3–0 lead at half-time, eventually running out 5–0 winners. In Barcelona they have a word, *fibra*, which means temperament. Chelsea's *fibra* cracked that night as the bombastic strike partnership of Fuste and Rife grabbed two goals apiece. Had Chelsea avoided defeat at the hands of Barcelona they would have met Real Zaragoza in the final. It was held over till the following season. I never did find out who won it.

Eighteen years later Venables was to return to the Catalan capital as manager, yet another twist to the plot of his pulp fiction life. At that time Barca were struggling frantically to emerge from the long shadows of Real Madrid. They had not won the league for eleven seasons, despite a bottomless pit of money, and there were serious doubts that the young Englishman was up to the job. Instantly those doubts melted away. Venables, as if sauntering into the Roma defensive wall, picked up the microphone and addressed the multitude in passable Catalan, a language he had been studying for two years after scouring London for someone to teach him. His first act was to axe the player recently voted the most famous of the twentieth century but already crippled by injury and drugs, Diego Maradona. Within a year the title was won . . .

The Diamonds were scattered like POWs escaping Colditz. As the Doc once told me, 'football was a rat race and the rats were winning'. Barry Bridges stormed out of the airport en route to Barcelona when Docherty turned up with his new capture, Charlie Cooke. He was sold to Birmingham along with Bert

Murray. Venables was sold to Tottenham and a few weeks into season 1966–67 George Graham was sold to Arsenal for £50,000 and a player called Tommy Baldwin, nicknamed 'The Sponge'.

In 102 games he had scored 46 goals and was top goalscorer in the two full seasons he played.

Chapter Five: London Calling

No one ever reaches a high position without daring.
Publilius Syrus

A Mears was a central figure in the second most famous crime of the century; when the World Cup was stolen! On 20 March 1966, a few days after Chelsea's pulverising victory over Manchester United, the Jules Rimet trophy was heisted from a showcase at the Stanley Gibbons stamp exhibition at the Central Hall in Westminster. My father Joe was chairman of the Football Association as well as Chelsea at that time. The Association had loaned the World Cup to Stanley Gibbons so that they could exhibit it as a special attraction, a case of life imitating art.

The whole crime was a comedy of errors that merited its own X-file in the internal Metropolitan Police archives. The file was closed for over 30 years but was made available in recent times. The trophy was insured for £30,000 (less than half of the fee paid by Tottenham for Venables), but its actual value was £3,000. The thief was a fellow called Edward Betchley, who gained entry into Central Hall by unscrewing a brass doorplate on the back door. Betchley then forced open the showcase by busting the padlock. (The World Cup was secured only by a padlock?!) England had a fantastic ironclad defence including Moore and Banks, which helped them to win the World Cup, but Betchley had found a gap in the defensive system. Amazingly, the two private security guards on duty had left the Jules Rimet unattended; one was sipping a coffee and the other was in the loo.

The country was in an uproar. Can you imagine it happening today? The reward would settle your mortgage. The media would be warning of a movement to undermine the foundations of society.

The next day Joe Mears received a mysterious call advising him that he would be receiving a parcel at the Bridge and that he should follow the instructions to the letter. The post was better in those days and the next day, sure enough, a piece of the World Cup turned up with the following ransom note. Excuse the grammar and the spelling – the note has been reproduced word for word.

No doubt you view with very great concern the loss of the world cup to me it is only so much weight in scrap gold so if you want to see it again i suggest you do as i say and follow my instruction.

First if the press or police are informed of this, this cup will go into the melting pot addmitted i only get a fraction of the money i want but i shall be safe and you lose the cup forever but if you are willing to pay me ££15,000 in £5 and £1 pound notes you shall have your cup back and you will be satisfied and so will the rest of the WORLD.

If you agree with this follow these instructions.

Insert in Thursdays Evening News Personal Column, Willing to do business signed. Joe.

Second contact will be by phone to Chelsea F.C.

Find enclosed top of World Cup. To prove Genuine.

IS TRESS ONCE AGAIN THAT THIS CUP IS ONLY SO MUCH SCRAP TO ME AND REPEAT AND DO NOT INFORM PRESS OR POLICE.

It would be a great pity to destroy this cup in view of its great history and beauty it porttrays.

If i do not hear from you by Thursdays or Friday at the latest issume its one for the POT.

Within ten minutes of opening the parcel Joe received a call from Betchley using the alias of Jackson. After confirming receipt of the note, he demanded £15,000 in £5s and £10s immediately. If he received the money on Friday he would put the cup in a cab on Saturday morning. My father went straight to the police. Detective Sergeant Jack Slipper was still chasing Ronnie Biggs and the rest of the criminals who had looted the Glasgow mail train three years earlier, so the case was put in the charge of Detective Inspector Charles Buggy of Scotland Yard's Flying Squad. He soon formed a cunning plan. Barclays Bank made up several envelopes to represent the £15,000 but the bulk was paper; that old gag used in every cop show.

On Friday Buggy went to my father's home in the Fulham Road. The plan was to pretend that my father was ill in bed with angina. This had an element of truth because his health was ailing and sadly he was to die within a few months of the theft. My stepmother was worried about the robbery and she wanted Ronnie Harris and his brother to act as minders. Mick Greenway had also phoned Chelsea to offer the services of the Shed in tracking down the whereabouts of football's most coveted prize.

When Betchley called a meeting it was scheduled for nearby Battersea Park. Betchley was advised that a family friend, a Mr McPhee (Buggy) would be coming off the subs bench to act as a representative and conclude the transaction with the cup thief.

Betchley was at first dubious but agreed to the meet in the shadow of the power station. The power station has stood empty since about the time I abdicated at Chelsea but to me it was the biggest icon in London. Perhaps it was the Pink Floyd album cover that made it so, or was it the Wonderbra advert that sealed its legend? Designed in 1931, the year I was born, by Sir Giles Gilbert Scott, who also designed the red telephone box, the power station was the most potent image of London. Driving over the bridge to the Bridge on an autumn evening with the drama of the power station in all its grandeur on one side and the lights of Stamford Bridge in the distance . . . You just felt uplifted.

The police had squad cars in the power station and plain-clothes officers in the park. Buggy drove my father's Ford Zodiac to the meet. Just like in the Tom Cruise movie *Jerry Maguire*, Betchley asked Buggy to show him the money. Buggy held up some notes and, seemingly satisfied, the cup stealer asked Buggy to drive him to St Agnes Place in Kennington. Buggy obliged, but Betchley became concerned when he spotted an undercover van that was trailing the Zodiac. The van was apparently shaken off by the detective inspector, but it turned up later at St Agnes Place. Betchley's nerve deserted him; he was no Harry Roberts. He jumped out of the fawn car and made an escape over some back gardens, but despite moving quicker than Tampling he was eventually cornered in an alley after a long chase and hauled away by the rozzers.

I do not know if Betchley was a Chelsea fan, but he followed the strict Headhunters code of silence and for the next 48 hours told the police nothing. The nation was in bowel-loosening turmoil while the cup was still missing. The police raided the houses of every known associate of Betchley but came up with nothing. The government were asking questions and the press spilt so much ink on the story that even the Beatles were relegated to the inside page. The police were slaughtered in the foreign press because the myth soon grew that they had been guarding the Jules Rimet trophy. 'A catalogue of bungling and astonishing ineptitude,' the French tabloids gloated.

Like I always say and Mariah Carey sang, 'then a hero comes along'. Pickles the dog became a national hero when on the Sunday night he found the parcel containing the cup under a bush in Upper Norwood, South London. How it got to be there nobody can tell you to this day. Draw your own conclusions about it. The story ended happily; the cup (designed by French sculptor Abel LaFleur) did not have a scratch, Pickles's owner copped the £6,000 reward and a few months later Moore went up the stairs at Wembley to lift the World Cup for the only time. Betchley appeared at the Old Bailey, pleaded guilty and drew two years.

SUNNY AFTERNOONS

At noon on Friday, 1 July 1966, whilst walking in an Oslo park, my father Joe collapsed and died. He had been chairman of Chelsea since 1940 and of the Football Association since 1963. His death at the relatively young age of 61 devastated me personally. For the club it was the proverbial string that once pulled, unravelled the skein of relationships that held the team together.

My father had accompanied the England squad on the pre-World Cup warm-up which included victories over Finland and Norway. He died less than a month before England won the World Cup and did not live long enough to see his beloved Chelsea's first Cup win. My father had attained his remarkable position in the game primarily as a result of his talents as an organiser. He always spoke in measured tones that appeared to convey great wisdom. Joe was been born in 1905, the same year that his father and uncle founded CFC. A goalkeeper for the Old Malvernians, he became the youngest director in football when appointed to the Chelsea board in 1931. So the young, soccer-mad whiz kids who later made it to the boardroom did not really start with Matthew Harding and Steve Gibson.

Joe always kept his feelings under control, win or lose, and he was on the wrong end of some truly atrocious luck at times. Never better than when entertaining post-match, he knew what to say and when to say it, whilst other chairmen were known to court controversy.

Docherty started season 1966–67 wearing the stunned expression of Count Dracula on a sunny afternoon. He could scarcely believe that his team had been involved in the public abortion of their dreams of honours for two successive seasons. My father's death had shaken him to the very core of his being. They had mutual respect for one another, and Tommy knew exactly how far he could push things like his career concerns with my father. Joe Mears's successor as chairman was Bill Pratt, 'Pratt by name, Pratt by nature', the Doc would always say. Docherty could barely conceal his contempt for him. The Chelsea manager was about to destroy his career and some of the team with his psychological war games.

Chelsea had no Europe open to them that season and already I had misgivings about the long-term future of the club with Docherty. I sensed my father also had some reservations. He had always kept the corporate insanity away from the players and the top brass at arm's length from the dressing-room. He saw that the young, impressionable players on whom Docherty had tried his theories of football were soon discarded if things did not work out and it worried him. I know he was sorry to see Venables leave the club. The hair-line cracks were appearing around that time. Morale was high amongst the fans, though, even after having suffered so many near misses. It had been a colourful odyssey and there was a feeling amongst most supporters that this could be our year. A trip to Wembley at least.

The opening fixture could not have been harder, away to West Ham at Upton Park. Chelsea had never won a league game there and they had been trying since 1923. World Cup fever was still raging, particularly down in the East End. The three players who had made the biggest contribution to the triumph were lining up in claret and blue that afternoon: captain Robert Chelsea (yes, honestly, it was his middle name, look it up) Moore; hat-trick hero and future Chelsea manager Hurst; and the other goalscoring hero of the most dramatic final in World Cup history, Martin Peters. The sellers outside the Boleyn pub had T-shirts proclaiming 'West Ham won the World Cup'. Who on that afternoon of Ethiopian heat could dispute that assertion?

Chelsea silenced the East Enders on the opening day of that extraordinary season with a tremendous display of attacking football. John Hollins smashed them ahead in the first half with a raking free kick that the departed Venables would have been proud of. Hollins's drive beat the Hammers' goalkeeper Jim Standen after an intricate charade involving Tambling, McCreadie and Terry's replacement, Charlie Cooke. Ronnie Boyce, who had scored a cup-winning goal, equalised for West Ham in a fast, epileptic second half. Near the end, Cooke opened his Chelsea account. Dribbling past one defender, Cooke then feinted to move down the line as Moore came in to tackle. Moore was still transferring his weight to his left leg in an attempt to follow. Meanwhile Cooke changed direction and headed inside with a burst of acceleration before cracking a fierce low shot into the corner of the net to win the game for the Blues. When Cooke had the ball there was only one thing on his mind, and that was to take someone on. The fact that it happened to be Moore, the only Englishman to lift the Jules Rimet trophy (thanks to Pickles the dog), the outstanding player of the tournament and the defender with the greatest appreciation of positional play ever, meant nothing to Charlie. It was the most audacious début by a Chelsea player I ever saw.

The World Cup success of '66 heralded the decline in wing play. Greater emphasis on possession and workrate made the dribbler a luxury. How did they get it so wrong? The Scot needed no space to operate in, for nobody had greater mobility on the ball. Modern footballers can play if they have acres of space.

This gives vital time to think and it also meant not acting quickly or having to make instant decisions. The same player that could do anything in ten yards of space would lose the ball and panic if they only had five yards to operate.

Cooke was born in October 1942 at St Monans, Fife. In the summer of 1960 he signed professional for Aberdeen from Renfrew Juniors. He made his début in season 1960–61 and later joined Dundee in December 1964. The following season he was voted their player of the year. He was around for a couple more seasons before the Doc swooped to sign him. At Stamford Bridge the gestation of his talent was instant. Cooke was the most perverse, cocky and mesmerising player I ever saw. He was always there at the right time, not too early, not too late. Charlie's prime role was vital to the team. If he released the ball too early then the midfield could not keep up, if he gave it too late then the speed went out of the attack. Cooke bound the whole team together. Although I felt that towards the end of his first spell with Chelsea he would play too far forward, in the early days he controlled the whole game and gave me some of my most cherished moments.

Cooke's contemptuous treatment of Moore was a challenge to the rest of the capital. Wasn't it brilliant? Charlie was the new kid on the block. Charlie had travelled south with a growing reputation and he had a point to prove. Venables had been the King of the Kings Road but Charlie wanted to rule London Town. The Doc was excited by his capture and hyperbole abounded. To him managing was like winemaking. The players were his grapes, some of them burnt, some of them not quite ripe; the sugar was not yet right. With a lot of sweat, though, you could make great wine.

In Docherty's cramped office there was a little picture of the Chelsea manager posing with his former captain, Venables, taken the night they won the League Cup. Since then the road had twisted and forked. Venables had gone one way, his peers for the most part had gone the other. The Doc had Cooke now, and the renaissance prince, Osgood.

A few days before Cooke had left Moore in rags on the Upton Park turf a man called Harry Roberts achieved cult status amongst the criminal classes by murdering three policemen in Shepherd's Bush.

THE TEARS OF AUTUMN

Following their success at Upton Park, Chelsea hit the front like Frankie Dettori chasing his seventh winner at Ascot that memorable day. Osgood hit both goals as Chelsea beat Forest before a packed Stamford Bridge. Around that time I received a letter from M.C. Webb requesting that the Fulham Road End be called the 'Shed' as that was the area where the fanatics stood. Reference was made to the fact that the Shed sounded a likely place for the 'Blue Submarine' to be housed. The Beatles had just put out their song 'The Yellow Submarine', which had been adopted by the Shed as a theme song. Of course they had repainted it.

Alex Stepney played his only game in goal for Chelsea in the 3–0 victory at Southampton in early September. Docherty was having problems with Bonetti and a new contract. Tommy had spotted the potential in Stepney, who was playing for Millwall at the time. Perhaps he was being a bit too clever for his own good, but he was anxious to sign Alex and begged the board to buy him. Docherty was a globetrotter and loved nothing more than taking the team to such far-flung places as Australia and all over Europe. To the married players such as Bobby Tambling (undergoing some religious upheavals around this time) and family man Bonetti this was not such an attractive prospect. Mobile phones were yet to arrive, and it also took that much longer to get anywhere. I always sensed a problem in the relationship between the trio. As well, Docherty's futuristic dream was to build up a super-strong squad of crack players. His idea was to play Bonetti in one game and Stepney in another, pre-rotation, pre-Vialli. Stepney was soon on his way to Old Trafford, where he carved out a brilliant career and won a European Cup medal. Stepney's incredible stop from Eusebio in the final's closing minutes of normal time set up the extra-time win. United fans always saw the purchase of Alex as a microcosm of the gulf between the two clubs (the brains and the brawn from the North and the greed and artifice from London, perhaps). Alex was a superb keeper but Bonetti was, well, Bonetti.

Tambling hit five goals at Villa Park as we crushed the Villa 6–2 to exorcise the ghosts of our two semi-final defeats on that ground. As Bobby sliced and diced the claret and blue defence I sensed a new purpose in our play. After James Greaves, Tambling was the greatest goal machine in the history of the club. Though the record individual score is still six goals, scored by George Hilsdon in 1906–07 against the mighty Glossop in a Second Division game (no, I did not see that one before you ask), it was Tambling's first five-goal performance in his career and equalled Jimmy's achievement in scoring all the goals at Preston in a 5–4 win. That was one of the most bizarre games I ever saw. Jimmy scored first, then Preston equalised, and that is how it went on. It was very disorientating for everybody concerned. When Preston made it 4–4 an angry Greaves berated the Chelsea defence, 'Whatsuup! [predating the Bud ad] Every time I score you give a goal away. When I get to five that's it.'

True to his word, Jimmy nipped in for his fifth goal and the embarrassed Blues defence held out. The Villa attack was not such a problem, although the big fellow, Hateley, who had kept George Graham out of the Villa attack, did give us some problems in the air and scored. That was George's last game for Chelsea. The following Friday he joined Arsenal for £50,000 and a young striker called Tommy Baldwin. Baldwin was spotted by an Arsenal scout playing for a Gateshead junior club and scored ten goals in 19 games for the North London side. Docherty had been impressed by Baldwin's display against Chelsea a few weeks earlier. The situation with Graham had deteriorated and a move was in the interests of both parties. It couldn't have got any worse.

Twenty-one-year-old Tommy scored at Maine Road the next day on his début as Chelsea thrashed Manchester City 4–1. There seemed no stopping Chelsea as they equalled their longest unbeaten sequence at the start of a season. They had gone ten games winning six and drawing four, the previous best had been also ten games in which only three were drawn and all the rest won.

Tambling scored his 150th first-team goal in the City game but the star of Maine Road, as he had been so far all that season, was Osgood. He was still a fledgling really, but in the Manchester City match he reached new heights, literally walking through the sky-blues' defence before picking his spot to score between their goalkeeper and the near post. Osgood was the axis of the team, he was a phenomenon. Peter has the lot; power, skill and pace. Above all was the deceptive speed that took him past defenders when the moment looked lost and it set Osgood apart from the other 'flair players' of that era. He had the acceleration of those zippy Mini Coopers that were roaring up and down the Kings Road in that golden summer and early autumn of 1966. John Cooper, who invented the Mini Cooper, died at Christmas 2000, but he lived to see his car immortalised on celluloid in *The Italian Job*. Osgood received a credit in the film, the famous 'Osgood is God' slogan daubed on the side of the gang's van. Michael Caine was the star of the film. I met him once in a Knightsbridge restaurant. A keen football fan, he lived in Chelsea Harbour near the birthplace of Alan Hudson.

On 5 October 1966, Chelsea were drawn to play Blackpool in the second round of the Football League Cup. The world was just an amusement park for Peter Osgood. He was the leader of the Chelsea set. An emerging Kings Road dandy, Osgood could take his place alongside those other London All Stars, Mick and Keith from the Stones, Caine in his 'Harry Palmer' glasses, Ron and Reggie in the Blind Beggar, a Hurst volley away from Upton Park. Swinging London lasted barely two years. Elitist, style-obsessed and narcissistic, it was destined not to flourish, like the talents of Docherty's Diamonds and one Peter Osgood. Chelsea had plugged into the Zeitgeist of the moment. The hard times of the late '70s were a galaxy away. Osgood had come a long way from the building sites of Windsor to the cusp of the big time. Like the hero in *The Great*

Gatsby, his dream was already behind him. The dream of being the greatest footballer this country ever produced.

Osgood broke his leg that starry night in a sickening clash with Emlyn Hughes. I never liked Hughes either as a successful player with Liverpool, or later as one of the Scouse 'Talking Heads' (today we have Messrs Hansen and Lawrenson) that perpetuated the myth of Liverpool Football Club. Osgood always had a strong sense of self-preservation. He had clashed with Hughes early in the game and was preparing for another crunching tackle. The break was very, very bad. Osgood, despite the great career he was still to have at Stamford Bridge, was in my view never the same player again. Those close to him would later notice a slight change in his character. On the field he was always looking for the tackle first. The quest for perfection ended that night at Bloomfield Road. The Chelsea striker never recovered the killer burst of pace he had before the accident. Osgood retained his own pavonine skills which were both arrogant and effortlessly brilliant, but they acted as a smokescreen for the psychological battle he had already lost within himself.

Peter had the skill to have become the greatest centre-forward ever to have played for England. Even better than Nat Lofthouse, Charlton, Shearer, anyone you care to mention, Osgood was amongst the greatest players who ever played for Chelsea; Greaves, Gallacher, Zola *et al*. World-class players like Vialli and Gullit have played in recent years, but that was at the end of their careers and whilst fans saw glimpses of their talent, it would be unfair to include them.

Osgood epitomised swinging London as much as David Bailey or Paul McCartney, celebrating and celebrated, inaccessibly cool. Perhaps it all went wrong that night.

Peter Houseman, whom Docherty largely ignored, scored the goal that earned Chelsea a draw that night, and also scored in the replay. Chelsea, unbeaten before Osgood's accident, were devastated by the tragic loss of their superstar. Blackpool knocked Chelsea out of the League Cup 3–1 and Burnley won by the same score at the Bridge to end the unbeaten league run. Blackpool was Docherty's Stalingrad. His master plan to rule the world with his young team came unstuck there twice. The previous year had seen him send the core of the team home in disgrace after the 'incident' and now his protégé left the seaside town with his leg smashed. It was so bad that I thought he would be lucky to walk again, let alone play at the highest level.

The Doc was quick to act to fill the gap left by the injury to the young emperor's leg. The press scented blood, another soap opera unfolding. The old 'Chelsea Crisis' headline was trotted out. Headlines come and headlines go whether it is concerning Thatcher, Clinton or Blair, but one that runs and runs and will still be used long after my time is 'Chelsea Crisis'. It covered every manager from Ted Drake to the chap that cannot speak English terribly well, Ranieri. Compared to someone like Jamie Oliver his English sounded passable enough!

Tommy signed Tony Hateley from the Villa for £1,00,000, a fortune for those times. As much in a way as Chelsea were to pay for Sutton. The fans would call both 'White Elephants'. The significance of the colour was lost at that time, but the elephant could have been applicable to the Hateley deal. The similarity does not end there; both had brief unhappy spells with the club. Hateley's spell might have been marginally more productive that Chris's. Tony had no equals in the air, he could head a ball harder than most players could kick it. When he headed a stunning goal against Sheffield United in the Cup, the following spring, those who were lucky enough to witness it literally saw the net vibrate, such was the power it was struck with. Hateley's problems started when the ball was played to him on the ground. His first touch was non-existent and I saw the bulldozers that knocked down the old East Stand turn quicker. Chelsea had to modify their style to accommodate him.

Christmas 1966 saw West Ham return to the Bridge and one of the most amazing games of all time was played out as a 5–5 draw. Even the connoisseurs of the many bizarre matches played out at Stamford Bridge left the ground totally baffled by the events of the afternoon. The game contained literally everything. Bonetti made perhaps the greatest save of his life to keep out a Peters header. Peter literally bent himself double to scoop out the World Cup hero's effort when it looked a certain goal. Martin's loping header dropped over the goalkeeper's head but somehow he cleared it. Later Martin scored a goal fit to win a World Cup. Chelsea ended up scrambling a draw from a game that they dominated from start to finish. They urinated on the Hammers defence from a great height. Strange as it may seem, for the first 25 minutes it was scoreless, a few missed chances then the floodgates opened. The scoring went like this: 0–1, 0–2, 1–2, 2–2, 3–2, 3–3, 3–4, 3–5, 4–5, 5–5. Chelsea scored the last two goals in the closing seven minutes.

My abiding memory of that crazy game is of Tony Hateley. With the scores locked at 5–5 and the referee looking at his watch, Charlie Cooke swerved past Moore again and crossed low to Hateley. Big Tony had beaten the Hammers' offside trap and was practically standing in the back of the net. All the ex-Villa man had to do was guide the ball over the line and into the net to win it 6–5, but instead he stooped to try and head it over the line! The ball was barely above the ground. He missed the ball completely and it rolled past an unguarded net and outside the post. Tony did a pratfall into a huge puddle as he tried to head it home. The crowd streamed away to their Christmas holiday trying to make some sense of it all. Pity it was never shown on TV. I recall

Sutton, making his Chelsea début, fell over in front of an empty goal twice but Hateley was even closer. A cold sweat pours over me when I recall it.

Once I tried to buy a young Liverpool forward from Bill Shankly. The lad was putting in some startlingly great performances but had a reputation for being a little dense, shall we say. 'All his brains are in his feet,' I recall Bill saying. You could paraphrase the Shanklyism and mention that Tony's brains were certainly where they should have been, in his head. Shankly actually bought Hateley from us. Wherever he went he scored goals. Today, with a crosser like Zandfer or Ginola feeding him, Hateley would clean up. Houseman would have been the perfect winger for Hateley but Docherty remained unconvinced of the Battersea boy's talent. Boyle replaced him in the side as Chelsea's motor spluttered. Three straight defeats over Christmas blew any lingering chance of the title. On New Year's Eve Sheffield Wednesday, our *bête noire*, crushed Chelsea 6–1 at Hillsborough to round off a turbulent year. Our only hope for the season was the FA Cup.

THE COLOUR OF RAIN

Chelsea had a tricky tie away to Huddersfield in the third round of the FA Cup. Houseman was back in the team and opened the scoring which helped the Blues gain a narrow 2–1 win over the Yorkshire side. Tambling was enjoying his best season and shot the second-half winner.

Tambling scored again in the first few minutes of the fourth-round tie away to Brighton. The old Goldstone ground was packed to the rafters as 35,000 jammed in. Receipts were a club record £8,500, which today would just about buy a few season tickets in the Matthew Harding Stand. Bobby's goal was spectacular even by his standards. The Chelsea man burst through from the centre circle leaving a trail of defenders in his wake, and machine-gunned home from the edge of the box. Chelsea looked set for an easy win. Boyle was sent off shortly afterwards though for fighting. All hell broke loose as the Seasiders tore into ten-men Chelsea. Their skipper Turner equalised after a terrific scramble in the goalmouth and we were lucky to hang on for the replay. Sporadic fights broke out on the terraces as Chelsea fans took on the locals. The atmosphere was very tense.

After the match the *Daily Express* chief football correspondent, Desmond Hackett, criticised Chelsea's performance and announced that he would walk barefoot from Wembley in the unlikely event of Chelsea wining the Cup. The *Express* had a superb cartoonist called Roy Ullyett whose caricatures of the game's leading characters gave a dimension to the coverage of the matches that is sadly lacking today. In the replay Chelsea butchered Brighton 4–0. Tambling thumped in two goals with his exocet left foot. Tony Hateley hit his first Cup goal and reserve defender Alan Young popped in the last.

Sheffield United were the visitors in the fifth round of the Cup. Tambling again scored his obligatory goal and then Hateley's wonderful net-bursting header clinched victory. Bobby limped off 20 minutes from time with a back injury. That spoilt his perfect attendance record and cost him a place in a Football League eleven against the Scottish League at Hampden. Tambling was taking a terrific pounding every week, which was to shorten his career. With the news on Osgood not good (his injury was even worse than feared and the bone was taking a long time to knit together) and Graham transferred, there was a terrific weight on Bobby's hunched shoulders.

In early March Chelsea visited White Hart Lane in what some shrewd critics saw as a rehearsal of the Cup final. Ian (Chico) Hamilton, at 16 years four months and 18 days, became the youngest first-team player in the history of the club when he made his début against Tottenham. The youngster took the place of the injured Tambling. In the second half Chico out-jumped Mackay to head home a corner for Chelsea's equaliser. Another record that is unlikely to be broken – the youngest player to score on his début.

Also playing for Spurs that day was a young winger called Keith Weller who gave Ron's brother Alan a torrid time with his pace and aggression. Ron Harris had his hands full too, marking Greaves, who had put Spurs ahead in the first half. Missing out on the World Cup final had broken his heart. His personal vendetta against opposing goalkeepers was even more vengeful that season as he rattled in goal after goal. Greaves now had the *joie de vivre* of a nineteenth-century Russian peasant. When the final whistle blew though I noticed Greaves was the first over to congratulate Chico on scoring on his début. I really need to employ the Vaseline fade used by the '50s film makers here, but I was wondering if Greaves' mind was going back a decade to another young Chelsea striker who scored on his début on the same ground . . . Then Greaves had been the 'new kid in town' but now he was the *numero uno* gunslinger and there was only one place to go from there.

Chico, Greaves' doppelgänger, was born in Streatham in 1950 one chilly spring afternoon. The young blond was a product of Houseman's old school, Spencer Park in Wandsworh. Discovered by Frank Blunstone, Chico (who got his nickname from a famous jazz musician of the day) was rated as good a prospect as the Hudson brothers. Many said he had a better temperament. Chico should have been the next Greaves, the instant replacement for the damaged Osgood, but injuries and inconsistent form blighted his Chelsea progress. Perhaps it had a lot to do with the egotistical attitude of his peer group. They dissipated their energy on drink and women. Chico carved out a long career in the game though, playing for Aston Villa and Sheffield United. To me he looked a dead ringer for the lead singer in a '60s pop group called Love Affair. Guys that pretty Chelsea typecast, and they often burnt out fast . . . Alan Birchenall and Teddy Maybank with their peroxided hair spring to mind, as well as Mickey Fillery with his trapezoidal cheekbones. They all faded like Roman candles after brief flashes of brilliance in the Blue. Perhaps they thought they had to play in a manner as stylised and extreme as their looks.

Peter Houseman was never a pretty boy, the Shed had nicknamed him 'Mary'. His predecessor in the team, Albert Murray (now exiled in Birmingham), was christened 'Ruby'. Pre-Beatles Ruby was the Britney of her day and highly successful. She was so famous that her name (albeit helped by the connection with the Chelsea star) passed into Cockney rhyming slang: Ruby Murray = Curry. Though not many of the Shed's inhabitants would admit to partaking such culinary.delights. This was still the '60s, remember. It was natural that anyone with that surname would earn the soubriquet.

Houseman's nickname, 'Mary', was just a reference to Houseman's manner and style of play, which certain sections of the crowd were at odds with. The football supporters of that generation preferred their role models to be bad boys. The '60s were the golden age of the 'Bad Boys' whether it be actors like Richard Harris and Oliver Reed, pop stars like Keith Moon and the football mavericks like Best, Marsh and co. Full-back Harry Cripps was the idol at Millwall and was succeeded by Terry Hurlock. They were the fans that played. Ron Harris is still the cult figure of Chelsea. Dessailly and Le Bouef were world-class players and World Cup winners to boot, but even amongst those younger fans who were not even born when he was meting out punishment, Harris had the stronger image.

Sheffield Wednesday came to Stamford Bridge in the sixth round and the fans could smell Wembley. It was a chance for Chelsea to exact revenge for their semi-final defeat. Wednesday's only intention was to force a replay. Their plan had worked perfectly up until the second minute of injury time. Near the end a half-fit Tambling limped off with a groin strain and with it our only chance of victory, or so it seemed. The Doc gambled with his last card, pushing McCreadie up front and bringing on ex-Hammers defender Joe Kirkup as cover. In the time added on for Tambling's injury Eddie broke for the corner flag and in desperation fired over a 'rocket launcher'. Hateley, anonymous throughout the rest of the match, rose above two defenders to nod forward to Baldwin. The Sponge lunged but did not connect properly, and the ball struck his shins rather than his instep. It flew down and bobbled on the muddy pitch. In goal for Wednesday was Ron Springett, a brilliant goalkeeper in his day. That had almost been his day. Springett had played for England but was kept out by Banks and Bonetti. All game he had kept Chelsea at bay. Expecting a volley from Tommy he threw himself towards the far post. He was a little premature. The spinning ball bounced over his clawing fingers and slowly into the net. The Bridge was in pandemonium.

I could not believe we had scored with such a freakish goal. All my thoughts were on how I could arrange another replay at Hillsborough. For the third year running we were going to Villa Park.

Chapter Six: It's All Over Now Baby Blue

We know what we are but know not what we may be.
Shakespeare, Hamlet, *Act 4 Scene 5*

Managed by Don Revie, Leeds United were seen as the emerging talent of the next decade. Over the years the resentment and jealousy between the two teams expressed itself in a series of bitter battles which finally culminated in the civil war of the 1970 FA Cup final. I can only speculate just how much the 1967 semi-final exacerbated the situation.

Just on half-time, with both teams yet to score, Charlie Cooke, restored to the side after some niggling injuries, picked up the ball on the halfway line and dribbled down the left wing. He was confronted by the late Billy Bremner. The Scots midfielder was the red-haired dynamo that drove the Leeds machine. Imagine a cross between Gazza and Vinnie Jones with a touch of Ginola. Bremner was Hughie Gallacher's love child, a player with an angel's touch and a streak of the Yauza in his character. He made ex-Chelsea skipper Graham Roberts (no relation to Harry) seem positively moralistic.

Cooke's dribble past Billy Bremner was as memorable as when Ryan Giggs scored his solo goal against the Arsenal defence in the 1999 FA Cup semi-final replay. Twice that season Charlie had produced dribblers of such movement, vision and technical expertise that they had reduced the world's best defenders to the role of mere onlookers. Cooke's run past Moore at Upton Park was exquisite, his virtuosity at Villa Park turned everything inside out, not least of all Billy Bremner. Cooke had the 'drag back trick' perfected by the hours spent in his childhood playing street football. Once a 'tanner' ball player . . .

The oldest trick of all, the one where the ball was shown to the opponent then dragged back, with the sole, as the defender charged in. As arrogant as Ali dropping his guard against Foreman in their 'Rumble in the Jungle'. Ali goaded the champ with 'Come on, George, try your best shot'. I could practically hear Cooke mouthing to Billy, 'Come on in Billy. Here it is . . . Want it?'

Well, do you, punk?

Bremner lunged again but Cooke was gone and instantly crossing to the far stick. A topspin lob. Not unlike the shots perfected by John McEnroe in his destruction of Björn Borg in the 1981 US Open.

Tony Hateley had a short Chelsea career. I suppose you could say that he was a flop of Suttonesque proportions. But for one shining moment he was a god like Ossie. There was not a player in the game better equipped to dispatch Charlie Cooke's cross. When the ball reached Hateley there were some Chelsea fans who were convinced that he was already hanging in the air like a Bell assault helicopter. Hateley had the priceless ability to meet any cross, no matter how hard it was driven, with perfect balance. Hateley's temple made contact. The ball flew past the Leeds goalkeeper Gary Sprake and into the goal. Tommy Baldwin followed it into the net. Tambling, the ace predator, was quickly on the scene. None of their services were required, so comprehensively was Sprake beaten. Chelsea had an army of 30,000 fans in the crowd of 62,378. Most of them were camped high up on the Kop at the far end, the end that Tony Hateley had scored. The same end that Chelsea had conceded two second-half goals in successive seasons. It would be safe to assume that the majority of the fans had made the two heartbreaking trips in previous seasons when Wembley was there for the taking or so it had seemed. This time Chelsea were playing a better side than their conquerors with a team that could be said to be inferior to the earlier version. All that pent-up emotion, frustration and disappointment was released in a huge torrent that seemed to sweep down from that mammoth terrace, Chelsea had scored just before the break, when they came out for the second half the fans were still jumping up and down. A case could be made for the goal to be ranked in the top three all-time Chelsea greats. The others? Try Osgood's at Old Trafford also against Leeds and Clive Walker's at Bolton.

The second half was an anti-climax. Docherty ordered that the hatches were to be battened down. The wall went up. John Boyle was kicked in the mouth by Gary Sprake in a rare Chelsea attack. In the last minute Leeds won a free kick on the edge of the box. The decision looked wilfully average to me. Leeds brought up their Howitzer siege gun in a last-ditch effort to salvage the game. Up stepped Peter Lorimer, who possessed the hardest shot of his generation. John Giles took a quick free kick and tapped it to Lorimer, who unleashed a thunderbolt from all of 25 yards. His shot completely beat Bonetti and whistled into the net. I knew he was going to smash it, the natural swing of his kicking leg across the body allayed by him pointing his opposite shoulder at Bonetti. Leeds celebrated saving the game. Thirty thousand Chelsea hearts sank, their brains frantically fast forwarding to how they were going to get the time off to see the midweek replay. There was no extra-time in those days. Truly this was an awful moment, the Villa Park hoodoo had struck again. But no, referee Burns had already signalled for the kick to be retaken because it had been struck before he gave permission. It was claimed that the Chelsea defensive wall had moved and had not been within ten yards of Peter Lorimer. Amazingly Leeds were penalised and the kick was ordered to be retaken.

Pandemonium broke out, there was a scuffle, and Leeds players harangued the ref and linesman. It went on for ages. The fans were stunned on both sides. After the fury of Leeds had abated Lorimer strode up to retake the kick. Docherty was on the line screaming for the Harris brothers to stand directly in front of Lorimer. I do not even know if they heard him. Peter hit this one with more ferocity than the first kick. Alan Harris threw himself at the ball and it struck his thigh and it flew straight up into the air, Eddie McCreadie hacked the ball away into a pen of blue and white Chelsea boys. When it finally descended, the Doc was punching the air on the touchline. The ref blew the whistle. The Doc was first on the pitch and ran to the Harris boys, who had never played better. The roar from the Chelsea end was louder than when Hateley scored. Chelsea were at Wembley and Spurs were the opposition.

Chelsea lost 2–1 to Tottenham in what was dubbed the 'Cockney Cup final'. It was a drab anti-climax of a match and lacked atmosphere, which I always found surprising. Perhaps it was because the game was so one-sided. To Chelsea fans it was a skin-crawling experience.

Tottenham had had an erratic trip to Wembley, the great Double-winning side had disintegrated and manager Bill Nicholson was still trying to rebuild a successful side. In those days Spurs were the cheque-book side of soccer. Of the 1967 Cup-winning side only two players, Frank Saul (the match winner) and ex-Wimbledon boss Joe Kinnear (voted man of the match), had come up through the ranks. The tax structure in those days encouraged successful clubs to buy expensive players. Transfer fees were tax deductible, ground improvements were not.

In the third round Spurs had been drawn away to Millwall. At the Old Den Millwall had gone 59 league games without defeat over 32 months. On the back of that, some time in the last century they rose from Fourth to Second Division. Spurs had scrambled a draw at Millwall and edged through the replay at White Hart Lane thanks to a solitary goal from ex-Dundee striker Alan Gilzean. The Scot was the equal of Hateley in the air, perhaps even better. Gilzean had the skill of being able to head the ball with industrial strength in any direction. Back headers were his speciality. In the cup final he dominated Chelsea centre-back Marvin Hinton, who at 5 ft 10 in did not have the height to counter the threat of Gilzean. It was a tactic that exploited the only difference in the sides.

Hinton was another player born out of his time. Had he been playing today he would be a sensation. Signed from Charlton in August 1963, the Croydon-born defender was one of the first 'sweepers' of the modern game. Gareth Southgate reminds me a lot of him. Hinton was the thinking man's player, the quintessential stylish defender. For a Chelsea analogy Hinton was more the elegant le Bouef (on a good day) than Mickey Droy or John Troy: a new Chelsea star.

Chelsea seemed to be overawed by their trip to Wembley. Tottenham's build-up for the final did not disrupt their usual pattern, and they were full of confidence as a result of a nearly four-month unbeaten run. Consequently they trained in the normal manner and had only one night away from home. Their studied diffidence was a pose worth watching, while Chelsea were nervy. Rumour reached the press that all was not well within the Chelsea camp. Money reared its ugly head. Tommy, before clearing it with the board, was promising handsome bonuses if Chelsea won the Cup. Bill Pratt was furious and no bonus was forthcoming. The players were upset, the problems were further compounded by disputes over ticket allocations. Mighty fine preparation for the biggest day in the club's history. Chelsea on the brink of success before internal problems wreck their chances; where have we heard that before?

It was beyond silliness. For Spurs it was their fourth Cup final in six seasons, for Chelsea it was a trip into the unknown. Their nerve ends were frayed, wired tighter than an old piano. The Spurs players watching television in their hotel on the morning of the match could almost smell the fear emanating from the interviewed Chelsea lads.

With the score 0–0 Charlie Cooke picked up a loose ball in the Spurs half and moved forward on goal, dipping his shoulders and dummying right and left. About 25 yards out he suddenly twisted and let fly for the roof of the Tottenham net. The corkscrewing run was superb, the shot even better, maybe not as powerful as Lorimer's, but Cooke was aiming for optimum rather than maximum power. In those days a single player could occasionally win for a team a cup they would not have normally won. (In the preceding final Everton's Mike Trebilcock won the cup with two fine strikes after McCalliog's Sheffield Wednesday had been two goals clear at one stage.)

For a split second it looked like Charlie Cooke had won the 1967 FA Cup final for Chelsea as the ball flew towards the net. Then fate intervened and it was to be three more strife-torn years before Ron Harris was to lift the cup. It was to be 30 years before Ruud Gullit was to lead Chelsea to victory at Wembley. Fate moved its giant hand. The hand in question belonged to a massive, gimlet-eyed Irishman.

In goal that day for Tottenham was Pat Jennings, signed by Bill Nicholson from Watford for £30,000 three seasons before. (He told me once that his wages were £40 a week when he signed.) Pat had played at Wembley once before. Northern Ireland had lost 4–0 to the England Youth side captained by Ronnie Harris. Up to that moment in the 1967 final he seemed so uninvolved he might as well have stayed at home and arranged the furniture, Jennings would be in most fans' list of the top three goalkeepers of all time. For a time he was probably the best shot-stopper in the world. Certainly the save he made to push Cooke's shot over the bar would have made the top ten of greatest stops ever. Somehow Ireland's most capped player kept the ball out.

'Life all comes down to a few moments and this is one of them,' said Bud Fox in Oliver Stone's film *Wall Street*. If life comes down to a few moments then you could say that the history of Chelsea would have turned out a little different if Cooke had scored. The apogee of a lot of people's youth would be different. It would have lifted the listless Chelsea side from their puerile mood and spurred them on to win the cup. Docherty, who was to leave the club within a few months (a strange echo of Vialli's departure from Chelsea within a few months of a disappointing Wembley), might not have gone. Sexton would not have managed the team. The Bitches' Brew of internal strife and financial woes which undermined and almost capsized the club would not have happened if Chelsea had kept winning trophies. There might have been no change of chairman. The possibilities are endless and unfathomable.

It was like the Ray Bradbury sci-fi parable, where the time traveller steps on a butterfly and when he gets back to the present things are not quite the same as when he left . . .

A butterfly flaps his wings in China. Pat Jennings saves a goal. Chelsea were always stranded on the carousel of time.

Five minutes before half-time Alan Mullery, now a nostalgic man who last I heard of was in a libel case with Alan Sugar, fired in a speculative shot. The ball bounced awkwardly off Alan Harris and dropped directly in the path of Spurs' Scots winger Jimmy Robertson. He was the 'nearly man' of Tottenham, always threatening but never quite fulfilling. He instantly knocked the rebound past the stranded Bonetti from the edge of the box. A feeling congealed around my heart like a cold vapour.

Midway through the dreary second half, played out in an eerie silence, Spurs captain Dave MacKay powered in a long throw-in (pre-Ian Hutchinson, who made it into an art form). Spurs centre-forward Frank Saul had his back to the Chelsea goal, but he pirouetted and hooked a low shot into the left-hand corner of Peter Bonetti's goal. It was to be Tottenham's last cup goal of the '60s but it won them the FA Cup.

Saul had scored the winner for Spurs in the semi-finals against the highly rated Nottingham Forest. At one stage the City Ground team looked like they were going to be only the second side at that time to win the Double. Saul was a player who, like his biblical namesake, threatened to slay his thousands and claim his kingdom. Like so many of his partners, Saul always seemed inhibited by having Jimmy Greaves alongside him. Chelsea were keen on signing him but Spurs would not even listen to an offer from outside West London. Greaves had a very quiet match, effectively policed by Ron Harris, the only Chelsea player to emerge from the Cup final with his reputation intact. Ronnie was the youngest player ever to skipper a Cup final side.

Great play was made in the media about the revenge factor involving Terry Venables. One article talked of Venables 'nutmegging' Charlie Cooke in the final. I recall seeing Best in a World Cup qualifier being closely marked by Johann Neeskens of Holland. Neeskens was a world-class player, but George was superb that night. The Irishman nutmegged the Dutchman so often that at the end of the match he offered Neeskens a tie-up from his socks to tie his legs together.

No degree of arrogance approaching that level occurred in the Cockney Cup final. The showdown–face-off never took place.

Terry was finding life hard at Tottenham, trying to plug the huge gap in their midfield left by the tragic death of John White. In a million-to-one accident the Scots genius had been killed by lightning on a golf course. The retirement of Blanchflower and the gradual decline in the warrior Mackay left Venables with a huge burden to carry. The ex-England coach was about as popular with the Spurs crowd in his spell as a player as Gordon Durie was with both sets of supporters in the '90s following his defection. 'Terry' at Chelsea quickly became 'that Venables' at Tottenham. That particular Venables was used to a faster, longer ball being hit to younger, fitter players than he found around him at White Hart Lane. The Diamonds were all about intelligent supporting runs. Terry tried to adapt his game to distribute shorter passes from around the centre circle. At Wembley his boyhood mates like Hollins and the Harris brothers swallowed up his efforts, though.

Five minutes from time, with the game reaching the boredom level of the 2000 Villa final, the immaculate Jennings punched a cross onto Bobby Tambling's head and the ball looped into the net. Instead of setting up Chelsea for a grandstand finish, it only added a curious air of unreality to the proceedings. The Stamford Bridge side's quixotic Cup campaign died not with a bang but with a whimper. The Cockney Cup final fizzled out, the dampest of damp squibs.

As the Chelsea fans limped home like a defeated army it started to rain. Not the *Bladerunner* downpour that lashed down on Matthew Harding's blue-and-white army after the 4–0 hammering at the hands of Manchester United in the

1994 final, but a steady, grey drizzle. Nobody at the Chelsea end stayed to see Mackay and his pals disconcertingly parade the cup. I saw Ron Harris collect his loser's medal and noticed him swallow slightly as though a piece of dry popcorn were caught in his throat. I had not seen that look since he had walked off at Villa Park after the Liverpool defeat, or was it the Sheffield Wednesday game? Some fans noticed that the famous 'Docherty's Diamonds' battle standard had been discarded and lay in the gutter of Wembley Way. Soon it was sodden with rain and trampled on by a thousand Doc Martens.

At least Desmond Hackett was saved the ignominy of walking barefoot from Wembley. The post-match banquet was a disaster, it was held in a room with an interior that looked like it had been painted with nail polish. Hardly anyone was eating but the drink was being caned. It was like a Mike Leigh parody of swinging London. Docherty had a smiling mask that he wore like ceramic. The speeches rambled on. Bill Pratt was talking some brain-dead inanity about past glories when the Doc, his eyes shiny and indolent with rage, grabbed the microphone and demanded with distaste creeping into his voice that the speech be about the current squad.

In the corner Peter Osgood was peeling the gold label off his beer bottle and rolling the pieces into tiny balls. He told my wife that 'Chelsea were going to be the greatest team London has ever seen'.

HOLIDAYS IN THE SUN

The 1967–68 season started predictably with a hangover. Chelsea had finished ninth in the table the previous season and had flopped bewilderingly in the Cup final. Most of the team resembled footballers at Wembley about as much as they did pandas. The late film director Stanley Kubrick was given time to create his masterpieces, but the Doc's time had run out before he could deliver his. He had bought a new centre-half, Colin Waldron from Burnley. Colin had a sparkle in his eye and a mop of fair hair. He looked not unlike Ricky Schroder, the young cop in *NYPD Blue*. Gilzean's mastery of Hinton at Wembley had convinced Docherty that he needed a catenaccio to stiffen the defence. Hinton was switched to that role, with Waldron filling the centre-back position. Tommy Docherty's tactics were slightly too clever for their own good. It smelt like old Gorgonzola to me.

The Chelsea programme for one of the opening home fixtures against Fulham (a tepid one-all draw) included an article complete with diagram about the renumbering of shirts. The number two shirt was now that of the sweeper and the number seven shirt (formerly right-wing–outside-right) now related to what they quaintly referred to as the 'deep forward' or the central midfield berth. The programme went on to explain that the concept of a winger was 'obsolete'. No leading side was regularly playing more than one winger and he was even having to double as a marking back wide midfield player. What was happening to my beloved wingers? Chased away by progress.

Featuring in the number seven shirt at the start of the season was Peter Osgood, back in the side after almost a year in the wilderness. He had spent agonising months trying to get match fit and had also endured painful rehabilitation on his shattered leg. I was shocked to see how much weight he had put on. Osgood had become something of a country gent in that time away. He was pictured in the football magazines wearing a strange fishing hat of the kind worn in recent times by members of Oasis and somebody called Chris Evans. The Wizard of Os was pictured with his gun, shooting whatever it was in the countryside. For a time Tony Hateley stayed in the Osgood household whilst the big man house-hunted. It was a clever ploy by the Doc and they became good pals. I used to see them around the Bridge together but they were destined never to play in the same Chelsea attack. Pity. Hateley's poor showing in the cup final and Osgood's return to first-team action prompted the Doc to sell him to Liverpool.

Osgood was peeved at not being taken on Chelsea's close-season sojourn to Bermuda. His gifts were once multiple but sometimes we all wondered and worried for him. The season started badly for him and Chelsea and it got worse. Docherty wore the hunted look of a man who looked into the future and saw an iceberg. Newcastle demolished them 5–1 at St James' Park and then Southampton came to the Bridge and whipped the Blues 6–2. Colin Waldron was getting a hard lesson in the rudiments of life at the top. Southampton had more aerial strike power than a squadron of B52s. Their forward duo of Ron Davies and Martin Chivers (soon to sign for Spurs in exchange for Frank Saul and a mountain of cash) shared all six of Southampton's goals. The Chelsea defence spiralled into oblivion. The only bright spot for a devastated Chelsea in a shambles of a match was that Peter Osgood scored both goals. One of them was a repeat of his slalom at Turf Moor, before he broke his leg. Incongruously wonderful – typical Chelsea.

The game was played on a wonderful late summer's afternoon. It was the hedonistic Summer of Love, of Itchycoo Park and Sgt Pepper. Two middle-aged season ticket holders were having a harsh row in front of the directors' box as the stunned Chelsea fans trudged home. One was slaughtering Osgood, saying that he was finished as a top-class player. He went on to say that Osgood was overweight, lacking pace and his overall performance was half-arsed without nerve or heart. This fellow was the colour of boiled ham, almost pink with apoplectic rage. His companion was extolling Osgood's virtues, saying that they had just witnessed one of the greatest goals ever scored at Stamford Bridge. Osgood was not the problem, he maintained, but a brittle, glaringly lightweight defence that had let in six goals at home. That was Chelsea, always stimulating. Like the punk rock group the Sex Pistols, you either liked them or hated them. There was no in-between, you had to have a view.

Once again Docherty had ignored Peter Houseman and he missed the final. John Boyle had retained his place at the start of the new season but Houseman was recalled for the home game against Sheffield United. He scored in an exciting 4–2 victory. Houseman scored again up at Liverpool but the Reds hit three and only world-class goalkeeping by Bonetti, in tremendous shape, kept the score-line respectable. Bonetti was given a wonderful ovation by the Kop. They had remembered his fantastic display against them in Chelsea's famous cup victory and always showed great affection for the man they called the 'Cat'.

THE DUSTBIN OF HISTORY

> You are pitiful isolated individuals, you are bankrupts, your role is
> played out. Go where you belong from now on – and the dustbin of
> history!
> *Leon Trotsky to the Mensheviks, 1917*

Hateley might not have had such fond memories of Chelsea from his time there but he exacted swift revenge. He was brought down for the penalty that led to the first goal and then scored twice in one minute early in the second half. One of them was an ostentatious diving header, almost at ground level, that even Bonetti could not stop. Hateley was not a player for half measures. Perhaps he was trying to repay for his fluffed chance against West Ham the previous Christmas. That performance against Chelsea was to be his swan-song at Anfield – he soon moved to Coventry for £80,000. That was 15 months after the Doc had persuaded Bill Shankly to pay £100,000 for him. Interesting to note that the fee was a world record for a non-international player. Today Hateley is almost an Orwellian 'unperson', erased from doctored photographs like Stalin's enemies. Perhaps this will rescue him from the dustbin of history. Hateley had more than enough nous to pass some on to his son, the rangy Mark, who went on to play for England. Chelsea's ace striker Kerry Dixon was around in those days and they were both vying for their country's number nine shirt. Mark had a long career in the game, which included playing alongside Ray Wilkins for AC Milan in the famous red and black. Hateley junior later played for Glasgow Rangers, where he became a cult figure. The focus of Kasparov saw him through some tough times.

Chelsea were approximately nowhere in the early autumn of 1967, with stumbling home draws with Stoke and Coventry sandwiched between a heavy 3–0 defeat at Nottingham. A 2–1 defeat at Middlesbrough had signalled the end of Chelsea's interest in the League Cup. This was in my view never a lucky cup competition for Chelsea. I was concerned about events as we continued to slip towards the bottom of the league. We had 11 points out of 30 and were sinking fast.

On 6 October Tommy was suspended for a month by the FA, following incidents on the close-season tour of Bermuda. The position for Docherty at Stamford Bridge had become untenable. The club was a Casablanca of gossip and unrest. Without Joe Mears as its stabilising influence a cognitive dissonance arose between him and the board. Bill Pratt was to die later in the season after a brief illness. For the second time in less than 20 months Chelsea were to lose the counsel of a dignified, experienced leader. Bill's father had been chairman for a short spell in the mid-'30s and Bill had been vice-chairman since 1952.

The exact circumstances of Docherty's FA suspension were shrouded in mystery. The 'incidents' were undisclosed, but he had been involved in some ding-dong rows with match officials in Bermuda. Hateley was sent off in one game and the incensed Docherty ordered the rest of the Chelsea side to do a 'walk out'. This would have had massive implications globally. Eventually the situation cooled down and the game resumed. Later the Doc abused the officials in a politically incorrect manner.

There was allegedly another breach of protocol when Lord Chelsea refused to attend a function. This earned him a backlash in the local press. Docherty was out of control. There is a fine line between cocking a snook at the establishment and simply being a clown. Docherty and players like Hudson walked it finely. Like George Best and Oliver Reed, to the younger generations Tommy was one of those 'legendary for being legendary' figures. As Chelsea manager he was almost iconic but became better known for being a talking head with an endless store of anecdotes.

I was not present on the Bermuda jaunt. Suffice it to say it was to prove to be the Doc's 'Bermuda triangle', into which his Chelsea career was to enter and disappear. In October 1967 Tommy was sitting at the apex of an inverted Stamford Bridge triangle. I had seen his behaviour on previous club trips when moderation, like mediocrity, had no place on the agenda. We had visited Australia a few months after the Blackpool incident. The Doc had some issues with Peter Osgood at that time. Os had been away with the England Youth squad at the time and had consequently missed the notoriety. As the Chelsea players disembarked the plane for a fuel stop at Bangkok, the Doc told him,

'Son, if you had been there, you would have been the ninth.'

Part of the itinerary in Australia included a trip to a wine-making factory. What genius dreamt that one up? When Tommy noticed that Osgood was not indulging he made a special point of going over to him and telling him to get a drink. A few minutes later my father arrived on the scene and engaged Tommy in conversation. The chat ended with Docherty pointing over to the young Chelsea star. Tommy angrily strode over and grabbed the flute out of Peter's hand. 'What the hell are you doing drinking wine at your age?'

After the visit and back at the hotel the Doc checked the Chelsea players for freebies. He unearthed enough Chardonnay to stock an Oddbins on Christmas Eve. Having seized the contraband, he gave it to the concierge to auction for charity.

EYES WIDE SHUT

The Doc suffered from air rage; there was something about long-haul flights that brought out the worst in him. Travelling back from Australia, the Chelsea team were on the same plane as the '60s pop star Crispin St Peter and his entourage. The Irish singer had just enjoyed a huge global hit with a song called 'You Were On My Mind'. The Doc had Van Gogh's ear for music and was always jeering at the players' tastes. He took an instant dislike to the long-haired pop singer and his trendy clothes. I think he wore velvet trousers and a Paisley shirt. The Doc spent the flight amusing himself by throwing bread rolls and pillows at Crispin and his chums. When they looked up Tommy would have his eyes shut, feigning sleep.

Sitting behind Tommy was the club physio, Harry Medhurst, famous for his somewhat protruding ears. Peter Houseman sat next to him, gazing out at the clouds; eight miles high. The Doc struck St Peter's head with a shot of Lorimer-type power. This was to prove to be the last straw, and one of the star's minders–roadies muscled up the aisle. This guy looked like he played line-backer for the Pittsburgh Steelers. He grabbed Harry Medhurst by the lapels of his Chelsea blazer: 'You big-eared c***. Do that again and I will knock you out.' Then he started on Peter Houseman, the most gentle, laid-back guy in football. 'Are you in on this?' It looked ugly, but just then Ron Harris stood up and asked Peter if he was all right. The heavy calmed down. I do not think he knew who Ron was, but there was something about his demeanour . . . Ron gave him what he thought was a smile and the heavy went back to his seat. The Doc appeared to still be in a slumber.

Coming back from Bermuda there were reports of another outbreak of bread-throwing. I do not know if there were any pop stars involved. Eventually the captain summoned the manager of the Chelsea team to the cabin. He read the riot act to Docherty and warned him that unless the rowdy behaviour ceased forthwith he would have no option but to turn back and put the team off the plane. Once again, imagine the tabloid headlines if that happened today!

A very conciliatory Docherty explained that he had been asleep and was unaware that his charges had been behaving so badly. He put it down to the fact that the team contained a lot of young players on their first trip abroad. He promised that he would keep them in order and that there would be no more bread chucked.

We convened an emergency board meeting. Top of the agenda was Tommy receiving his P45. Bill Pratt asked Docherty to sit down. 'We just can't go on like this, Tom,' he said gravely. It did not come as a shock to the Doc, in fact he had been waiting for it since Frank Saul's goal at Wembley. Before Pratt had time to tell him he was sacked Tom chipped in. 'Mr Chairman, gentlemen, can you excuse me a second?' He popped outside the boardroom and soon came back with some bottles of champagne. He shrugged and grinned that famous Tommy grin. 'I thought this was going to happen. Fancy a drink?'

So that was how it ended. We sat for a long time sipping champagne and chewing the cud. Tommy was never officially sacked – he quit. The most exciting episode in the history of the club ended as it had started; with the style and class of Tommy Docherty.

To consign Tommy Docherty to a '60s Jurassic Park is a little cruel. His flamboyant ultimate failure was better than the benign success of Vialli. David Mellor once called Docherty a dinosaur in his newspaper column when Docherty had the temerity to query the goings-on at present-day Chelsea. Mellor, in his self-appointed role as Chelsea's media spin doctor, was quick to attack the Glaswegian. Funny, because in all the time I was at Chelsea I never once saw Mr Mellor at the club. That must have been when he was supporting Fulham. The famous QC George Carman, who died of prostate cancer, once said of Mr Mellor that 'he behaved like an ostrich and put his head in the sand, thereby exposing his thinking parts'. Whatever history says of Docherty, his contribution to the club was 1,000 times greater than that of Mellor and his ilk.

In my view Docherty should have his own statue in the Village complex. Only Gullit in his short spell at Chelsea created the same sort of impact. The parallels are obvious. Both joined Chelsea at a time when the club was becalmed. Both managers triggered huge changes in the team by audacious moves into the transfer market. Both men believed in the introduction of a youth policy, neither suffered fools gladly and both were to fall foul of the structure that their cocksure proclamations had outgrown and eventually alienated. Both were like free-range chickens let out of the coop to run around the barnyard and imagine they were free, but when they ceased laying eggs, they were slaughtered.

Morrisey advises us that celebrity is a form of revenge. Gullit was the first foreign coach to win the cup when Chelsea beat Middlesbrough. When Ruud took Newcastle to Wembley to face Manchester United (on their way to the Treble), a pre-match interview revealed that he could not recall what he had done with his medal.

The stats indicate that Tommy Docherty had a managerial win rating of 58.6 per cent, while his replacement Dave Sexton's record was a fractional 0.9 per cent better. Perhaps Docherty had tired of living inside his own vision and destroyed it. Oscar Wilde wrote that whom the gods wish to destroy they first give what they desire. This was never truer than Dave Sexton and Chelsea during the tenure of his seven-year reign from 1967 to 1974.

Chapter Seven: All Tomorrow's Parties

The world never hears of its greatest men, the men it calls great are just ahead enough of the average to stand out, but not far ahead enough to be remote.
Raymond Chandler, April 1955

The defeat at Birmingham effectively ended Chelsea's challenge for honours in the 1967–68 season. Once again it was to end as empty as a sneaker on the side of the motorway. West Bromwich Albion lifted the cup with a scrappy 1–0 extra-time victory over Everton. The final had come a little early for the Scousers who were bedding down their wonderful midfield trio of Alan Ball, Howard Kendall and Colin Harvey. Jeff Astle fired in his goal of the season to seal an unimpressive victory for the Throstles. A generation later Astle took on the role of buffoon in the Baddiel and Skinner spoof soccer TV show. At that time he was one of the most prolific scorers in the history of the game. Astle started his career at Notts County, where ex-Chelsea legend Tommy Lawton gave him tutelage in heading. This was like a young hoofer getting dancing lessons from Astaire. Astle's cup final winner meant that he had the unique record of scoring in every round of the cup. Only one more player was to achieve this in the modern game and Peter Osgood's astute sense of timing ensured that the twentieth century would never see it happen again.

Manchester City took the league title by two points from United. In terms of movement and passing the present Chelsea were perhaps no better than the all-English City side coached by Allison. It was just faster. Liverpool finished third just ahead of Leeds, with Chelsea nudging sixth. They had lost only seven of their last 31 games and qualified for the Fairs Cup as London's highest placed team. United's home defeat at the hands of Chelsea cost them the title that season. Chelsea were the scourge of Manchester, City were beaten 1–0 at the Bridge, reversing a narrow Good Friday defeat at Maine Road.

The set-back at Stamford Bridge jolted City's title hopes. Alan Birchenall hammered in a superb goal after he was put in by Marvin Hinton's through ball. Hinton was as unflappable as ever. If he had been on the *Titanic* he would have ordered more ice in his gin and tonic. City spent the rest of the game camped in the Chelsea half and did everything but score. Bonetti had a private battle with Francis Lee, throwing himself all over the goalmouth to beat out his many attempts. The geometry of the City passing was exquisite. New boy Webb was outstanding, blunting the threat of the fiery Mike Summerbee, whose 14 goals from the flanks paved the way for the title. Chelsea were made to look second-rate against City that night, despite the fact that they won the game. So often the history of Chelsea reveals that they lost games they should have won, and vice versa. Chelsea had made rapid progress under Sexton. However, as he watched the City midfield overwhelm and eventually strangle the Chelsea engine room, he knew there was still much work to be done, especially in the creative areas.

Peter Houseman kept his place in the side till the end of the season. It was his most consistent spell so far in the first team. John Boyle, who seemed to get the nod over Peter in the Docherty era, had suffered head injuries in a car accident. Bobby Tambling was hospitalised again for a second stomach operation and concerns were growing for his long-term fitness. The toll was beginning to tell on him. Around that time he was undergoing a spiritual change, and the other players noted how withdrawn he had become, like a fugitive from a Graham Greene novel.

Meanwhile Houseman made the cover of the Chelsea programme against Burnley with a picture of his goal against Tottenham at Stamford Bridge on Easter Saturday. The competition between the two sides and the sets of supporters was even more intense following the Cockney Cup final. Chelsea had no complaints about the result but bitterness arose between the two as to who were top dogs in London. Some of those feelings still reverberate from that year.

Arsenal were at the same stage of rebuilding as Chelsea, trying to insert new players into the existing framework. Like Chelsea after the regrouping period, their star was about to ascend. Spurs were further back in the process of evolution. Venables was still finding the going tough at Tottenham, with the crowd on his back. In his own laconic manner he pointed out that they had given him all of three games to acclimatise to the Tottenham way. In the encounter at White Hart Lane, at the start of the winter of '67 Chelsea had been easily brushed aside 2–0 (with headers from Cliff Jones and our friend Gilzean) in a game marred by crowd trouble. The game was actually stopped as supporters spilled onto the pitch following fighting in the Park Lane end. That was the legendary 'walking stick' battle, when hundreds of sticks painted in club colours were used in a re-enactment of a medieval battle. Police photographs of weapons confiscated after the match include axes, kung fu stars, butchers' knives and chains.

Charlie Cooke had just won the Joe Mears Memorial Trophy, awarded to him by the Supporters' Club as the Chelsea footballer of the year. My father would have liked that. Cooke had completed a double, lifting a similar award at Dundee shortly before his transfer to London. Spurs, as they would find to their cost in the future, had no answer to him in such zestful form. He surged past Cyril Knowles, the Spurs full-back who died of a brain haemorrhage shortly after retiring from the game after a colourful career. Knowles desperately conceded a corner and Houseman volleyed it high into the roof of the net, although he was in the midst of four Spurs defenders. Despite his slightly awkward-looking frame, Houseman packed a tremendous shot. The goal, scored in front of the future site of the Matthew Harding Stand, was probably the best he had scored so far in his sporadic career at Stamford Bridge.

Houseman and Cooke tormented the Spurs defenders in the second half and it was no surprise when Baldwin notched a further Chelsea goal after Jennings had saved McCreadie's free kick. The ball spun loose and the Gateshead-born striker rolled it back into goal.

Houseman made another goal for Baldwin in a home win over Burnley. Despite the attentions of two defenders, he found Tommy with an immaculate centre and the striker scored with ease. Baldwin finished the season with 15 league goals. Tommy's winner in the last league game of the season at Birchenall's old club, Sheffield United, clinched the European spot. The Shed was surfing, The Sexton oligarchy was moving Chelsea forward, and Houseman was determined to be a part of Chelsea's promising future. He did not care if he did the wood-chopping and water-carrying for the Cookes and the Osgoods. Boudewjn Zenden reminds me a little of him. The Dutchman is faster than Peter was but Houseman was special.

Chelsea fans were always impertinently cynical about their favourites' chances for honours. Sexton spent the summer diligently applying himself to sorting the wheat from the chaff. He spent hours checking out the youth teams and reserves, and every player had their progress monitored. It did not escape his meticulous attention that Alan Hudson had returned to the fray following a long injury. In April 1968 the 16-year-old apprentice had played his first game for a year against Crystal Palace in a South-East Counties League (junior division) first-leg Cup final. He had been ordered on the eve of that season to rest for a year because of a knee condition, but now he was ready to go. His brother John's apocalyptic hopes of a career in the big time ended when he left Chelsea after a bust-up with Docherty and his considerable talent was lost to the game. He ended up cleaning windows and eventually moved to Italy.

If you turned on the radio that drowsy summer you could hear Richard Harris crooning Jim Webb's opus 'Macarthur Park'. The BBC was showing the first episodes of *Dad's Army*. The summer of 1968 was notable for the student riots in Paris, and Martin Luther King and Bobby Kennedy were assassinated. Andy Warhol was also shot. Warhol said that everyone would be famous for 15 minutes. David Webb was rapidly attaining cult status and a blaze of publicity which was to last for more than a quarter of an hour.

GOOD OLD WEBBY

The Shed had many famous characters, each with their own nickname. They read like a surreal version of *The Beano's* Bash Street Kids. The roll of honour for the class of '68, a good year for the Shed and all who sailed in her, includes many humorous nicknames. Courtesy of Mick Greenaway's notebooks try this for just some of them . . .

Lofty, Eccles, Jesus, L.A., Greasemonkey, Tarback, Foamback, 007, Ivanhoe, Screamer, Ken Dodd, Bernie the Milkman, Porky, Robbo, Little Jock, Celtic 'D', Bendy Wendy, Bristol Pat, Mandy, Pudsey Dave, Braddy Dave, Braddy Tommy, Celtic Angie, The Golden Goals Twins (Dave and Alan) Primo, Kosty (pause for breath) Garrison, Goofy, Happy, Grimsby Roz, Bristol China and dozens more.

One of the most famous characters was a chap known as 'Good Old Webby'. He started appearing in the Shed about the time David Webb joined Chelsea from Southampton. Joe Kirkup, the solid full-back, forming part of the deal. The Shed acolyte would just utter 'Good old Webby' every time his hero was on the ball. That is all he was ever heard to say. I used to spot him all over the country following David Webb, wearing the same check tweed overcoat and always chanting the mantra. Time goes by in leaps and bounds but espying the figure in the tweed coat shouting 'Good old Webby' was as iconic an image as Cooke nutmegging Cyril Knowles.

David Webb was yet another East End boy who ended up with the West End girls and a steady job down the Fulham Road. To this day he still radiates the mischief and seductiveness of a man who needs to be the centre of attention. He was born in Stratford in April 1946 and became a West Ham schools player. He later joined Orient as part of the groundstaff and played for the first team then managed by Dave Sexton. In the spring of the World Cup winning year he moved to Southampton and helped them win promotion.

Standing three-quarters of an inch under six feet he weighed in at 12st 12lbs. He sported in those days a crew cut and had a cleft chin and piercing eyes. Fans noted a perceptible likeness to the singer Glen Campbell. His biting tackles and timely interventions soon made him a favourite with the Shed. Harris and McCreadie were two of the hardest tacklers that ever dished out leather. The Chelsea crowd like their defenders tough. Marcel Desailly was always more popular than the others. No one could doubt Webb's authority. Marvin Hinton was an imperious defender. He was the man who arrived to break up opposition moves, and when he had possession no attacker could get near the ball. Webb and Harris were the pillars of the defence though. Webb also had an advantage over most defenders, he had an eye for goal and loved going forward. Dave was the most versatile of all the players on Chelsea's books. He could play at right-back, centre-back or even as a striker, his one weakness was that he lacked real pace, which would preclude him from being a modern wing-back. In some Chelsea games Webb would appear to be just everywhere.

An analysis of Premiership player stats for the last season of the twentieth century indicated that Gianluca Vialli strayed offside every 34 minutes. Chelsea finished third in the table for the team that had most shots (481). Without the aid of laptops, videos and databases no figures were available for the seasons of Dave Sexton's management. I would bet Zola's BMW 7 series though against a bottle of Becks that Webb had more shots and headers in a season than Le Bouef. He also put more forwards down than the Gallic clothes-horse. If Webb crash-tackled a player it was like being hit by a Connex Express. (When they run.)

In 1968–69 Webb scored eight goals which included a hat-trick against Ipswich. The three goals he scored at Portman Road on Boxing Day were the first he scored for the club. Webb did nothing by halves. It was a memorable performance and when the snow began to fall the Chelsea crowd began to sing the famous 'Jingle bells, jingle bells . . . Oh what fun it is to see Chelsea win away'. Webb was Chelsea's only ever-present player playing in all 54 games and was voted Chelsea's player of the year. Bill Shankly knew the mind of his beloved Kop inside out. 'The whole of my life what they wanted was honesty,' he said to me once. 'They were not so concerned with cultured football, but with triers who gave 100 per cent.' Webb could not have had a better CV. Like the man said, 'Good Old Webby'.

By the start of the 1968–69 season Peter Houseman had played in a total of 61 league games and had scored six goals. He established himself in the team and consolidated his position in what was a somewhat chequered season for Chelsea. The main disappointment was their early exit from the Fairs Cup. The competition had grown in stature and the field of runners was regarded as the strongest yet; it included the cream of Europe amongst them Fiorentina, Atletico Madrid, Sporting Lisbon, Hamburg S., Dynamo Zagreb, Feyenoord, AS Roma, Real Zaragoza and AC Napoli.

Chelsea were matched against the Scottish team Morton in the first round and went through 9–3 on aggregate. They slammed five in at home without reply and won the second leg 4–3 with Houseman scoring his first goal in European competition. The only thing memorable about the games was the garish kit chosen by Morton. Today fans are used to the acid house, dayglo, psychedelia of replica kits but in the sixties sober strips were commonplace. The 'Inter Milan' strip, blue and black striped shirts, black shorts and black socks had caused a stir in the ill-fated semi-final defeat against Sheffield Wednesday. The fans were always writing in asking Chelsea to play in them but the players regarded them as unlucky and shunned them.

The second round gave Chelsea a tie against DWS Amsterdam. Dutch football was undergoing a revolution at that time. The performances of the young Johan Cruyff, then playing for Ajax, were drawing envious glances from the top teams in Europe. Amsterdam had no players with the class of Cruyff or Neeskens but were highly focused and well drilled defensively. Both their backs were as pacy as Hakkinen and David Coulthard. They denied Chelsea any real chances at the Bridge and that was the same story in the second leg in Holland. Both matches ended without a goal and Chelsea went out on the spin of a coin. Ron Harris had called correctly to dismiss AC Milan in Chelsea's previous Fairs Cup run but the 1968–69 sojourn ended abruptly. Such an end to a lucrative European venture would be unthinkable today. Immensely greater financial rewards have produced infinitely greater pressures, like penalty shoot-outs and golden goals, but imagine Sky TV analysing a Beckham flick-up of a coin . . . Keane could receive a red card for arm wrestling the Bayern captain as they fought over a best of three, the possibilities are endless.

Speaking at the time Ron Harris lamented Chelsea's exit in such a manner. He felt that all the effort Chelsea had put in against the Dutch had been for nothing.

'Spinning a coin, flipping a disc, choosing an envelope from the referee's hand – these things should have no part in deciding who goes into the next round. Even the World Cup could be won on the toss if the final is still level after a replay and extra-time.'

Chelsea fans thought that their team should have gone through as they had some of the biggest tossers in the game on their books.

Newcastle went on to win the Fairs Cup in bizarre circumstances. They had finished only tenth the previous season but had scraped in under the 'one club per 'city' rule. Four English clubs were invited to participate: Chelsea, Liverpool, Leeds and the Geordies. They overcame Ujpest Doza of Hungary in the final and to this day have never won a major honour since. I hope my dear loyal friend Bobby Robson can change that. Ujpest had the finest centre-forward in Europe playing for them, Ferenc Bene – a player whose skills would make even Osgood or Cooke seem ponderous. Newcastle fought like tigers though to take the cup 6–2 on aggregate

Newcastle met Chelsea early on in the season still awash with emotions after their European triumph. The Blues stormed to a two-goal lead by half-time. Bobby Tambling cracked his 150th league goal with as sweet a left-footed drive as he ever scored. Osgood set up the chance and laid on a second for Birchenall to run into the net. Chelsea were strolling it, or so it seemed. Newcastle tore into the Londoners in the second half, Chelsea were in a careering, nihilistic mood that night. Tommy Gibb scored from 25 yards to leave Bonetti helpless, then a player called Brian Robson hit two late goals to rob Chelsea of victory. Brian was known as 'Pop' because of his premature balding head. In recent years the bullet heads of Vialli and Rio Ferdinand have dominated the game but in the '60s the sight of a bald head would always get the chants going. Robson was in Astle's class as a marksman but was sadly neglected by England. Strangely, he was to finish his career at Chelsea. We had a real bargain and he still scored match-winning goals. The dying breed of strikers who only scored goals. Solskjaer is the nearest throwback we have in the modern game to such a player. The match stats reveal he scores a goal every 71.08 minutes. Greaves' figures would have been interesting.

A few days later Chelsea put aside the hiccup at Newcastle with an amazing 4–0 win at Old Trafford. It is still Chelsea's biggest win at the Theatre of Dreams. Baldwin put Chelsea ahead in 42 seconds and they never looked back. United fielded eight of the team that had won the European Cup at Wembley on a night as emotional as anything the late dramas at the Nou Camp evoked.

Houseman was deputising for Cooke, who had taken a bad knock at Newcastle. Cooke's vintage performance (as sweet as Chateau Margaux 1957) at Manchester in March had masterminded United's first home defeat in nearly two years. Houseman chipped in with a marvellous performance. He blistered the Reds full-back, a young chap called Kopel whose name was almost the same as that of the awesomely talented winger who played for them with such distinction under Tommy Docherty.

Houseman made a second quick goal for Tambling to sweep home and then Bobby created an opening for Baldwin to shoot his second and Chelsea's third just on half-time. A blockbuster from Birchenall after a clever decoy run from Houseman completed the scoring for Chelsea. Near the end Webb blasted in a tremendous shot that ex-Chelsea keeper Alex Stepney turned onto the post. Webb was cursing his luck all the way home. He dearly wanted a goal at Old Trafford . . .

The 4–0 thrashing sent tremors around Old Trafford that did not subside.

It signalled the end of the great United side that had ruled Europe. Most of the team had passed their sell-by date and the youngsters were left to fend for themselves in the isolated, ruthless world where reputations were there to be shot at. Having gone downhill fast United were soon to go over the edge. It was a path I was to learn about eventually. Chelsea fans were given a police escort out of Manchester as enraged United supporters tried to attack them. Chelsea had committed regicide. When the travelling Shedites had arrived at Manchester Piccadilly they were greeted by gangs of Manchester United supporters, hooliganism was reaching different proportions. That season saw the emergence of the skinhead cult that was to cast a shadow over the game for many years.

Chelsea never really struck a consistent vein of form in the league. They thrashed newly promoted Queens Park Rangers 4–0 at Loftus Road in a game played out in torrential rain. Baldwin scoring twice, Osgood rapped in a penalty as the rain fell in silver sheets, Birchenall wrapped it up with a glorious diving header. A run of three consecutive away defeats at Burnley, Stoke and Liverpool slowed our momentum. Even in the most lamentable games some of the team were never less than watchable. Houseman stopped the rot by scoring the only goal of the game at Highbury. He was taking on more responsibility with each match I had noted, making and taking goals.

Chelsea's away record over the last five seasons merited examination. In 105 games they had won 43 games, drawn 26 and lost only 36. Had there been some sort of league based on the away performances Chelsea would have won it from Manchester United. United's record reflected 39 wins with 30 draws, they lost 36 games also. It was the home form that had let Chelsea down. Sexton had commented that in a big open stadium it was not easy to contain the noise generated by supporters. Chelsea fans had gained the reputation as being amongst the most fanatical in the game.

The Shed was second only to the Kop as the most famous end in football. The United fans who packed the Stretford Road end of Old Trafford would argue against this, along with the inhabitants of the Arsenal North Bank. If the Shed had an equivalent in pop music it would have been the Cavern Club in Liverpool, birthplace of the Beatles. The Shed was designed to give cover to the bookmakers and punters who had flocked to Stamford Bridge for the greyhound racing. Today the Shed is long gone, replaced by a new stand and a leisure complex of luxury flats, bars, restaurants and a hotel. Ironic that the site of Chelsea's most virile image is now a young professional's wet dream.

Chelsea had an abbreviated run in the Football League Cup. They returned to St Andrews in September for a tie against their Cup conquerors, Birmingham.

Compared to the dramas of the previous encounter the game was a non-starter, Chelsea scrambling through courtesy of an own goal. The next round saw Chelsea drawn against Derby County, who that season were to blast their way out of the Second Division. Derby were managed by Brian Clough, one of the youngest managers in the game who was just embarking on his majestic career. The 'Rocket Man' was about to set the heavens ablaze as he took his teams to the stars and beyond. Nottingham Forest eventually honoured Clough by erecting a bronze bust in the main reception area and renaming a stand after him. Clough led Forest to European Cup success in 1979 and 1980, a feat that seems even more unbelievable with each passing year. Say all you will about his towering ego and his unorthodox manner, he came through victoriously.

Clough as a player was a goal machine second only to Greaves in the scoring stakes. For example, in the season 1959–60 he scored 39 league goals for Middlesbrough. That did not include the five he scored in one match for the Football League against the Irish League in Belfast. The following season he scored 34, before his transfer to neighbours Sunderland. At Middlesbrough Clough scored 197 goals in 213 league games. Clough was as fast as a puma but tragically a horrific injury sustained in a goalmouth collision ended his career and he turned to management almost in despair. Clough was an attacker all his life. He built his teams around fast wingers pumping over crosses for his goal-hungry strikers to convert. Simple but devastating.

Clough for some reason disliked Chelsea, perhaps it was the image of the London 'wide boys' that upset him. He used the quaint expression of 'spivs' in reference to a particular London side who employed, in his view, questionable tactics. Venables was the personification of this 'London flash' in Clough's view and they were to clash many times over the years as their respective managerial careers entwined. Chelsea were always a thorn in his side. The Blues beating Forest a couple of unexpected times when they were on their unstoppable push from the foot of the Second Division to the European Cup. Chelsea were interested in purchasing his son Nigel at one stage but the family blocked the move. Shame.

Derby drew 0–0 at Chelsea in the first game. Clough had recruited the old war-horse Dave Mackay, whose swansong for Spurs had been the Wembley victory over Docherty's Diamonds. Mackay was to finish the season as joint footballer of the year along with another hard driving skipper, Tony Book of Manchester City.

Derby blocked all Chelsea's moves that night, Mackay's legs may have all but gone but his football mind was as sharp as Garry Kasparov in the Sarajevo grandmaster chess tournament. In the replay Derby blew Chelsea away 3–1. I think the expression 'not being at the races' would cover it.

Above: EUROSTARS
Ronnie Harris looks for
the hallmark on the Cup-
Winners' cup, Athens
1971.
© Hulton Getty

Left: OOPS UPSIDE YOUR
HEAD
Harris clatters Stan 'the
man' Bowles of QPR.
© Hulton Getty

Above: CHELSEA V LEEDS 1970
Peter Osgood almost wins it at Wembley.
© Hulton Getty

Above: Osgood has just equalised in the replay at Old Trafford. The
wizard is mobbed by Houseman, Cooke and Baldwin. Note the
young Shed boy on the left.
© Hulton Archive

Above: 'THE CHAPS'
The squad that won the FA
and European Cup-Winners'
cup.
© Hulton Deutsch

Left: GENIE IN A BOTTLE
Jimmy Greaves – the greatest
goal scorer of all time.
© Hulton Deutsch

Above: YESTERDAY
ONCE MORE
Jimmy Greaves
circa 1957. Note
the badge.
© Hulton Getty

Right: VIALLI! VIALLI!
Sacked after
Chelsea had won
the Cup by beating
Aston Villa.
© Allsport

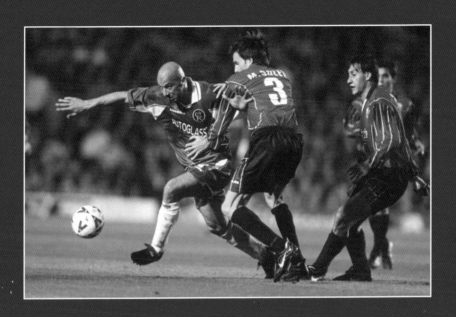

Top: MR BLUE
Vialli in action.
© Allsport

Above: THE WISE GUY
Dennis was Chelsea's most popular player in the '90s but was
discarded by Claudio Ranieri.
© Allsport

EL DORADO
Terry Venables – the Diamond Geezer.

NUMBER NINE DREAM
Jimmy Floyd Hasselbaink – the new Greaves?
© Allsport

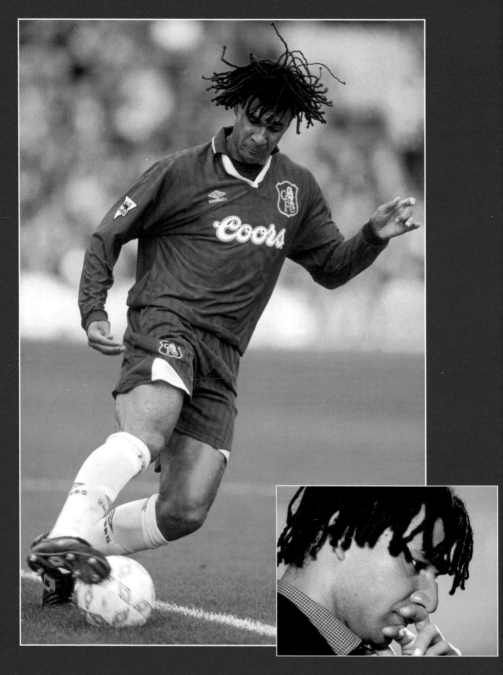

Above: BUFFALO SOLDIER
Ruud Gullit – Chelsea was the swansong of his glittering career.
© Allsport

Inset: RUUD BOY
Complex and elegant, blessed with the ability to find
the next big talent.
© Allsport

Sexton was worried that Chelsea lacked the cutting edge to unlock subtle defences like Amsterdam's or iron-clad back fours like Derby's. Osgood was slowly coming back to something approaching his best. Peter was taking the penalties now to boost his goal tally. Birchenall worked hard and chipped in with his share of goals. The same could be said for Baldwin. Chelsea were criticised that season for being too cautious, yet Docherty played with a sweeper both home and away. Sexton was still looking for the X-factor that would give Chelsea that extra dimension up front. Agression with something else that would terrify defenders.

THE UNFORGIVEN (IAN HUTCHINSON)

Some would say that Clint Eastwoood's cowboy movie *The Unforgiven* was his best work. Eastwood played the part of Will Munny, a ruthless gunfighter who, following the tragic death of his wife, retired from gun-fighting to be a pig farmer. With his farm facing financial ruin he is forced to take one last job . . .

Halfway through the film he is in conversation with an aspiring gunslinger who is describing the death of one of his hapless victims.

'He had it coming,' the kid tells Munny.

Eastwood pauses and replies as only Clint can, 'We all got it coming.'

Ian Hutchinson was the Clint Eastwood of Chelsea. The quiet man with the air of violence. He rode into town and cleaned it up just when it was needed most. He leaves soon afterwards, possibly badly hurt. Perhaps he had it coming.

Ian had the good looks of a western hero with the long hair and sideburns, plus he had the physique of a movie star. At first he seemed dull and unobtrusive, lacking the foppish violence of Osgood or the glitz of Birchenall. Underestimating Hutchinson was a big mistake defenders made. They failed to see the hungry wolf look in his eyes till it was too late. Sexton signed him for £2,500 from Cambridge United at the end of the 1967–68 season. It was without doubt the best signing he ever made for Chelsea. Sexton was proud of Hutch, if Osgood and Hudson were reprobates then Ian was just the naughty schoolboy. He could outdrink the pair of them. We have discussed the fine line between cocking a snook at convention and simply being a sad drunk. Well, this line was well walked by all of them. Whenever they met they greeted each other like something out of *Goodfellas*.

Hutchinson is best remembered for his long throw, one of the oldest methods of attack that was used a lot by the Spurs double-winning team. Dave Mackay had, before the emergence of Hutch, the longest throw-in in the game. He had even engineered a goal against Chelsea in the Cup final with one. In the contemporary game, Vinnie Jones had a useful throw but the practice seemed to die out when the ex-hod carrier defected to the Hollywood Hills seeking a career on the silver screen. He was gone in 60 seconds almost.

It was simplicity itself. Hutch would throw to the furthest unmarked Chelsea player, often this would take several opponents out of the game at a single stroke. There was no real counter to it. He just threw the projectile. The trajectory of his throw making it impossible for even the tallest of defenders (ie Jack Charlton) to head clear. Ian had height and distance. Sometimes he would wind himself up, bending almost in half to whiplash over a throw, but more often than not it was a flick.

His heading ability was in the Hateley class. That skill of hanging in mid-air that all great headers possess was part of his game. How many goals would he have scored had he been on the end of one of his own throws? If only he could have chucked them higher and run faster! His bravery was his undoing. Hutchinson was the desperado who never came to his senses. He played in only a handful of major games for Chelsea, Audrey Hepburn made only 20 films. At the end of his brief career he was simply battered into retirement. At that time Ian looked like he was generated by a computer from parts of car-crash victims. He would go for simply anything, the spring-heeled Jack of Chelsea, but when he had a winger with the precison of Houseman alongside him life was easier. The crosses were laid on for him. Peter Houseman's greatest skill was that of being able to cross accurately even when under pressure. At £8 million, Chelsea's purchase of Grankjaer made him the most expensice in Danish history. His accuracy made him worth that. Houseman was a product of a school of thought that football was played with jackets for goal-posts and that the object of defenders was to get stuck in as quickly as possible. The Chelsea of Cooke passed the ball as near to perfection as makes hardly any difference, but as videos show, Cooke and Houseman had noticeably more time and space than, say, David Ginola. Yet the contradiction occurs of harder tackling, Giggs's marvellous solo goal against Arsenal, which won them the semi-final, would not have been scored against the Leeds or Chelsea defences of the late '60s. Giggs would have been chopped down long before he progressed far enough into the penalty area to explode home his blistering shot. Some of the Arsenal defenders looked like they were wearing surgical boots as they trailed in his wake that night.

Houseman, in the words of Cruyff, was a winger who 'liked the chalk of the touchline' visible on his boots. That was his killing zone, the area where he did his best work. When Hutchinson joined CFC the mosaic was almost complete.

Hutchinson scored his first goal for Chelsea in one of the most amazing fixtures that they ever played. It was the goal that never was because the game was abandoned due to 'floodlight failure'.

In a bitterly cold first month of 1969, Chelsea travelled to Preston for a fourth round FA Cup-tie. In the third round Chelsea had beaten Carlisle 2–0 at home, Osgood and Tambling scoring their customary Cup goals. The rumours were still circulating the Bridge that Tambling was close to quitting football for a future in the Jehovah's Witness movement. The record Chelsea goal-scorer had fallen heavily under the spell of the Jehovah's. I never spoke to him about it.

The Preston match ended goalless, only noticeable for the appearance of full-back Stewart Houston. The young Scot's Chelsea career was plagued by injury but he had a successful time with Manchester United. He really made his name though when he turned to management and became assistant to George Graham at Arsenal and later Tottenham.

Hutchinson scored in the replay and Birchenall added a second but the floodlights failed in the second half and the game was abandoned. It was rescheduled for the following Monday afternoon. Today any hint of floodlight failure brings rumours of Far East betting coups but in those days it was all down to the power supply when a generator gave out. A few years later and the fans may have thought we had been cut off for not paying the bill. Sandwiched between the Preston matches was a trip to Southampton. An injury-hit Chelsea side were hammered 5–0 by the Saints, who seemed to enjoy using Chelsea for shooting practice. In two games they scored 11 times! Hudson made his Chelsea début that day.

On the Monday afternoon 36,522 took the day off school or work to watch the daylight replay of the Cup match. It was daylight something, more like robbery! Preston took the lead and held it till the last 90 seconds. In the closing minutes, Preston's rising young star, Archie Gemmill, nearly put Preston into an unassailable lead. He crashed a powerful shot against the underside of the Chelsea bar which left Bonetti beaten all ends up. Seconds later the Preston keeper made an incredible save from a point-blank effort from David Webb. It was more than most Chelsea fans could take and they headed for the exits. Perhaps work would have been a better option for them.

David Webb never knew the meaning of defeat though whilst he wore a blue shirt. In the closing minute he crashed the ball home with a stupefying volley from two yards out after a frantic scrum in the six-yard box. There must have been 20 players in the penalty box. Those fans that were left in a freezing, half-empty Stamford Bridge went crazy. The thousands down in the Fulham Road, dreaming of a warm fire and worrying about work, heard the roars and turned back to see what was happening.

Straight from the restart the tireless Charlie Cooke intercepted a sloppy back pass from a Preston forward and surged downfield. The Preston defence were like rabbits caught in the headlights of a car. As cool as if in a five-a-side game he shot home an unlikely winner. The crowd were uncomprehending. The scriptwriters must have hijacked it for the European Cup final that won Manchester United the treble.

It would have been nice to record that from that 'Great Escape' Chelsea went on to lift the Cup, but Chelsea being Chelsea found a way of blowing it. Even Steve McQueen on his stolen motorbike would not have found a way around or even over the human wall of death that the West Bromwich defence put up in the sixth-round tie at Stamford Bridge.

In the previous round Chelsea had overcome Stoke 3–2 in a thrilling night match. This time the lights stayed on. Osgood continued his one-man war against Gordon Banks, who had joined the Potteries side from Leicester City. City had a young goalie called Shilton who they were expecting great things from. Osgood fired two shots disdainfully past the goalkeeper who was soon to be acknowledged as the finest in the world. The winner was a cheeky strike after John Boyle's intelligent chipped pass had beaten the Stoke offside trap. Stoke fought like tigers that night and their manager, Tony Waddington, felt his side was unlucky not to force at least a replay. Birchenall had been the other Chelsea scorer, he was feeling increasing pressure from the presence of Hutchinson.

A WHITER SHADE OF PALE

Once again Chelsea had a colour change for the quarter-final game. They wore the alternative strip of yellow shirts, blue shorts and yellow socks. They had worn the same colours when they beat Sheffield Wednesday with Baldwin's goal. West Bromwich wore all white. In the '60s white was a highly popular Cup strip. Tottenham had worn it on their European jaunts. The previous home game had seen Chelsea slaughter Sunderland 5–1. Birchenall had given Chelsea a first-half lead but Bobby Tambling stole the show scoring four goals in 18 minutes. A devastating spell between the 56th and 74th minutes took the Jehovah's Witness to a total of 199 goals. Houseman had a hand in three of the four Bobby Tambling goals. Peter wore the 11 shirt whilst Bobby had the legendary number ten on his blue shirt. Chelsea poured down the left-hand side of the field and completely overwhelmed the Sunderland backs Palmer and Harvey. Only superb goalkeeping by Jim Montgomery kept the score down. Montgomery was to go on to make one of the most historic saves of all time to rob Leeds in the 1973 Cup final. His save from Peter Lorimer (had some bad luck in his career, what with his disallowed goal at

Villa Park) was on a par with that of Banks's stop against Pelé in the World Cup. Ian Porterfield, who later managed Chelsea, scored Sunderland's match winner.

Also plugging the numerous gaps in the Sunderland defence against the Houseman–Tambling typhoon was Colin Todd. Colin was destined to become second only to Bobby Moore as the most stylish defender ever to play for England. That was the strength of English football in those days. Class players everywhere you looked. Sunderland stayed up by four points that season. QPR accumulated 18 points, still the lowest-ever total recorded. Geoff Hurst smashed six goals against Sunderland at Upton Park in October. The following month Jimmy Greaves equalled Tambling's four-goal haul against them. Sunderland were no wazzocks though.

Sexton was switching the players all the time, trying to find the combination that would give him the thunderball lottery win. Against Sunderland Osgood played in a four shirt, with the usual occupant Hollins wearing the number eight. Birchenall was the central striker, with Cooke drifting and foraging on the right. Houseman's nimble crossing was the bonus, their accuracy and variation set up chances galore.

In the early summer of 1999 Johan Cruyff gave a damning verdict on Kevin Keegan's England team, describing them as 'technically poor' after their inept 1–1 draw against Bulgaria.

'The game was no good,' said the former Barcelona manager. 'It was too slow, the passing was poor and technical qualities were very bad. The crosses were very poor. A country like England should not have to rely just on Beckham to cross the ball. There must be some more people in English football who can do that but, if not, you had better start teaching others. England put in maybe 25 to 30 crosses aginst Bulgaria and only one good one. It's not a very good average, is it? If the crosses are poor it's always difficult to score goals.'

After the hammering given to Sunderland the Bridge was packed and the talk was of another semi-final. Chelsea got the flyer they wanted. Tambling scoring early to set the Bridge alight. A fourth semi-final place beckoned. Villa Park again? But . . .

Osgood had an airball soon afterwards as the Cup holders clung to the wreckage. Another of Cruyff's maxims was that it was harder to concentrate when you had the ball than when you were without it. It was a throwback to the twin disappointments of the Villa Park defeats in 1964 and '65. Chelsea froze, the prize was so close, they had entered the bank vault, picked up the wedge and now all they had to do was walk out and stay calm . . . But a bell was ringing somewhere.

West Brom were battle-hardened by Cup success and public Cup failure.

QPR (then in Division Three) had humiliated them at Wembley in the League Cup a few seasons before. Two goals up at one stage and then Rodney Marsh started to play. Undaunted they had gone back to Wembley and lifted the FA Cup. They were used to fighting against the odds, unfashionable and underrated. They had some old professionals at the back, weary, vastly experienced, a throwback to a bygone era, but still mean. Very much the old guard. The Sheffield Wednesday defence that had snuffed out the Diamonds of Docherty were similar hard men. Chelsea never liked mixing it with teams like that. The same is true of their twenty-first-century counterparts.

Peter Houseman, who had tested the penetrability of the Albion rearguard early on in the contest was clattered twice within a few minutes. He was perceived as a threat and the supply route to Tambling. The Midlanders' midfield started to contest ground previously vacated. Gradually they pushed the ever-increasingly anxious Chelsea back. Goals from the deadly strike duo of Tony Brown and Astle tore the game from out of the Londoners' hands. What they dreaded most had happened, West Brom had come back from the dead and had their noses in front.

In the last 15 minutes Chelsea unleashed one of the most intensive bombardments ever seen at Stamford Bridge. To say West Brom never got out of their penalty area would not be an exaggeration. I recall Webb's arm pumping the air to inspire the Shed. Most of the last quarter was played out in the six-yard box. In the dying seconds Webb appeared to bundle the ball over the line. Osborne, the West Brom keeper, sat on the ball not really knowing where he or the ball were. John Boyle's response was to try and hack ball and keeper over the line. The whole ground was just shrieking, or so it seemed. Fans charged down the aisles near me.

The game ended in an uproar as another terrific scrimmage ended with the ball hitting the side netting amid a mêlée of fists, kicks and elbows. The Shed was in an absolute fizzer all game, from Chelsea's opening strike to the grandstand finish. As the hysteria reached epic proportions the elongated fragility of Houseman was to incur its full wrath. After the bitter Cup exit Houseman was quoted as saying:

> I can't understand why, but I seem to have been getting the bird for as long as I can remember. If you are having a bad spell – and every player suffers those – you expect to be criticised. But the Stamford Bridge fans seem to go for me no matter how I am playing.
>
> There doesn't appear to be a logical explanation for this sort of thing. Either the crowd like you straightaway or they don't. It's almost as if the fans need someone to have a go at, it happens on other grounds as well.

I understand Terry has been getting a lot of stick at Tottenham.

I thought that the criticism was rather unfair after the West Brom defeat, even though I was not particularly surprised by it.

The more you are in the game the more chance there is of making a mistake. But I've no intention of resorting to hiding. My only hope is to play my way into the crowd's favour.

Chapter Eight: The Winger Who Came in from the Cold

My favourite unrecorded song of all time is the single refrain of a chant that I heard one New Year's Eve in the last year of the '60s, whilst waiting by the East Fountain in Victory Square for the bells of St Martin in the Field to chime midnight.

There is abroad this night a holiday spirit, predominantly one of Caledonian aspect, and being a mild sort of evening for the season a great body of citizenry convene in the locality to exchange mutual demonstrations of goodwill.

Circumspect in the revellers' midst, among them but not of them, stands a vanguard of the metropolitan gendarmerie (Old Bill) regarding the festive multitude with unusually benign humour.

Ostensibly, their presence here tonight is a vigil against any milieu potentially inimical to the public peace.

Shortly before midnight, the abrupt turning of many heads in the crowd signals the arrival on the scene of some two dozen or so youthful skinheads, flanking the public throng by the negotiation of the North Steps. Lately unleashed from that enclosure of the Fulham Road designated the Shed, this juvenile corps advance on the square with the relentless purpose of a Mr Bobby Tambling, the truculent swagger of a Mr Peter Osgood, the parsimony of a Mr Eddie McCreadie, the devitrification of a Mr Peter Houseman and the haircut of a Mr Ron Harris. Assembling at the Charles the First Monument, they gave lusty voice to an original rendition of the celebrated 'Stamford Bridge is falling down' thus . . .

From an uncredited article in the citizen column of the NME circa 1977, courtesy of the archives of Cockney Rebel fanzine.

You may like to know that West Brom used up all their luck at Stamford Bridge in the sixth round. They went out in the semi-finals and Manchester City eventually took the Cup, thanks to a goal from Neil Young. About that time he was getting his band together to appear at Woodstock – or am I getting confused?

Leeds won the 1968–69 title after more near misses than even the Diamonds had. They only lost two matches all season, none at home. Don Revie was using the new 4–3–3 system to dominate the league, like Manchester United do today. The cornerstone of his success was the deeply demonised defence and a ruthless midfield mercilessly overworked by Revie. Chelsea trailed in fifth place, 17 points behind Revie's marionettes. Osgood had only scored nine times in 35 games but Sexton had been playing him in midfield for long stretches in a desperate, some would say foolish, attempt to find the right balance.

A band called Thunderclap Newman had a huge hit with a song called 'Something in the Air' which could have been the theme song at Stamford Bridge. I certainly felt that there were good times ahead. Elsewhere things were not so bright; British Troops started patrolling Catholic areas of Belfast, Colonel Gaddafi mounted a coup in Libya and the Kray brothers were jailed for life at the Old Bailey.

The season started badly for Chelsea, hit by injuries they crashed 4–1 at Liverpool in the opening match. It was another scalding hot day and Anfield was the pressure cooker that baked a rattled Blues side. Hutchinson scored a brave equaliser early in the second half but, lacking Webb and McCreadie, the defence cracked as Liverpool poured forward. Even the elegant John Hollins picked up a booking.

The World Cup duo of Hurst and Peters were on target as a drab Chelsea lost at Upton Park a few nights later. The sky was the colour of wet cardboard as the coach drove home, the old 'Chelsea crisis' headlines were being written already but Sexton steadied the ship as they won two and drew five of the next seven. Houseman was still floating around in the attack. Sometimes he wore a number 10 shirt, other times it was the more familiar 11. An accurate Houseman cross provided Hutchinson with the only goal of the game in a League Cup win at Coventry. Houseman shot his first goal of the season in the 2–0 home victory over Burnley. As he walked off he gave me a little thumbs-up like the young RAF pilots used to when they entered the cockpits of their Spitfires. Peter liked playing against Burnley, he once told me.

The early autumn saw the first of the epic gladiator battles against the champions, Leeds. The Blues were to lose the first of these encounters in a league game at Elland Road. John Giles, their midfield general, scored the first from the penalty spot after John Hollins had handled. Lorimer wrapped the points up for Leeds with a thunderbolt from 20 yards near the end. This one was allowed to stand. Lorimer was bitterly upset by the events at Villa Park two years before and the full ferocity of his shooting power was always felt by Bonetti.

By a quirk of fate Chelsea went back to Leeds only four days later for a League Cup tie. As so often happens in football, the form was reversed in just a few days. A marked improvement saw Alan Birchenall shoot Chelsea in front 20 minutes from time. Shortly afterwards Tommy Baldwin went down on his knees for a loping header from a Houseman cross and saw his effort crash against a post and ricochet into the hands of the Leeds goalkeeper Sprake. I thought we had pulled off a rare, shock win at Leeds, but in the dying seconds Leeds' Paul Madeley scrambled a draw with a messy goal. Madeley was 'Mr Utility' for Leeds and was able to fulfil any role for them. Like David Webb he was often pushed up front because of his versatility in times of crisis, with a brief to salvage what he could.

The replay took place on a balmy October night and Chelsea ran out worthy, easy winners. Charlie Cooke was the hero of the evening as his form came flooding back in waves. It was a triumphant return to form by the 'Double C'. Always the extraordinary chameleon, the cult of Charlie Cooke was already under way but that season saw him mature to being the greatest entertainer in the game. Towards the end of last season his form had dipped alarmingly and the first rumours of his emotional distress were circulating. Poor Charlie had a calamitous inner life. It provided twist and torque to his football. Against Leeds Cooke was unstoppable, scoring the first and setting up Birchenall to drive in the decisive second. In season 1969–70 the image of Cooke was set in stone. Like the entire team, he had flashes of brilliance.

Chelsea should have cleaned up that season. For a team so associated with chaos, though, things could never run smoothly. In the next round Chelsea travelled to Carlisle, the furthest point north that they could have visited. More recently, Carlisle only managed to stay in the league thanks to a goal scored by their goalkeeper in what appeared to be the last moments of their league career. The Brunton Park side had a knack of spoiling Chelsea's parties, though.

In 1974 they won their first-ever game in the highest echelon, scoring twice at Stamford Bridge. It also happened to be the day that we unveiled the East Stand, at that time the most expensive and controversial in the history of the game. Comparisons to the *Titanic* might be justified. The stand siphoned off millions with the kind of ostentatious architecture only billionaires would dream of constructing.

Chelsea wore yellow and blue that night. The colours reminded me of the china in Monet's dining-room at Giverny. Osgood and Birchenall frittered away chances like City boys tearing up tenners and showering them on world debt protesters. Bonetti had been hit by a missile midway through the first half and was feeling groggy. It later transpired that some meathead in the 18,513 crowd had chucked a slate at him. It was heavy enough to have caved his skull in, but as we all know cats have nine lives. The following week saw Peter break the all-time Chelsea record for Football League appearances set by Ken Armstrong between 1945 and 1957.

At Carlisle Bonetti was strugging. The floodlights flickered like strobe lights and his vision was blurred. The Chelsea defence protected him as best they could and hacked the ball away from his goal at every opportunity. Nobody played better than David Webb, who was down to take over in goal should Bonetti collapse. Chelsea were very much in control, with Hudson probing all over the park. A Chelsea goal looked likely at any time. Carlisle could only mount sporadic raids and were reduced to long-range shelling of Bonetti's goal.

The referee told the crowd over the public address system that he would not abandon the match, no matter what the score was, but that he would clear the crowd and finish the game in an empty ground. Bonetti looked increasingly uncertain as the game wore on. Near the end Carlisle won a free kick 25 yards away from his goal. The wall of Chelsea bodies partially cleared but the Carlisle full-back Hemstead tried a speculative shot that ended up in the back of the net. It was a shot Peter Bonetti would normally have sneered at, lacking pace and accuracy, but it was enough to dump Chelsea out of the League Cup. Roared on by the hardcore Chelsea supporters who had made the 600-mile round trip, Chelsea charged at the Carlisle goal. Webb was thrown forward but it was Houseman who so nearly saved it. Seconds from the close of play he spun and fired in a thumping shot that skimmed the Carlisle bar. It was the last Cup game Chelsea were to lose for a long time.

The circumstances of Chelsea's defeat saw a call for a change in the substitute rule. As the laws stood Chelsea would have had to continue without a specialist goalkeeper.

PATH TO THE ABSOLUTE

Sexton was disappointed at the result, but kept the faith. He regrouped his forces and saw out the autumn and early winter. Birchenall was hit by a bizarre knee injury in October that took months to clear. Hutchinson seized the chance to make that place in the team his own. Sexton was seeking extra cover for certain positions and added the defender Paddy Mulligan to the squad. The 24-year-old Republic of Ireland half-back or full-back signed from Shamrock Rovers. He was whippet-thin and fire-eyed, and had a generous, sympathetic spirit. A black mop of hair made him look more like a singer in a show band than a footballer. He gave up a job as a salesman in office equipment to join the Kings Road Club. Mulligan was a great character whose genial personality instantly gained him popularity with fans and players alike. Sexton was keen to maintain harmony in a dressing-room of disparate temperaments. Houseman was slowly establishing himself in the aggressive atmosphere of the dressing-room but his treatment at the hands of the Shed fuelled his insecurities. Tricky displays of wing play and spectacular goals helped. In the year Houseman made his début John Le Carré wrote his seminal espionage novel *The Spy Who Came in from the Cold*; perhaps Houseman, like the agent Leamas, was now coming in from the cold.

Houseman scored against Derby in a game sandwiched between the League Cup games. It was a typical effort, left foot from 20 yards, that the 51,000-plus packed into Stamford Bridge warmly applauded. The game finished 2–2 and Chelsea were lucky to keep their home record intact. Clough's burgeoning side was already causing ripples in the big time with their powerful running and elegant passing. It prefigured what was to come in later years from his teams.

Leonard Withey died in the autumn after giving up the Chelsea chairmanship because of his deteriorating health. Withey had been particularly adept at financial matters and had been deeply involved in negotiating the new lease, which had been of major concern. I was then appointed chairman and my life was never the same again.

Life was good for Peter Houseman. His son Matthew Peter was a year old, he had acquired a Vauxhall Viva Estate car and he was enjoying a lot of Chinese cuisine, along with his other favourite, scampi and chips. His favourite TV show, Morecambe and Wise, topped the ratings that year. Houseman's hobby away from football was football. Docherty had cracked that one at his interview and it opened the door. He coached a team of boys in his local village, Oakley near Basingstoke. He would coach them on Monday evenings and on Sunday afternoons could be found watching them play in a local league. Tea was the strongest beverage going in the social scenes he frequented. Houseman's schedule was relaxed, middle class, white collar, not unlike that of the thousands of young men who followed Chelsea. Despite their growing reputation as the toughest of fans, the truth was that the majority were middle-class boys from good homes. 'Middle England', as Blair's spin doctors say. The variety of backgrounds of the Chelsea fan-base was unique. Whilst most clubs' support in those days came from the working class, a fair percentage of Chelsea supporters were middle-class office workers. Houseman led the life of a typical office worker. Today a star player has a career run on business plans and military-style promotional campaigns. It would be no understatement to say that fame rapes its victims in the new century. The gap between Beckham and his fans is a yawning chasm, while Hudson and Houseman were the local lads who played instead of watching.

Houseman would always wear his club suit on Saturdays, though players were only required to wear suits to away games. The style thing was taking hold of the other players through the influence of the young Hudson. Hudson had broken into the side at the start of the season as a result of the long injury list and he was there to stay. No player had ever wanted the ball as much as Hudson did in the early days. His fashion antennae became more finely tuned than those of his fellow players. For those who care about such things, the haircut he sported around the end of 1969 was the finest that ever adorned a footballer.

As an icon, Osgood was gauche though enthusiastic. Hutchinson looked like he had potential as he slowly grew into his gunfighter demeanour, carving a niche for himself as the ultimate warrior forward. A gaunt shadow would come to haunt his face in later years as the injuries took their toll, making him look totemic. Ruud von Nisteleooy reminds me of him.

Houseman was very superstitious. He never drove himself from the hotel to the ground before a home match. The team would always lunch together as part of the pre-match build-up, so Bonetti or John Hollins would drive his car for him. Houseman never really enjoyed being in a car and more often than not he would be seen after a game catching the tube from Fulham Broadway. His relationship with the crowd was still a little uneasy – a letter appeared in the Chelsea programme from a fan wondering why Houseman never waved to the Shed when they chanted his name.

At Christmas 1969, Chelsea had climbed to fourth in the table. December had been a good month for the Londoners. They had started it off with their customary win at Old Trafford. Hutchinson blasted two first-half goals to set up their third consecutive win over George Best and co. Best was the only United player still capable of raising the Manchester crowd to any real level of excitement. The ex-Cambridge United striker headed the first from a long cross from Hollins and then drilled in a rebound after a great run and shot by Charlie Cooke. Houseman had another fine game, ensuring that he preserved his record of never finishing on the losing side at the Theatre of Dreams.

Wolves had rolled Chelsea over the following week scoring three times without reply. It was their first defeat in 12 games and at times the defence had looked very vulnerable down the middle. Sexton was concerned, but they bounced back with Webb scoring twice in a 3–1 victory over Cup holders Manchester City. Christmas must have suited David. He was always in the thick of the action, poaching goals. Hutchinson also hit another double as they beat Southampton by the same score on Boxing Day. The confidence Sexton had shown in Houseman was paying off as he rained in crosses for the goal-hungry Hutchinson, Osgood and Webb to convert.

Chelsea's last league match of the '60s took them to Selhurst Park to play the struggling Crystal Palace. Palace took a shock lead with a freak goal scored by their striker Gerry Queen. Phil Hoadley, whose name Chelsea had cause to remember in later years, pushed the ball through for the Queen of Palace to dash onto and score. Centre-half for Chelsea that day was John Dempsey, who had been signed from Fulham the previous season. Dempsey, funnier than

Frasier, whom he looked not unlike, managed to get his boot to Queen's shot but the ball took a massive deflection and spun crazily upwards. It dipped over the advancing Bonetti and fell into the Chelsea goal, rolling slowly against the back of the net. The record attendance for a Palace game, some 49,498, went crazy. Chelsea equalised ten minutes before the break, Hollins powered in a shot that Palace keeper John Jackson could only punch out and Osgood headed lazily back in.

The second half was delayed for eight minutes while a linesman with a pulled muscle was replaced. Hoadley, whose thunderous shooting had troubled Bonetti, was also substituted suffering from double vision after a clash with Harris. Chelsea applied the pressure, with Webb surging upfield at every opportunity. Houseman engineered Chelsea's second goal with a perfect centre. The stalwart defender Hynde got his head to it, but only succeeded in heading the ball over his own goalkeeper. Osgood, running in on the blind side, helped himself to a late Christmas gift. That season Osgood not only played with tremendous power, but his goal sense was never more acute. The half-chances were gobbled up along with the great goals. In this respect Jimmy Floyd Hasselbaink had something in common with him.

Shortly afterwards, a tremendous skirmish in the Chelsea goalmouth ended with Pinkney's corner being smashed against the post after the ball had bobbed about for ages. Pinkney was making his début as a replacement for the injured Steve Kember. Kember was Palace's star midfielder and a player admired by Sexton for his workrate and efficiency. Kember was a player seen by many as being force ripe – a footballer mature in certain respects but underdeveloped in others. I could see Sexton scribbling notes about him every time he played.

The mêlée ended with Osgood chasing the Palace defender McCormack upfield. Osgood had to be restrained by his own team-mates; even Bonetti left his goal to cool the white-hot situation. The sight of the undemonstrative keeper involved in the fracas set the Chelsea fans' hearts racing. The referee called the two captains together and told them to calm down the players.

Osgood exacted his revenge as Palace ran out of steam. The Chelsea midfield, with Hollins playing outstandingly, was using the increasingly desperate Palace attacks as a springboard for their dangerous breakaways. From one of them Cooke flicked over a centre that Jackson could not hold and the 'Wizard of Os' claimed his first Chelsea hat-trick. It was a simple goal; the ball dropped at his feet and he thrashed it home.

He wasn't finished though, clipping in his and Chelsea's fourth two minutes later as Chelsea ransacked the winter Palace. Most sides would have cruised, but Chelsea accelerated. Sexton appeared on the touchline, immaculate in a dark overcoat. The Shed boys who had caught the bus to South London gave it up for their king. Perhaps Sexton too was overcome by the emotion of it all. He was involved more than anyone in the resurrection of Osgood's career. Sexton had never lost faith in him, even when his leg took so long to heal. The appetite for self-destruction that was to symbolise the Chelsea of the '70s was a long way off. The great side of the early '70s came of age that afternoon in the crucible of Selhurst Park.

Houseman garnished the banquet with the fifth and best goal of the game. An exquisite diving header from Webb's cut-back cross. Houseman heading home full length from Webbie's centre! It was that sort of game. An even more incongruous sight was Harris leaving the dressing-room with a bouquet for his wife; apparently Palace treated all captains that way.

Palace's only bright spot that day was a loan deal which was set up to take Bobby Tambling to Selhurst. Bobby was unable to regain a first-team place following his cartilage operation and the Blues generously lent him to the South London club. It was to signal the end of his goal-strewn Chelsea career, but Hutchinson had by now muscled into contention as the number one strike partner to Osgood. Even Birchenall, himself hit by a string of niggling injuries, was having to look to his laurels.

1970

The third day of that momentous year saw Chelsea drawn at home against Birmingham in the third round of the Cup, a cup many expected them to win. The bookies had made Chelsea favourites. A shrewd Chelsea fan could still get about 10–1 for their chances. Birmingham included two old Blues Brothers in their line-up, Bert Murray and the wandering minstrel Tony Hateley who had joined the Brummies from nearby Coventry. Big Tony had the composite batting record. Barry Bridges had by this time left St Andrews to return to West London, playing for QPR.

Birmingham's tactics were pretty much the same as they had used to dismiss Chelsea from the cup in Sexton's first season as manager; defend tight and hit Chelsea with high balls. Hateley was countered by Dempsey, though, and the only real threat was posed by Bert Murray, a prototype Houseman. Early on in the game he gave the crowd a brief spellbinding moment from the 'diamond era', when a quick shot on the turn flew over the bar. A goal then may have disrupted a curious if not stilted Chelsea performance. Osgood started on his Cup record, scoring the first of the campaign just on half-time. Charlie Cooke put Hudson clear along the left wing and Osgood timed his jump to perfection to head the ball between Scottish international goalkeeper Jim Herriot and defender Bobby Thompson.

Chelsea played well within themselves, dominating but unable to convert their superiority into goals. Harris, venturing upfield on a rare search-and-destroy mission (minus flowers), almost made it 2–0 with a fierce drive brilliantly caught by Herriot. The second half was an anti-climax as Chelsea cruised, the crowd shivering in the freezing weather became restless at them. Near the end they finally stirred themselves and found a higher gear to wrap the game up with. Cooke flicked a pass inside to Houseman, who instantly turned it on to Osgood. Two defenders moved in on the centre-forward and he appeared to overrun the ball on the touchline only to regain control at the last moment, juggling it and turning for Hutchinson to crash in. It was his first-ever kosher Cup goal. In the last minute Hollins hit a huge centre over the retreating Birmingham defence to the far post, where Hutchinson hammered in his second Chelsea Cup goal and the game's third. After the match Sexton passed me on the staircase with a rare smile on his face; we both knew it was working.

The Cup draw saw Chelsea at home to Burnley in the fourth round, but before that they had the little matter of a visit from Mr Revie and his Elland Road shocktroops. Chelsea were lying in third place in the table with 34 points, six behind Leeds who had played a game more. Everton led the table with 41 points. The match was billed as the clash of the season. Just before kick-off Chelsea ruled Bonetti out with the flu. His place was taken by the reserve goalkeeper Tommy Hughes. Tommy had played only a handful of games despite his almost reckless courage, due to the continued excellence of Bonetti and his remarkable level of fitness.

Hughes had signed in July 1965 from Clydebank in Glasgow. Golf-mad Tommy was well over 6ft and heavily built, but had not yet been tested in the real heat of combat. To make things worse he had a bad dose of flu himself and felt only marginally better than Bonetti. Tommy had recently put in for a transfer, feeling that his career had little chance of advancement with the brilliant Bonetti blocking his progress. He was Scotland's Under-23 goalkeeper, if that counted for anything.

Chelsea stormed at Leeds from the start. It was an awful day, bitterly cold with pouring rain; no wonder everyone had the flu. Hutchinson's throws were of particular concern to Leeds. It was now official that Hutch had the longest throw in the league, probably the world. In a testimonial match for Bobby Tambling, Ian had won a long throw contest with an effort of 115 ft, a foot longer than Malcolm McDonald, a goal-scoring legend, future drinking partner of Hudson and a man who wore some serious sideburns. Supermac, as the Geordies were to christen him, was just starting to make his name at Luton. Sexton had him down as a prospect but he would not have got a game with the talent available. Hallelujah, what a time.

Leeds' counter to the menace of Hutch was for their star striker Alan Clarke to run up and stand as close as he could to the Chelsea chucker in an attempt to restrict his range. Clarke, whose namesake was lead singer in the fabulous pop hit machine that was The Hollies, made his England début that season and went on to score ten goals in 19 internationals. After failing to impress Aston Villa as a schoolboy he joined Fulham from Walsall. At Craven Cottage he was a constant thorn in Chelsea's side and went on to score vital goals against them throughout his career. He left Fulham as England's most expensive player when he joined Leicester for £150,000. His two brothers, Frank and Derek, were also useful players. Alan became England's costliest player for the second time, hotdesking clubs when he joined Leeds for £165,000 the previous summer. He had what all top strikers needed at that level, tenacity and a mean streak. Law, Hughes and Vialli all had those qualities, and Osgood developed them after Blackpool. Hutchinson and Hasselbaink were both naturals; there's no rationality about it.

Clarke was a deadly part of the hit squad that played for Leeds up front. He had a shot like a Kalashnikov rifle in his right foot and scored many with his head. Just as Billy the Kid was a left-handed gun, Clarke was never more deadly than when he could get the ball on his left side. He tested Hughes early on with a speculative shot from 20 yards that zipped over the sodden turf. It ended up amongst the paparazzi behind the goal but Hughes seemed slow to react as he went down by the post. Then Bremner fired in a shot that Hughes again looked unprepared for.

Clarke struck soon afterwards. Bremner put Mick Jones in for a close-range shot that spun off Tommy Hughes' body and, like the Osgood goal at Selhurst, flew wildly into the air. The Chelsea keeper should have caught it but Clarke, anticipating events, ran behind him and tapped the ball into an empty net for a disastrous goal.

It was Clarke's twelfth goal of the season and soon afterwards he had the ball in the net but again it was disallowed for a foul against Hughes. Poor Tommy was reeling, as if like Bonetti he had been hit with a lump of Carlisle slate. Leeds sensed blood and streamed forward. Norman Hunter was spoken to for taking a kick at Hutchinson near the corner flag as the Chelsea striker lay prone.

Clarke collided with Hughes as he raced in to meet a cross from Lorimer and fell badly. Soon afterwards he limped off, to be replaced by Mick Bates. Chelsea seemed in disarray but regained control with a two-goal burst just on half-time.

Hollins equalised with a terrific solo run, suddenly powering forward after picking his way through the midfield. John raced between two white shirts to fire in a tremendous shot. Sprake managed to get a hand to the ball but could only flip it up into the roof of the net. The crowd were delighted; Hollins was perhaps the most popular of all the Chelsea players of that era. Though never in the superstar bracket of Osgood or Cooke, and lacking the range of skills of Hudson, his more finite talent was supplemented by his tremendous workrate and the fact that he was the most consistent performer. His goals were always greeted with great enthusiasm by the Shed, who had a mistrust of really great players for some reason. They preferred primitive footballers to the complexity of players like Hudson. The emergence of young, home-grown talents like Terry and Jon Harley was always of more interest to the supporters than the purchase of world-famous mercenaries. Harley later went to Fulham.

Within seconds Chelsea were in front with the move that Leeds dreaded. Hutchinson, still seething from the hostile Hunter challenge, took a throw-in that could have ended up in the next millennium, Webb backheaded, John Dempsey, up on an assault on Sprake's goal, nodded the ball on and Osgood leapt like a jaguar to scissor-kick a magnificent goal. It would have graced any ground in the world. If the Versailles Palace had a pitch, that would be the goal.

Leeds buckled under the onslaught of two quick, fabulous Chelsea goals. We had them reeling on the ropes, but as so often happens in boxing the nearly vanquished were saved by the bell. The heat of the Chelsea attack was canned. Half-time gave Leeds time to gather their thoughts. As always with Chelsea, when given too much time to think they tended to freeze. Hughes' flu was giving cause for concern. Sexton decided to play Cooke and Houseman in a more withdrawn role to give more protection to his backs. The rampaging Hollins was told to curb his foraging to help shore up the centre of midfield. The powerhouse play of Leeds meant that we were being overrun by Giles and Bremner. Clarke was off the field but Sexton was worried by the threat of full-back (today he would be a wing-back) Terry Cooper. Revie was using him to play across the front line for long spells in the game. Cooper was a brilliant player, years ahead of his time.

Meanwhile, Revie was refusing to panic; he guessed correctly that Chelsea would fall back on defence and decided to go for a quick equaliser to unsettle them. His prayers were answered within two minutes of the restart. Terry Cooper, who was formerly a left-winger, scored a typical winger's goal of opportunism and verve. Cooper dribbled to the edge of the Chelsea box then pivoted and angled a fierce shot across Hughes and into the far corner of the net. Maybe Bonetti would have seen it, but it was unlikely that he would have got anywhere near it. For the rest of the game Leeds ate us up alive.

A freakish penalty put Leeds ahead. A lofted shot from Giles was judged to have been handled by Dempsey and the Irish midfielder beat Hughes with his sidefooted gimmick from the spot.

The roof was falling in for Chelsea – the contentious penalty decimated what little confidence they had left. David Webb was having a poor game against the Leeds wingers and his clumsy pass-back to Dempsey was intercepted by Lorimer. By now you will realise that Chelsea were anathema to Peter. He must have dreamt of this chance. He took the ball up to the advancing Hughes, sidestepped him and dribbled it into the net. It was one of the few goals he did not score with his whiplash shot and another act of revenge for Lorimer. He scored 168 league goals for Leeds in his two spells with them but it is doubtful if he celebrated any of them with more glee as he taunted the stunned Shed.

The exasperated Chelsea fans were already heading for the exits when Giles and Bremner tore a gaping hole in the Chelsea rearguard again for Mick Jones to hammer in number five. The game ended with brawling and harsh disputes amongst the two sets of players. Some Chelsea players started to get irritable and fists flew. A Leeds midfield player spat in Osgood's face as he took a throw-in. Harris strode around the Chelsea box trying to restore some semblance of order as the Leeds pressure took its toll. Ron could always be counted on in times of crisis, he was cut from a different cloth. Leeds took their foot off the throttle as Chelsea fell by the wayside.

It was a bitter defeat for Chelsea, their heaviest of the season and the first home loss. Like the Red Queen in *Alice in Wonderland*, they now had to run faster and faster to stay in the same place. It was natural selection; Chelsea and Leeds were each progressing so fast that each time they met one side staggered away wondering what they had to do next to keep pace with the other.

The Hughes problems aside, the centre of the Chelsea defence had been exposed as lacking pace and indecision. Against crafty wingers, the full-backs had been overrun for long periods. The midfield dominance Hudson had enjoyed all winter was eclipsed by Bremner and Giles. Houseman's contribution to the game had been virtually non-existent. The aggressive Leeds defender Paul Reaney was cited by Houseman as one of his favourite opponents for the tussles they enjoyed. That afternoon there was no modus operandi. Houseman was starved of the ball by the wrecked Chelsea midfield. That unforgettable match set up the climactic Cup final battle.

Sexton had to rebuild morale for the visit of Burnley. First, though, he had a trip to Highbury for a vital league game. Bonetti, now recovered from the flu, was restored in goal, with Baldwin deputising for Cooke, who was suffering from dental problems. Charlie always had a sense of grandeur about him but he seemed very aloof sometimes. Arsenal were in the throes of rebuilding their side. The following season they were to become the first team to take the League and Cup double since the fabulous Spurs of Blanchflower and White. The accomplishment of winning both Cup and Championship has become somewhat devalued by the unparalleled success of Manchester United, but the achievement of Arsenal should never be diminished. There was a more even distribution of talent in those times. The fact that a superb side like Chelsea never came near winning the league even with the vast talent available to them speaks volumes of the strength and quality around.

Arsenal fielded two 18 year olds in the Derby game, midfielder Eddie Kelly and a striker called Ray Kennedy, who was making his league début. Kennedy was to have his days against Chelsea but not on that occasion. Trouble delayed the start of the game and hundreds of young fans took refuge on the pitch as Chelsea's hooligan element tried to storm the North Bank. Another Arsenal legend, Charlie George, was to come on as sub later in the game. George was just emerging as a top-class player and idol of the terraces.

London was a cornucopia of breathtaking talent in the new decade, but most of the attention was centred on a player called Peter Marinello, Arsenal's glamorous £100,000 signing from Hibs. Marinello was tipped as the next George Best. London's media needed another Best clone to fill up their column inches. Fame as a profession was just beginning in football. Marinello was, like the title of the second Elvis Costello album, *This Year's Model*. He was a product of his time, as prepackaged as a '90s boy band. He had longer hair than Hudson and was prettier than George (Charlie not Graham). Marinello also had a nice line in expensive, flowing Cecil Gee raincoats. As a player he never had a chance to really prove himself. Very few talents could flourish in that hothouse environment. Even Best's career eventually crumbled in the furnace and at one time he was arguably the world's greatest player.

FRIDAY ON MY MIND

Robin Friday had his career lionised in the last decade. Described as the greatest player you never saw, the late Friday was given a trial by Chelsea when he was 13. He was a talent greatly admired by Harry Medhurst and was actually taken as a guest by the club to the 1967 Cockney Cup final. Perhaps that particular performance was enough to put the youngster off Chelsea for life. For whatever reason, he never made it at Chelsea. I do not recall him but I must have seen him play, because I watched hundreds of Chelsea trials and junior games. This was at the same time as Houseman was fighting his way up the ladder. Marinello was technically as good a player as Houseman and probably better than Robin Friday, yet only one of them had any tangible success. Houseman lacked the bravado of Friday and his image was not as trendy as Marinello's. It would be true to say that none of them could handle what fame represented.

Eddie McCreadie sat tight on Marinello all afternoon. The rain had persisted all week and the going was not to the liking of the speedy little Scot. You could compare him to a young Charlie Cooke. Peter showed touches of skill and grace but Chelsea, still licking their wounds after the Leeds débâcle, were in no mood to give auditions to young hopefuls. There were no stars in his eyes that afternoon. Eddie McCreadie described the winger after the game as 'a very good player'.

Marinello had a hard time at Arsenal, starved of the ball by his jealous team-mates. Even then there was so much pressure and envy. I cannot imagine what it must have been like for Vialli or Gullit. Once you have a certain level of press coverage everybody is gunning for you. The money someone like Beckham generates 100 people could live off, so these players automatically make enemies.

Marinello was eventually sold off to Portsmouth and ended up running a pub like so many of his fellow football-playing superstars. It was to be 13 years till another speedy, elegant winger with a taste for flowing raincoats was to hit the trail from Scotland to the bright lights, big city. Pat Nevin had an even greater impact on the media and a highly successful spell with both Chelsea and Scotland.

Chelsea crushed Arsenal 3–0 with almost effortless ease. After 40 minutes Hollins' miss hit cross confused Bob Wilson in the Arsenal goal and the ball ended up in the net in front of the North Bank. Nick Hornby must have been traumatised by the whole afternoon as worse was to follow.

After that it was Wilson against Chelsea. Twice he made point-blank saves from Osgood, who was through with the goal at his mercy. Hudson, playing immeasurably better than the previous week, set up the second for Hutchinson. Ian thumped home with his head after a huge trampoline jump that Eddie the Eagle could not have equalled even at the peak of his illustrious career. In the dying seconds Baldwin stabbed in the third goal from Osgood's lavish cross.

Chelsea, still buoyant from their stroll at Highbury, raced to a 2–0 lead against Burnley in the fourth round of the Cup. The first half was tense, Chelsea were still missing Cooke and Osgood was carrying a knock after his running battles with the Arsenal defence. After an hour Hollins put Chelsea in front with his third goal in successive matches. His low drive beat goalkeeper Mellor (no relation) from 25 yards. Osgood scored the second and his obligatory Cup goal in the next minute with a header that appeared to settle it.

Burnley were always tough adversaries of Chelsea. The economics of football were finally catching up with them and their glory years of winning titles were behind them. Each year they were forced to sell one of the many star players that their élite youth system had produced. The downward curve that was to take them within one match of going out of the league (like Chelsea's League Cup conquerors Carlisle) had already started, but they were not going to be beaten easily. Their defence scorched earth whenever they came to London.

Martin Dobson was a player in the mould of Hollins, equally at home in midfield defending or attacking. Burnley used him as the situation demanded. Two down away from home, the situation demanded that he was pushed up front. It worked a treat. Burnley scattered our defence with some powerful runs and scored twice in the closing minutes to force a replay on the following Tuesday. Once again the Chelsea defence had shown frailty at a crucial point in a match and Dobson had skewered them. Worse was to follow – Osgood took a further knock on his ankle and, despite intensive treatment on the Monday, was ruled out of the Turf Moor showdown.

It was time for Peter Houseman to come in from the cold.

Chapter Nine: Then a Hero Comes Along

All the world is a stage, most of it is miscast.
Oscar Wilde, Lord Arthur Savile's Crime

Eighteen minutes from the end of their fourth-round FA Cup replay against Burnley and Chelsea were heading out of the competition. Osgood, despite intensive *ER*-type attention in the treatment room on his ankle, was ruled out of the Tuesday night showdown. Charlie Cooke returned after his dental problems though, with Tommy Baldwin wearing the Wizard's number nine shirt. A strangely nervous Chelsea side trailed to a first-half goal from Ralph Coates. Throughout the early part of the game Coates had tormented the Chelsea defence and caused constant problems. The contest was unsophisticated and featured some brutal tackling, Chelsea conceding 11 physical fouls in the first 25 minutes. Coates was singled out for most of the punishment by the Chelsea defenders. Harris and McCreadie both earned bookings for reckless challenges on him. Coates, to me, was very much a 'one-trick pony' and flopped when transferred to Tottenham. That night, though, he was the fulcrum.

Hudson hit the post early on in the game but after that it was nearly all Burnley. The turbo-charged Coates concentrated on attacking down the left-hand side of the field and comprehensively exposed a weakness in the Chelsea side. Chelsea floundered in the wake of his sheer power and pace. After 35 minutes he suddenly switched to the right flank and cut inside; he often found it more preferable to cut inside onto his stronger foot. At the corner of the penalty box he unleashed a left-foot shot that whistled past Bonetti and into the net, making the score 1–0. And that was how it remained, with less than 20 minutes left.

Cooke was finding the going hard, as he was not 100 per cent fit. Hollins was driven deep to cope with the threat of Dobson. Sexton had given strict orders that he should be shadowed wherever he wandered. Up front, Ian Hutchinson was having a guerrilla war with the central defenders in the Burnley rearguard. Tommy Baldwin, a lower-maintenance Birchenall, was

119

having an unhappy evening. Houseman switched inside to find more space. Time was running out but Chelsea were ineffectual and undistinguished.

Meanwhile Chelsea's all-time greatest fan, Mick Greenaway, stood on the terraces with a band of Shed loyalists. Jeering Burnley fans surrounded them, but they knew better than to attack the London Boys. Mick grew up in Billing Street, which is literally in the shadows of the East Stand. Today it is an enclave of pretty little cottages with a fleet of BMWs and Jeeps outside. As you walk to the game it is the little side street with the barrier like Checkpoint Charlie outside. Hudson was born a few hundred yards away near Chelsea Harbour. No player personified Chelsea's image on the pitch better than Hudson. No fan demanded more respect of it than Greenaway. By this time Greenaway was the undisputed leader of the Chelsea hordes. The best-known 'non-famous' man in London, he was born in June 1945 at the end of the war. Over the years I came to know him very well. He became the fans' representative and was frequently in the office. His grandfather attended the first game played at the Bridge in 1905. There was always a Greenaway on the terraces and his father was a huge fan of Hughie Gallacher. Gallacher was Chelsea's first superstar of the 1930s. He died a terrible lonely death.

Gallacher had broken the mould of ordinary, subservient players and laid down a blueprint for the rebel superstars that followed decades later. Mick's favourite Chelsea players of all time were Osgood and Hudson. The rebel image appealed to Greenaway and sowed a seed inside him which was to ferment. Mick started to watch Chelsea during a golden period for the game. The post-war years were a boom time for football attendances and the gates were anything from 50,000 to 70,000, depending on the opposition, but despite the massive crowds, Mick's first impression was how subdued these Chelsea crowds were.

Perhaps the cosmopolitan nature of the spectators had something to do with this. The local community was drawn from all over England and Europe, while the bohemian contingent gave the area a certain decadence that was eventually to be reflected in the team. West Ham and Millwall were based in East London docker communities and this made for a more passionate atmosphere. These clubs were always intimidating places for visitors, with their tight compact grounds and fanatical support. In the years before the Shed, the crowd at Stamford Bridge were less of a bonus for the home side. Before the development of the ground, the spectators were separated from the pitch by a dog track. With impartial support and the vast open spaces there was a resulting lack of atmosphere. In the days of Jimmy Greaves, it was commonplace for the opposition to be clapped when they scored a goal and for the home team to receive only scant applause for their efforts. This state of affairs puzzled young Mick.

At that time he was standing on the vast terrace that later became the site of the West Stand, which in turn was torn down to be replaced by the structure housing the millennium boxes. The best vantage point was a spot high up on the mound adjacent to the halfway line. Soon groups of youths, attracted by the excitement and din coming from this area, began congregating here on match days. Songs and chants were emerging as they started developing a sense of unity. Songs relevant to London became popular and I distinctly recall hearing Chelsea versions of Flanagan and Allen's 'Strolling' and 'Underneath the Arches' from that vicinity. Flanagan and Allen, a music hall act, were early stand-up comics. (Mind you, we had enough of those at Chelsea down through the years.)

Greenaway's lasting achievement was that his strength and self-confidence enabled him to unite the band of loyalist Chelsea fans and various radical groups and shifted them to the covered end of the ground. He correctly guessed that the roof would make the noise reverberate and increase the atmosphere. Thus the Shed was born . . .

Mick, along with thousands of other Chelsea fans, had taken the day off work to make the long trek north. The gates were locked before kick-off and many Londoners had to stand outside trying to interpret the sounds of battle. Greenaway was defiant. He felt like it was finally Chelsea's turn that season. To paraphrase Noel Coward, 'for years they had been unspoilt by success'. It was an exciting time to be a Chelsea fan, far more so than today. CFC seems so institutional now. Just another shopping mall with expensive merchandise. The values seem frail and the stars are pre-packaged. It is a conveyor belt of imported talent and there is an inherent, insidious snobbery about what players have cost, with many still to prove their passion for the club. That cup-winning season the fans could watch talents like Hutchinson, Hudson and Houseman emerge from their chrysalis. They could exploit the emergent tendencies of rebellion and glamour when things were still simple enough for a few individuals to carry the weight alone.

Twice in the '60s Greenaway had been badly hurt by rival fans when they had tried to annex his beloved Shed. When Manchester United had stormed the Shed with their Red Battalions he was struck by a crowbar. The blow was intended to crush his skull but he dodged the full impact and received a busted shoulder. West Ham fans had bottled him in a similar assault on the hottest piece of property in football. The terrace was like 'Hamburger Hill' in the Korean War, bitterly contested for and the scene of much violence. Although badly cut by the aled-up East Enders, Mick returned to watch Chelsea fans retake their citadel. On another occasion Mick was hurt in his local Chelsea pub, the Ifield. The Ifield was a pub steeped in the heritage of Chelsea Football

Club and was used by both fans and players. A few doors along David Mellor's actress friend lived and I recall that the tabloids reported how he would spend some evenings enjoying her company wearing a replica Chelsea shirt. Ambushing Greenaway in the pub some Spurs fans decided to replicate a pitch invasion by ripping up chairs and throwing the splintered legs high into the air over the bar. Mick took another beating but nothing dimmed his resolve. His belief in the cause of Chelsea was as deeply entrenched as the beliefs of any freedom fighter. No Chelsea fan ever questioned it. Football was political and the politics were about Chelsea's style and content.

On the foggy pitch the game went quiet. Burnley had punched themselves out, Coates was exhausted and limping, Harris was catching him now and McCreadie was trailing him everywhere, Hudson started to prompt. Chelsea emerged from beneath the hatches they had battened down at the height of the Burnley storm. After taking all the punishment that was dished out the time had come to strike.

Greenaway and Hudson were both brought up by Stamford Bridge. It was written in Maitland's history of London that this was the point where Julius Caesar and his army forded the River Thames chasing the retreating Brits. (This must be the only time that London boys ran from an Italian crew.) That part of Chelsea was always lively. The Clash, those old punk rockers, lived in a squat overlooking the river and frequented Hammersmith Palais.

Although Maitland did not record the incident, *The Times* in August 1898 carried the following story about an event that happened on a Bank Holiday:

> In one disturbance that received wide publicity, a policeman had stumbled across a gang of about twenty youths, said to be known as the CHELSEA BOYS, who armed with sticks and stones were fighting a contingent of similar young ruffians from Battersea at Cheyne Walk by the river.
>
> A 17-year-old paper-stainer, James Irons, was brought before the magistrate described by the police as a ringleader and by his mother as a 'good boy'. It was said that he had used disgusting language and discharged a number of stones larger than walnuts from a powerful catapult to the common danger, he was found to have four previous convictions against him for gambling, disorderly behaviour and stone throwing. Regretting 'that he had no power to send him to prison without the option of a fine' the magistrate imposed a fine of 40 shillings or 21 days' hard labour.

Watching Chelsea at Burnley was certainly hard labour for Greenaway. His mind honed by hundreds of Chelsea games, he could sense a change in the pattern of play. Few fans had his knowledge or insight into football. Chelsea needed lifting, they were still in the game but now it had to be taken by the scruff of the neck. Mike unleashed a tremendous cry of 'Zigger Zagger'. If ever a particular football chant is locked into a certain period of time then 'Zigger' is as much a part of that era as Baddiel (another nouveau Chelsea fan) and Skinner's 'Three Lions – Football's Coming Home' was part of the last few years of the twentieth century. The chant was discovered, purely by chance, in the same part of England as Burnley. Greenaway had travelled up north a couple of years earlier for a Chelsea away game that was postponed due to bad weather. Rather than face a wasted journey he travelled on to Blackburn Rovers who entertained Leeds, though the word 'entertain' should be used lightly; the game was insipid and boring. It finished 0–0, and Greenaway spent the game wincing at some of the tackles made by the embryonic Leeds defence. The crowd grew increasingly restless in the Lancashire chill and the draw was played out in almost complete silence, occasionally punctuated by the chant of 'Zigger zagger, zigger zagger, Oi Oi Oi!'. This seemed to galvanise the fans and sounded completely different to anything Mike had ever heard before.

The roots of the chant are shrouded in mystery. Greenaway researched the matter and discovered the existence of a Stoke fan called 'Zigger Zagger' Pat who was thought to be the author of the song. The true origin is buried deep in some football X-file. The Kop sung it for a short period before the Gerry and the Pacemakers version of 'You'll Never Walk Alone' was played over the tannoy system as Liverpool took to the field. The rest, as they say, is history.

The 'Zigger Zagger' chant only came into its own when a play used it for its title. It was first performed by the National Youth Theatre at the Jeannette Cochrane Theatre on 21 August 1967 with a cast which included the late Simon (*Hi-Di-Hi*) Cadell. The play was written by Peter Terson, who grew up in Manchester in the '30s when City were the golden team of the era. *Zigger Zagger* was set in Stoke (which gives credence to the theory that the chant originated from that area). Terson tried in the play to compose a statement about the malaise of the time, avoided the cumbersomeness of the traditional social play but could find no other structure that would give coherence to his visions. It was still front-page news, the first study of the roots of football hooliganism. Terson tried to embody his keen if unstable vision in a story about people whose huge dislocation of experience and feeling would, by the very nature of their extreme dislocation, come to seem significant, a subject which has today spawned a whole cottage industry. Most of the so-called experts were only spectators outside the milieu where there is at least some awareness of the issues, whilst the real gang leaders, or 'Chaps', found it hard to get their factual versions published. Art imitating life? Eat your heart out, Nick Hornby.

Terson's work charted the progress of an 'average lad' who goes straight from a dead-end school to a dead-end job. Peter was not writing only about football, His real concern was the emptiness and futility facing so many youngsters pitched out of secondary school at 15 with only the prospect of dead-end jobs. 'This is about a boy who leaves school,' wrote Terson, 'with wasted years behind him, with nothing in front of him, except a factory job and a family, and the only immediate present – The Football.'

One of the controversial items of the play was its parody of psalms and hymns. 'Onward Golden City' was used at Stoke by the Victoria Ground's fans and 'God Save Our Gracious Team' was another Kop jukebox favourite. It was 'Zigger Zagger' that was the showstopper, though. Still is.

Greenaway, without any ideological delusions, made the chant his own, a theme song almost. Frank Sinatra immortalised the song 'My Way', but it was Paul Anka who wrote it. 'Ol Blue Eyes' made it his theme song though. 'Zigger Zagger' was the first post-modern statement in football.

'One Man Went To Mow' came much, much later, another Mick Greenaway arrangement of a traditional nursery rhyme. Mick told me shortly before he died that he had heard a drunk mumbling this as he dozed on an aeroplane. Mick was returning from a long-haul Chelsea trip and the nonsense stuck in his mind. The two all-time great Chelsea hits were both courtesy of Mick Greenaway. If he'd had a royalty fee every time Chelsea voices sang them he would have been as rich as Sir Elton, my old team-mate in the charity side.

The refrain of 'Zigger Zagger' bounced down the terraces and across the pitch that freezing February night. A cluster of dispirited Chelsea fans scattered around the main stand heard the battle cry and picked up on it. Some Chelsea boys isolated high up in the Burnley end started chanting the mono version of 'Chelsea, Chelsea, Chelsea'. It sounded like a funeral dirge but it always upset the other side. I heard the mantra from the directors' box. David Webb, fresh from another bruising clash with the Burnley hard man Kindon, also heard the chant. His craggy features split into a grin. Harris raised his clenched fist to shoulder height and yelled for more effort. Ronnie always was the toughest kid on the block, driving on his troops. Contrary to the media's often-expressed view, 'Zigger Zagger' was not a signal for trouble to erupt but a rallying call. Down on the Turf Moor pitch, Chelsea moved forward.

Peter Houseman lifted his head up and ran into the centre circle. I often think of him now. Peter was the purest, most idealised expression of English heroism, marred by tragedy. He was thriving in the floating role Dave Sexton had given him in the second half. Like all instinctive players he displayed a far better passing range when allowed to roam free. Burnley's defence had dropped deeper. It denied the space behind them to Baldwin and Hutchinson but it also meant that Houseman could run further with the ball without entering into congested zones.

An unnecessary defensive error let us back in. Houseman robbed Burnley defender Brian O'Neill of the ball, O'Neill had pulled the ball down and tried to beat the Chelsea forward as he ran at him. Houseman crossed the halfway line and picked up speed. Jimmy Thomson, the blond Scot, once a Docherty Diamond, was now a Burnley player. Houseman accelerated quickly to throw off the challenge of the ex-Chelsea back. People forget he had an engine on him like you had never seen. He raced on through midfield not so densely populated as it had been earlier. Mud and guts. Charlie Cooke appeared out on the right, a tiny yellow-and-blue smudge shrouded by smoke and a slight mist. The thought flashed across his mind that he should pass to the Scot and then go for the return. Something told him to keep going though. So on he ran deeper into the Burnley half, Cochise leading the braves from the front.

Ian Hutchinson was quoted later that year as saying 'being fit is not enough, unless you are also willing to go on making runs again and again, there comes a time when players begin to tire and start to wonder whether it is worth going off on another big chase'.

Other players may have hesitated, but Peter Houseman did not. At the edge of the box he cracked in a furious drive. Peter Mellor was well over 6 ft tall and weighed in at 13 st, but he looked like a dwarf in goal as Houseman's shot hit the back of the net. The Burnley crowd was stunned. The Chelsea supporters were silent at first, scarcely believing what they had just witnessed. Then they became almost hysterical with relief and joy. For the first time in his career Houseman had mesmeric power over his fans; they screamed, surged, adored.

Houseman stood alone, his right arm held aloft. Mellor tried to get up but slipped. The ball bounced around in the back of the net. It took ages for the first Chelsea player to reach him, a true solo effort. I will always remember him standing there under the gold glare of the floodlights – ''scuse me while I kiss the sky'. Hutchinson and Cooke engulfed him, then they were coming from all parts of the pitch. The mêlée signified for Houseman acceptance, opportunity and eventually tragedy rushing at him in those running figures on the Burnley field. Houseman's success was also to be his destruction – it started then.

THE SELF-PRESERVATION SOCIETY

The match should not have gone to extra time. Chelsea unleashed a blitzkreig. Hutchinson crashed a shot against the underside of the bar, which flew out. For a moment I thought we had scored. (There wass never a Russian linesman around when Chelsea required one.) Baldwin missed from close range. Cooke's drive ricocheted off Jimmy Thomson with Mellor beaten.

In the third minute of extra time Houseman found space on the left. Red Bull was not available then but he played like he had downed a barrel of the stuff. Peter instantly dispatched an inch-perfect centre, Himalayan in height, for the onrushing Baldwin. Tommy was still suffering from the long-term effects of a knee ligament injury suffered in December 1968. Apart from his recent tap-in at Highbury, his only other goal so far that season was also against Arsenal, scrambled in a 3–0 home win. It had been a dark time for Tommy and many other players would have quit. But as they used to say in the Shed, he was 'staunch'. He had been limited to a handful of games but was slowly regaining his sharpness and desire. A less experienced player would have flicked the header downwards but Baldwin nodded it up and over Mellor, high into the net. Chelsea were in front again and this time they stayed there. Burnley were splitting at the seams.

Greenaway was hoarse with exhorting Chelsea on. Sexton demanded that the workrate was maintained. Cooke, not having a good night, missed the easiest chance of the two ties but Burnley were a spent force, dead on their feet. Houseman was dazzling, shooting and passing, running and harrying, like a shark darting through water. It was fitting that he clinched it for Chelsea four minutes from the end, shooting in the third goal off a post. It was the same post Hudson had hit in the first half, a lifetime ago. This was Houseman's first-ever two-goal performance for the Blues and it propelled him to a new stratum of celebrity. Things were never going to be the same for him or Chelsea. That night was mystical, an incredible combination of chance and talent.

Chelsea returned to Selhurst Park in the fifth round of the Cup. This was just a whistle stop for the Wembley Express. The record of receipts Chelsea had set at the Christmas Osgood goalfest was broken again that day. Osgood continued his one-man vendetta against the Palace defence by heading in the first from Peter Houseman's corner.

Palace equalised early in the second half, Roger Hoy catching Bonetti wrongfooted with a header. The South London side tore into Chelsea and missed a couple of half-chances in goalmouth scrambles. For a while it nourished the delusion that they were in the game with a chance of putting Chelsea out. The pattern of the match was identical to the league encounter. Chelsea took the lead, were pegged back with a bizarre equaliser and then encountered stiff resistance from the home side. But Chelsea clung on and, once again, in the last third of the match found the will to push their bodies to the absolute limit. It was all down to determination and grit.

John Hollins lofted a mighty free kick into the Palace box and John Dempsey, surrounded by tough defenders, scored with a majestic header. As Palace reeled Osgood smashed a flamboyant volley through a crowd of players and onto the post. The terraces were like a battlefield. Things began to get hysterical.

By the 72nd minute it was over as a contest. Peter Houseman scored his third Cup goal of the season and slashed Palace's defence to pieces like some blue-shirted Hannibal Lecter. The goal was yet another variation of the oldest trick in the Chelsea repertoire, but one that few teams could counter. This time Webb took a free kick, Dempsey, on the rampage throughout the second half, flicked the ball on and Houseman, the gazelle, finished with a colossal shot.

Then Hutchinson machine-gunned in the fourth, obviously thinking it was worth while making another chase and the game finished with Chelsea, as our friends the Clash would say, in 'Complete Control', their fusion of power and class the final confirmation of their startling rise. We were all intoxicated by the experience of winning. That year we didn't know there was a tomorrow – now we do.

ONCE UPON A TIME IN THE WEST (OF LONDON)

QPR were next on the hit list as the draw kept Chelsea in London. Out came the yellow-and-blue shirts again after their little trip to Turf Moor. The parallels between the Crystal Palace and QPR games are interesting. In both matches Chelsea hit four goals and finished strongly, but they had to overcome stubborn opposition from the home side. The late Sir Alf Ramsey visited Loftus Road. I never really got on with Sir Alf as I found him very aloof. He never gave much of himself. It was as if he was too good for football, as if dealing with the players was beneath him. We never connected personally or professionally. The World Cup holders manager was there to check out Osgood's form with an eye to the upcoming defence to be held in Mexico that summer.

Ramsey had said, 'If we are going to keep the World Cup in Mexico we must improve our technique. We must learn to kill the ball more cleanly. There is a need for players who can do this quickly. We are short of this type of player.'

Once again Osgood did not fail to deliver, scoring a hat-trick and dominating the game. Ramsey could hardly fail to have been impressed by the form of Hudson, who had easily his best game in the Cup run. All his strengths were stunningly focused into one performance. It was after this game that Ramsey made his famous quote: 'There is no limit to what this boy could achieve.'

Ramsey, not known for his effusive praise, never said a truer word. At that time there was no limit to what Hudson could have done in the game. I think he was potentially the greatest player London ever produced. Ramsey's words were a harbinger of the unprecedented worship and attention he was to receive for an all too brief time, at that time the praise kept coming. Peter Marinello, the 'new George Best', was getting the hype down at Highbury, but soon it was to switch to Hudson. On the field he was a necromancer.

It is also interesting to note that a future England coach was in direct opposition to Hudson that day and was instantly impressed. Terry Venables was now plying his trade with the Rangers, his first unhappy spell at Tottenham being concluded by a transfer across London. Terry, being Terry, was unfailingly diplomatic about the whole thing. He was back in his old stamping ground of West London. QPR turned out to be a good move for him; he recaptured some of the brilliant early form shown at Stamford Bridge and the stability was helping him plot his managerial career. Venables, being Venables, was always one jump ahead. At this time his impact at QPR was largely misjudged. He was the most gregarious man I ever met. Today I can see it accentuated his greatness.

That day Chelsea blew Rangers away, playing superb controlled football in short devastating bursts. They were reminiscent of the great Liverpool side of the early '80s, running, passing, cruising, attacking, cruising, attacking, coasting, passing, running, always running. Chelsea were two up in ten minutes and booking their place in the semi-final, or so it seemed. David Webb smashed the first of his Cup goals after an intricate move down the right between Cooke and Hollins. Cooke had missed the Garden Party at the Palace and was making up for lost time. Sixty seconds after Webb's goal, Charlie set Osgood up for a second goal. Charlie threaded an immaculate pass through the heart of the QPR defence and 'The Wizard' did the rest. Two nil! No wonder Osgood grinned wickedly and gazed up at Ramsey and his retinue.

Another old Chelsea boy still had a part to play in the melodrama. Barry Bridges had joined QPR from Birmingham and took up where he had left off at St Andrews by giving Eddie McCreadie a melting. Coates had exploited McCreadie's pace, which was slowly being diminished by time and injury. Despite that, he remained the team's best blocker. After 25 minutes Eddie pulled down the double B flying machine and the referee gave a hotly disputed penalty. Ron Harris led the protests, as only he could, but the referee was not swayed. Venables scored with a penalty taken at the second attempt to narrow the score-line. Terry's first effort was saved by Bonetti but the referee made him retake it, judging Bonetti to have moved. Venables, always the consummate dead-ball artist, beat his old mate Peter with a crisp drive. Hasselbaink hit them harder, but Terry placed them better.

Chelsea were breaking more box office records than *Star Wars* that season – 33,572 packed into Loftus Road. Outside the touts were making a killing. Tickets worth £2 were going for ten times their face value. At Highbury for a recent Chelsea clash the touts were selling £25 tickets for three times their face value. Football is more expensive these days then?

Just before half-time Bridges came within inches of scoring with a header that another ex-Chelsea number nine, Tony Hateley, could not have bettered. Bonetti could only watch as the ball scraped the foot of the post. A goal then might have changed things. Across town and a few miles north, Watford were dumping a shot-shy Liverpool out of the Cup.

Chelsea took an instant reprisal. Hollins fired in a murderous shot that spun off the Rangers keeper Mike Kelly and Osgood instantly smashed in the third. With almost an hour gone Osgood rapped in the fourth and his first FA Cup hat-trick. Peter Houseman's swerving cross had caused havoc in the QPR penalty area. The Rangers back Dave Clement failed to clear the centre. Osgood pounced to precisely control the ball. Almost in one flowing movement, he shimmied the unfortunate Clement and fired a ridiculously hard shot past Kelly to bring the score to 4–1. Osgood followed it into the net. When I saw him do that I knew how serious he was. Chelsea fans had taken over three sides of the ground. They always overran QPR – what a bunch! All hell broke loose on the terraces. Tambling, Venables, Graham and co. had established the first generation of Chelsea fanatics, now Osgood and Hudson had the second wave to propagate the idea of Chelsea. After that it just got into a mess. The peculiar ritual of mass adulation was at its most acute during those legendary Cup matches.

Osgood was never more confident, he cavorted in front of his audience. The England manager, and still the only man to win the World Cup for his country, watched still and impassive from the QPR directors' box. Sir Alf had witnessed two talents in Osgood and Hudson that were on a par with anything his squad was to meet in Mexico. He received terrible flak from the media for suggesting that the eventual winners Brazil had taught him nothing. The misconstrued point that he was trying to make was that he saw nothing he had not seen before. I always felt a lot of antagonism from him towards Chelsea. Later I was on the committee that fired him.

Osgood's hat-trick meant the game was effectively over, but Barry Bridges was not finished and he ran through to pull a goal back. Even the Rangers' goals that day were hallmarked Chelsea. Both sides made and missed more chances, but that was how it stayed.

At the end of the match I caught Venables looking at Hudson the way we all look at people we admire. The baton passed from Greaves to Venables, Venables to Hudson, Hudson to Wilkins, all the way down to Zola and Frank Lampard, who recently joined for £11 million.

One last thing about that game – Dave Clement, the QPR defender, was to commit suicide a few years later. He was a buccaneering full-back and a fitness fanatic. I recall a fine game in Rome in 1976 he had for England, when we lost a vital World Cup qualifying game. The pressures of the modern game drove him crazy.

Chelsea were through to the semi-finals, their fourth appearance in six seasons. They were drawn against Watford, thus avoiding Leeds and Manchester United. Chelsea's win over Rangers confirmed that their slow transition from also-ran status was total and irrevocable. They were no longer a flamboyant decoration.

Almost 30 years on Manchester United were slowly strangling the FA Cup by their decision to opt out and plump instead for some Brazilian New Year gimmick. Perhaps they had something to learn. Arsenal Manager Arsene Wenger was furious that Manchester United were 'slowly killing the FA Cup. And why? To play in a tournament nobody's heard of.'

The season before Arsenal had narrowly lost to Manchester United in a semi-final that embodied the richest tradition of the world's premier club cup. The three matches described in this chapter were as good in their way as any Cup games ever played. Chelsea were technically superior to their opponents but the tremendous fighting spirit that the Cup engenders lifted them to such heights that the games became very evenly balanced for a long period. Today the gulf between the haves and have nots (even in the Premier League itself) is so great that matches of that type are not nearly so commonplace. The French manager was convinced that the semi-final had been so emotionally charged that had his side won it, Manchester United would have ended their campaign with nothing. Yet in the high summer of 1999 Manchester United were prepared to ditch it in favour of a world club cup he described sneeringly as a 'business tournament'.

'Business.' Wenger spat out the word. It was psychological warfare as he went on to say,

> If football becomes only business, it will kill the real love for the sport
> and after that the attitude would be spread out to the fans as well. I am

not saying money is not important but it must not become the only thing. My main concern is that what should make the big player today is, first, a love of the game.

Houseman loved football, Osgood loved football, and so did Hudson. Their success was their destruction. The whole point of this period is that it was a revelation, but by its very nature it could not be sustained.

Chapter Ten: Once in a While Forever

A man has only one destiny.
Michael Corleone, The Godfather Part III

It was the wet spring of 1970. A 24-year-old George Best signed an eight-year contract with Manchester United worth £10k a year. The average fan earned £1,200 a year. In the next 12 months Chelsea would win two major cup competitions, the Beatles would split up, Apollo 14 would have a moon landing, and Jimi Hendrix and Jim Morrison would both die. Simon and Garfunkel were number one with the classic 'Bridge Over Troubled Water' but at the Bridge the waters for once were calm.

As the Chelsea machine purred on to a semi-final clash at White Hart Lane against Watford, Everton, the underachievers, consolidated their thrust for the league title. Peter Osgood slammed in a hat-trick against the perennial fall-guys of Sunderland. This was a few days after the exciting Cup win at Burnley, which he had missed with ankle problems. Peter Houseman made the first goal with a lofted, swirling centre that deceived the Sunderland keeper Jim Montgomery. The Sunderland goalkeeper managed to hold the ball two-handed but the devilish spin on Houseman's cross meant he could not retain it. Osgood was on hand to thrash the ball high into the net.

Hudson created the second for him, tricking two defenders for Charlie Cooke to nudge into the path of the striker. Osgood glided into the box like a top-of-the-range BMW and fired a waist-high drive wide of Montgomery. It looked that easy. Perhaps it was. Osgood was dispatching goals so quickly then. His speed of action was second to none. It was forward play of another dimension. Completely brilliant.

Joe Baker, the Sunderland centre-forward that afternoon, was once on Chelsea's books as a youngster. I recall him very well, he had an interesting personality, very laid back. Never really verbalising his feelings, Joe was another small centre-forward in the mould of Gallacher who learnt his trade playing street football with a tennis ball in his gutties (a Scottish word for gym-shoes or plimsolls). Baker was born in Liverpool of Scottish parents and he went on to win eight caps for England, partnering Greaves on occasion. He once scored ten goals in a cup-tie for Hibs and had a highly accomplished career. Joe was one of the first British players to play in Italy. He was transferred for £73,000 to Turin.

Whilst in Italy he narrowly escaped death in a horrific sports car crash. His companion was Denis Law and the game nearly lost two of its biggest stars just when they were set for stardom. They lost control of their Alfa Romeo, which was a complete write-off. Italy was an exciting but dangerous place for a young British footballer, as Greaves would confirm. When Law and Baker became obstreperous they were on their way home. Joe returned to England for a hugely successful spell with Arsenal. At Highbury he teamed up with schemer George Eastham, the ex- Newcastle United star.

Baker was an all-time great at Highbury and easily stands up to comparison with Frank Stapleton, Ian Wright and our old pal Ted Drake. By the time he was playing for Sunderland Joe Baker was past his best but he still had enough tricks in the bag to worry the Chelsea defence; Sexton was always telling Dempsey to be more vigorous against ball-players like Baker. After a long-range shot had hit the bar, Baker knocked in the rebound to pull a goal back for Sunderland midway through the second half. Sunderland included Mick McGiven in their defence. Mick was later to work on Chelsea's coaching staff. The Wearsiders (or as they are now known the 'Black Cats' or something equally ghastly) briefly threatened to salvage the game, but Osgood completed his first league hat-trick 12 minutes from time.

Houseman was fouled out on the left-hand touchline, Hollins arched over the centre and when it landed Osgood hammered the ball first time into the roof of the net. He was on fire at that time, just phenomenal. No other striker compared with him for unpredictability, ingenuity and range of imagination. Osgood radiated power like Clark Kent before a bad kryptonite binge.

Comparisons could be drawn between Osgood and the former England captain with those butterscotch eyes, Alan Shearer, who also suffered a career-threatening injury whilst at Newcastle. The injury to his ankle was sustained against Chelsea and after a long absence of over six months he returned with his once-awesome powers diminished. At Blackburn he scored 112 goals in 138 Premiership games but in his first season back after injury he only managed eight in open play. A strong element of his game was the ability to get to the ball first. As his strength and power declined he became frustrated and petulant. A niggling streak seemed to have been added to his game. Shearer had an increasing tendency to use his physique and lean into defenders, which made him unpopular with the opposing fans. Osgood disguised his shortcomings in pace with increased stamina and his goalscoring prowess.

A few days after their exertions at Loftus Road Chelsea were held to a goalless draw at home by a rugged Newcastle United. Excessive demands were being made on their squad already. I did some research into exactly how many players Chelsea used in the last four decades. It makes some interesting reading: 1960s, 79 players; 1970s, 67 players; 1980s, 81 players; 1990s, 97 players.

What the figure will be for the 2000s is anybody's guess. The pattern is of a steady increase. Of course the turnover is now greater and the huge influx of overseas players has increased the size of the squads,

Osgood and Bonetti were away on England duty. Ian Hutchinson was injured. (Already so early into his fledgling career on the cutting edge of the game he was picking up more than his fair share of knocks and blows.) This meant a comeback for Alan Birchenall. It was the striker's first game for four months but it ended in hospital. The 'Birch' was detained in nearby St Stephen's Hospital with a bad gash below his left knee after he collided with Newcastle goalkeeper Liam McFaul. Alan Hudson crossed and as Birchenall tried to head home he was injured in an ugly clash with the Geordies' custodian. Like Hutch, he was game for anything. He was a huge man and Sexton once described him as 'a helluva good runner off the ball'.

UP WHERE WE BELONG

Paddy Mulligan substituted for the injured Birchenall and David Webb was pitched forward. Chelsea had little return for all their effort. Towards the end they lost a little concentration. Newcastle's rugged defence, battle-hardened in Europe, held out despite heavy pressure from Chelsea. Tommy Hughes played in goal for the Blues and kept a clean sheet, which was an improvement on the score-line for the Leeds game. Hughes' next stint between the sticks was to prove not so satisfactory.

The injury effectively ended Birchenall's career at Stamford Bridge. His dilemma was that he loved the club, but there were so many great players around that it was hard for him to get a game. The following summer he took the well-trodden path to Crystal Palace where Chelsea recouped the club's £100,000 outlay on him three seasons before.

My favourite story concerning Birchenall happened shortly before he left the club. Chelsea had travelled to Venezuela for a tour. My wife June and some of the players went off to water-ski. I stayed behind, doing some vitally important thing a chairman of Chelsea would have to do in Venezuela, when I was interrupted by Alan. He had a mischievous twinkle in his eye.

'Chairman, what do you want, the good news or the bad news?'

I always asked for the worst news first. Still do.

'The bad news was your wife fell into the water without a life-jacket. The good news was I dived in after her and saved her.'

Alan knew all about diving, of all kinds, as a disputed penalty he subsequently earned for Palace against his ex-team-mates was to prove. Needless to say I feigned annoyance; 'Call that good news? This settles it, you are going on the transfer list. Today!'

After the Birch left the Bridge he became another hired gun. His stay at Palace was thankfully short and he was soon transferred to Leicester City (another rest-home for ex-Chelsea players: Dennis Wise and the idiosyncratic Frank Sinclair was there, last I heard). The Birch's later clubs included Blackburn, Luton, San Jose Earthquakes and Memphis Rogues. At all these clubs he performed his usual impeccable duty of holding up the ball before bringing others into the game. What many fans did not understand was that Birchenall could take away two, or sometimes three, defenders on his own because of his vision.

It is interesting to note that Birchenall was entitled to a £5,000 signing-on fee when he signed for Chelsea. His basic wage was £65 a week plus the £30-a-point bonus. Alan had started his working life covered in grease as a £6-a-week apprentice fitter in a bus garage. Football had enabled him to buy an £8,000 detached house near Ascot racecourse. At the time of writing, Mr Beckham's weekly wage demands would buy a dozen of those houses.

Birchenall was aroused by fame's first kiss and was determined to carve out a career with a big club. For that reason he had earlier turned down a move to Ipswich, but his prospects at Chelsea were limited by the emergence of long throw king Ian Hutchinson, then at the height of his powers. Sexton had noted the renaissance of Tommy Baldwin. Birchenall was good for morale, full of vim, laid back. Seemingly carefree, he had the *chutzpah* of a market trader and a streetwise, sarcastic sense of humour. Like Terry Venables before him he fancied himself as a crooner. He told stories of his time in Sheffield when he would sing on stage with an up-and-coming singer called Joe Cocker. Cocker went on to become one of the biggest recording artists of that era; he had a world-wide smash hit with a duet called 'Up Where We Belong'. Alan was not on the record, as far as I know. Actually it was a lady called Jennifer Warnes. I recall that on a trip up north I heard Alan and his estuarine drone singing a Tom Jones song. If he had not been so serious it would have been funny.

The East Ender was always a popular character in the Chelsea dressing-room, ever since his initiation by Ron Harris. Harris had crash-tackled him in one of the infamous five-a-side games. These were played on Friday mornings, on the forecourt behind the Shed, where the Chelsea Village now stands, and were the scene of some fierce challenges. Joe Fascione had warned the new boy to watch out for Harris. Legend had it that he drowned newcomers in a soup of their own backbones. Ron worked on the theory that if you messed with the bull you got the horns. He wanted all newcomers to know who was the top man, the hard boy of London – reputation was everything. Still would be; ask Vinnie how it works. Before the internal problems tore the side apart, that was the set-up. Birch shrugged off Little Joe's warning, feeling he was being over-solicitous. His words went unheeded because a few minutes into the five-a-side the bullet-headed Chelsea skipper sent Birchenall catapulting six feet in the air before he crashed to earth. There were plenty of stars in the Chelsea car park that winter's morning, but Birchenall could only see the ones that shone at night. Harris, short-haired and hyper-impatient, stood over him and berated him with, 'That will cost you £65.'

Harris knew what everyone earned at Chelsea. The pugilist of this parish was as economic with his money as he was with his scything tackles. Osgood used to give Ron a lift to training and would pick him up at the sweet shop he ran with his pretty Cockney wife, Lee. As Harris prepared to leave for his day's crunching, the 'Wizard of Os' would help himself to juicy pear-drops or a few of the succulent wine gums contained in the heavy glass screw-top jars on the counter. Who could resist such treats? Harris was always quick to remind his centre-forward and unpaid chauffeur of the price of the confectionery and to charge him accordingly.

Both Harris and Birchenall went on to have successful careers when their football exploits had ended. Naturally the sweet shop entrepreneur became a millionaire due to property speculation, whilst Birchenall is now one of Britain's top shoe salesmen. Alan imports and sells millions of pairs of shoes every year and has a bigger collection than Imelda Marcos. It has been said that he is such a sharp salesman he could sell even Marcos a pair of flip-flops.

THE SWEET SMELL OF SUCCESS

Osgood was back for the visit to Coventry on the Saturday following the draw with Newcastle. Chelsea won at a canter, 3–0. Most of the game was spent in the Coventry half. Baldwin drove them ahead from Hudson's cross after he made the centre-back look an idiot. Then 'Good old Webbie' repeated the trick from Osgood's turnback from near the corner flag. Again, the goals were made inevitable by pressure. Chelsea tore the spine out of Coventry with their sheer power. Alan Hudson, the match star, scored the third with a solo run. It was a fantastic goal, he graced every match he played at that time. Sexton was encouraging his young star to run at defences and finish. It would have been interesting to have been a fly on the wall in the meetings between them. Even then I always sensed an animosity between them – nothing too overt, but there was always tension there.

Houseman was nearly booked for a clash with Ernie Hunt, the chunky Coventry midfielder. Hunt, who had earlier crocked Hudson with a fierce challenge, then held back Houseman as he raced through on goal. In a rare outburst Houseman retaliated with a firm push in the back and only the timely intervention of Hudson, who restrained Peter, saved the moment and stopped the violence from escalating. Houseman had a lecture from the referee for his trouble. Houseman never had an unpredictable fuse like Osgood. Since his terrible injury defenders sensed that Osgood was wound particularly tight. To them he had the air of someone who could just as soon settle matters with a punch to the mouth as a handshake. Coventry were wiped off the board. I always sensed the hatred of Chelsea at towns like Coventry. We were regarded as upstarts. Hudson was seen as being nouveau riche, morally unacceptable and ill mannered. The studied nonchalance of Graham Le Saux invokes the same feeling today. It is worse now because the key players are foreign. That is why it is so hard for them to win away; unkempt teams like Bradford and Southampton raise their game to a very intense level.

The week before the Watford semi-final, Chelsea slipped further behind in the title race. When the gods seemed to be on our side they could only manage a 1–1 draw at home to Nottingham Forest. Once again another vital home point was squandered. Chelsea were playing better away from home. After months of poor weather the match was played out in bright spring sunshine. The kaleidoscopic jumble of the Chelsea attack was not on display that afternoon though. The dog-days of the Cup run seemed far away as Chelsea struggled to gain control over a mediocre Forest side. Tommy Baldwin fired Chelsea ahead with a controversial goal in the eighth minute. Paddy Mulligan, playing instead of Dempsey, was standing just outside the centre and drilled the pass of the season through to the Chelsea striker. Tommy juggled with the ball and then smashed it past Dave Hollins, brother of the more famous John. Forest appealed for offside, though it was doubtful whether they knew what hit them.

In the second half, Osgood missed two golden chances – perhaps the sun caused him severe myopia. The first was created by Hudson, then Cooke set him up to put the game beyond doubt. Forest stole a point with a late equaliser. Any outside chance of the league title went with the home points surrendered, but Chelsea's eyes were on the Cup.

THE WATFORD GAP

After just four minutes Chelsea were ahead at White Hart Lane against Watford of the Second Division. Hudson started the move, interpassing with Peter Houseman down the left, Watford scrambled the ball away for a corner but Hudson instantly centred from the flag kick. Beckham is the only player in the modern game that hits a comparable corner. John Dempsey, restored to the side, rose unchallenged to head down towards the foot of the far post. David Webb, up on another of his commando raids, had timed his run to perfection and was on hand to slam home. He slid into the net behind the ball. Webb was always in the trenches when the blue square was under pressure but also he scored so many vital goals. That moment was glorious. What a spectacular start! The Shed Boys were everywhere and threw their fists in the air and screamed with joy. The air was filled with a sense of conviction of certain victory. Webb jumped high in excitement, Cooke danced a jig on the touchline, the Chelsea fans saluted the goal with a tickertape greeting like Charles Lindbergh received in New York. Only Sexton was a little dubious, hunched on the bench, chewing gum.

Watford had other ideas though, refusing to be completely obliterated. They had conceded an early goal against a side capable of *Terminator*-like destruction. The Tottenham Hotspur pitch was in an awful condition. It had always suffered from drainage problems because it was so enclosed. A combination of the harsh winter, heavy rainfall all that week and tons of sand had turned the pitch into what resembled a giant carpet of Ready Brek. Chelsea had been forced to play on some awful surfaces so far in the competition and Loftus Road could be considered to be the worst of a bad lot. Nothing was as bad as what they encountered that afternoon. Ken Furphy, the shrewd Watford manager, guessed that the pitch would affect the intricate passing of the Chelsea midfield. His game plan was to stifle them from the start and to grab a goal when the opportunity arose. It had worked earlier in the giant-killing dismissals of Liverpool and Stoke. To paraphrase Danny Blanchfower, who had adorned the Tottenham field when it was playable, 'our plan was to equalise first'.

Equalise they did when their nippy forward Garbett scored a surprise goal. Ken Furphy had immediately switched his wingers Scullion and Owen after Chelsea had scored. This meant that McCreadie and Webb were forced to switch to opposite sides of the field, an action that unbalanced the Chelsea defence, which creaked alarmingly in the early stages of the game. A delicate arc of a pass almost chipped McCreadie out of position on the right side of the pitch. The Scot managed to get his head to the ball but he could only direct it (in the best tradition of Frank Sinclair) into the path of Garbett. The Watford man moved forward and shot hopefully towards the bottom right-hand corner of Bonetti's goal. Exactly what happened next is not completely clear. Possibly the Watford forward topped his shot, perhaps the ball took a deflection off the uneven surface of the pitch. Whatever, the ball spun crazily in front of the Chelsea keeper and bounced over him and into the net. The only comparable goal was Baldwin's last-minute match winner against Sheffield Wednesday in the quarter-final tie at Stamford Bridge two seasons previously. As Graham Greene's Harry Lime so correctly observes in that classic spy novel *The Third Man*, 'It is turmoil, violence and injustice which gives birth to genius.' This point was never so convincingly made as in that bizarre semi-final.

Chelsea were stunned by the Watford equaliser. Shortly after Garbett's goal, Scullion found his left-winger with a wonderful raking pass. Owen swept past Webb and hit over a huge, dipping lob. Bonetti redeemed himself for any lingering doubts about the Watford goal with a great catch. He grabbed the ball two-handed and held firm as two Watford forwards waited to pounce on any crumbs.

Watford took the first half on points, narrowly. Chelsea made a few chances but the yellow shirts held firm. We had the Blue back on. The Watford goalkeeper Walker made a smart save from a snap shot from Hudson. Walker's son Ian grew up to play for Tottenham and England but his father gave as good a performance as his son ever did on that famous ground.

Webb surged forward and burst into the Watford box to hammer a shot against Watford's central defender, Lees. The ball bounced clear and Houseman fired the rebound first time over the top with Walker scrambling to regain his feet. It was another chance that went begging. Chelsea were peppering the Watford defence with more shots than the FBI took at Bonnie and Clyde.

Cooke pumped over a centre as two defenders snapped at his heels. Osgood, desperate to score to maintain his goalscoring record, flung himself at the ball. He narrowly failed to connect. In frustration he hacked Lees from behind. Os was lucky to escape a booking as the Watford crowd hurled abuse at him. Just on half-time Houseman had a golden chance to put Chelsea ahead. Watford forced a corner, which Chelsea messily cleared away. Houseman took possession, he had an eye for goal and, head down, made straight for the Watford penalty box. His run was even further than the epic Burnley effort. The crowd sensed something special as the winger burst into the Watford half, scattering defenders in alarm. Houseman feinted one way and found space the other. The cloying pitch delayed his run. Vaulting a tackle, he shot from about the same range as he had scored from at Turf Moor. The shot was hard but not as cleanly hit. No shot could be. Walker was diving quickly and saved it, Houseman should have scored, he knew he should have hit it quicker, one small detail, but that was big-time football. The whistle blew for half-time. The Chelsea players looked across at one another but Houseman was already down the tunnel; he believed in goal karma and was waiting for his next chance. Watford fancied their chances of pulling off a shock on the mish-mash of sand and mud that made up the pitch. Goaded by the Chelsea fans, lifted by their own supporters enjoying their brief Warhol moment of fame, the Watford team were in high spirits, their confidence high.

Once again Chelsea stood on the edge of the abyss, at Burnley they were only a few minutes away from a shock exit. At White Hart Lane a strange lethargy had crept into their play at the end of the first half and chances were missed. The midfield in particular looked sluggish. Watford were given space and too much possession. Now was the time for Chelsea to stand up and be counted.

HOUSEMAN'S GREATEST MOMENT (FEAR AND LOATHING AT WHITE HART LANE)

For Sexton it was time for a word up, but he sensed that his team were edgy and his brief advice was a panacea for their jangled nerves. Docherty would have been screaming and chucking teacups. Chelsea were playing against the wind but he correctly guessed that it would help with their build-ups. He told Hutchinson to get busy with the Watford centre-backs. He wanted him to be the demolition man. Hutchinson was keen to download the Watford defence. Hudson was anonymous for much of the first half; he was active all over the pitch but the end product was missing. He was playing too deep. Instinctively he knew when to hold the ball and when to give it to someone else. In the first half he gave it too quickly for Hollins and Cooke to keep up. This ignored Sexton's fundamental principle that a good pass presents the man receiving it with no problems of control.

Chelsea went at Watford from the start. The sun peeped over the horizon like a nervous sniper. Hutchinson started to dish out punishment to anyone in range. Like Eastwood in his classic *Unforgiven* role, no matter how high the odds he was there, taking them all on. Soon he was climbing to a Cooke centre and Walker was called to make a back-breaking stop. Watford's yellow backline regrouped but it was only a prelude to their destruction; the Blue Army was about to overwhelm them. Sexton yelled for more speed, he sensed Watford were about to crash. The fans picked up on the buzz. Everybody in blue was pulling towards Wembley.

On the hour Chelsea scored a majestic goal to trample down Watford's lingering hopes. It was like a thunderclap around White Hart Lane. With half an hour left and a Cup final up for grabs, the team were still searching for their rhythm. Osgood started it and finished it. He flicked a pass out to Hutchinson, who immediately rolled it to Hudson, Alan feinted to move into a posse of Watford defenders but then turned and swept the ball to Houseman, far out on the left. Houseman controlled it instantly and then hit a centre of geometric precision into the box. Walker, sensing the danger, was off his line quickly. But he was not quick enough. Osgood was already waiting, like Tony Hateley at Villa Park three long years ago pouncing on Charlie Cooke's cross. At that time Osgood was out of football with a busted leg and a wounded psyche, one step away from oblivion. Now he was back and indispensable. He wanted that Cup-scoring record so badly he could taste it. Hateley had headed his goal harder, but I doubt if even Big Tony had put such accuracy in a header. Pictures of the goal show Ian Hutchinson in front of Osgood and behind the airborne Walker waiting for a rebound to fall or a ricochet from the posts. It never happened. The ball hit the back of the net with a whoosh and Osgood followed it in. A famous image of that era was of Osgood swinging from the net, celebrating along with half of London.

Lee Mavers of The Las, a classic Liverpool '90s band, once talked about 'not being a musician but passing on a feeling'. At that moment, frozen in time, Peter Osgood was not a footballer but someone passing on a feeling. It was a pivotal moment for him, before he left in a cloud of bitterness and dispute. You could feel the relief sweep up from the pitch and onto the terraces. Chelsea were then, as they always were and always will be, a team of moods. It had to be 100 per cent Blue for them. I still am.

The wall was smashed, the Castle Watford had fallen in the siege. Now Chelsea really started to play; they opened up. Cooke and Houseman were interchanging, taking away defenders, popping up all over the pitch and causing havoc. Watford were unable to resist, though try to resist they still did. Chelsea tore them apart, piece by piece. Cooke started an avalanche on the terraces when he threaded the ball past three defenders with some amazing technical dexterity. The molotovs were raining down on the Watford defence and the cocktails were a heady mixture of class and venom. Webb, sensing blood, pushed up. Thirteen minutes after Osgood's strike Houseman scored Chelsea's third with a goal fit to grace any match. It was even more spectacular than the Burnley effort, and very intricate. Receiving the ball on the right, he shook off defenders Walley and Packer and dribbled across the face of the penalty box. Houseman dribbled around Lugg, skipped past Lees and, as Duncan Welbourne moved in to tackle, sent in a blistering shot that left Walker helpless in the mud. Houseman's goal was a testimony to his tremendous stamina on the mudheap of White Hart Lane. Never was such an important game played by Chelsea on a surface that resembled the surface of Mars. His sheer power and determination, backed by the superior morale and discipline instilled by Sexton, won through. The Watford defenders were strewn like autumn leaves around a lamppost.

Diagrams and photographs show that Houseman had Osgood and Hutchinson close by, but his mentality was such that he took responsibility to find the space and take the goal. The other, more prosaic point to make is that Houseman's performance was not bad for someone initially seen as a provider of chances. He beat defenders with good lunges who came back relentlessly with bone-shattering tackles. This was not an age where the footballers fear of the yellow or red card dominated their defensive priorities.

Houseman had won the game for Chelsea in the space of 15 minutes, with the immaculate cross for Osgood's goal and his breathtaking solo effort. Chelsea were at Wembley; the pipers were at the gates of dawn. Watford were now systematically destroyed by Chelsea. Perhaps it was because they had put up such stubborn resistance that they had to be made an example of. Personally I think it was the arrogance of that side that made them determined to put anyone who defied them to the sword. On the first day of the 1999–2000 season, Zola created a goal for Poyet with an exquisite chip that only Charlie Cooke could have matched in terms of quality. Gianfranco stabbed his left foot under the ball and Poyet finished the move with a shot of power and venom. It reminded those lucky enough to have seen him at his zenith of Osgood. Zola had the same combination of strength and beauty, savagery and finesse. Chelsea could still produce an act of genius. That is what endures. The image of Poyet and Zola will be as vivid in three decades as Osgood swinging from the net or Houseman skipping over the sand.

And then a hero comes along . . .

SLAUGHTERHOUSE FIVE (APOLOGIES TO KURT)

Hutchinson scored the fourth 120 seconds after Houseman's goal. The final symbolic act was to demolish Watford. Hudson was bursting to get into the act. Long chestnut hair flowing, he took a short pass from Osgood and set off through the wreckage of the rag-tag Watford defence. Hudson was as fit as a flea, skimming across the sand and the mud to feed his giant striker. Like all great players he insisted on making an easy pass whenever he could. Perhaps that is why Bill Shankly rated him so highly; the Red Messiah of Anfield always claimed football was a simple game. A swivel and Hutchinson hit the net with a rising magnum shot of staggering power. Walker could only watch as the ball whistled through the air.

Now goals are timed like racing cars. The top ten lightning strikes of season 1998–99 is headed by Hasselbaink's (then at Leeds) goal against Arsenal, a shot that effectively deprived Arsenal of the title and set Manchester United up for the Treble. It was timed at 80.4mph and for the record was struck from 22.3 yards. Goldbaek's brilliant strike at Tottenham for Chelsea the same season was timed at 66.1mph, from a greater distance than Jimmie Floyd's, some 33.6 yards. Hutchinson's explosive fourth goal, on the same ground, was from closer range but more viciously hit even than Hasselbaink's.

Houseman clinched the semi-final with his second goal and Chelsea's fifth. Hutchinson had a big hand in this goal, exchanging passes with the winger in a classic Chelsea move. Dave Sexton loved his team to play one–twos. Nobody played them better than his blue-shirted forwards, though perhaps for strategic considerations, too often a move broke down with an over-elaborate pass. Chelsea held the beat a little too long sometimes, bearing in mind Sir Alex Ferguson's dictum about extravagance.

The near-paraplegia of the Watford defence allowed Hutchinson to set up Houseman for another excellent finish. He was never more decisive than in that period.

A carnival atmosphere took over the closing stages. Boredom replaced anger for the Stamford Bridge men. Bonetti, reduced to a spectator in the second half, suddenly made a wonderful diving save. This was from an armour-piercing free kick hit by Lugg, so Bonetti was to deny Watford even scant consolation. Osgood appeared to score in the dying seconds, but it was disallowed due to his shouting. It was a surprise that he could be heard over the din of the celebrating Chelsea Shed boys, who had turned the Tottenham Shelf (Spur's answer to the Shed) into an anthill of desperate emotion. Chelsea were through to the Cup final and a sensational clash against Leeds.

But first there was league business to attend to. Stoke City came to Stamford Bridge three days after the suppression of Watford. The gate was 29,000, a healthy enough figure but the second lowest gate of that epic season. The fact that it was a freezing, rain-lashed night didn't help. Once again it was a late goal that won it and it was Houseman who engineered it. In the last minute of a disappointing match, Houseman ran clear on the right, checked enough to make the centre with his more favoured left foot and found Charlie Cooke hurtling forward. Cooke met the centre first time and volleyed a wonder goal left-footed past Gordon Banks. In a few short months Banks was to make the save of the twentieth century in Mexico from Pelé. Voted the player of the twentieth century, though, Diego would have something to say on the subject, Banks was arguably the greatest goalkeeper of all time. He was certainly in the top three, and Bonetti was not far behind him. Events in Mexico were to slightly tarnish his golden reputation but to Chelsea fans he was the greatest goalkeeper ever.

Bonetti was only 5 ft 10 in, as opposed to de Goey, who clocks in at 6 ft 6 in, and is currently the tallest goalkeeper in the Premier. David James, who gifted Chelsea the Cup in 1999, was the second biggest keeper, being one inch shorter. Banks was just over 6 ft. Both Bonetti and Banks had great footwork. De Goey did not seem to have the agility because he was more cumbersome. In the three decades that were to follow, nobody at Stamford Bridge has come close to Peter Bonetti's level of consistency or his spectacular style. Petar Borota had the flamboyance of a young Bonetti but not the safety factor. Borota was the goalkeeper Chelsea plucked out of what was then known as Yugoslavia. He had a marvellous unbroken sequence of first-team appearances before falling out with manager John Neil and captain Mickey Droy. Borota was a vastly underrated goalkeeper. As far as he was concerned, goalkeeping was all about agility and style. He hated waiting statically on his goal-line and loved to play a long way from his goal. When performing as a partial outfielder, Petar gave Chelsea half an extra player on the field. Today Borota would have been seen as a necessity for the attacking side, not the luxury many regarded him as. His replacement was a teenager called Steve Francis, who was tipped by many as the new Bonetti. His confidence was eroded by playing in too many struggling teams, behind fragile defences. Disgruntlement turned into stagnation and he drifted down the league. Nobody ever had a God-given right to a golden future. The ones that did not make it fascinated me, all those nearly men. People ask me about Osgood and the select band of greats like Greaves, but the Steve Francises were characters also.

Peter Schmeichel has dominated the modern game utterly; Seaman has performed well for his country but had the benefit of playing behind the greatest domestic back four ever. Bonetti played behind a hard but often eccentric defence. Modern strikers would be heartbroken if they came up against goalkeepers of the calibre of Bonetti and Banks every week.

Cooke's winner against Banks highlighted the stamina of Chelsea. In reaching the final, Chelsea had scored 21 goals, and significantly 15 of those came in the second half. Of those 14 were netted after more than an hour's play.

Osgood missed the Stoke match because of a cold that also prevented him from playing for the Football League side. Bobby Tambling deputised for him; it was the first time that he had played for the Chelsea first team for seven months. His loan spell at Crystal Palace had not really prepared him for the rigours of a first-team spot at Chelsea. Tony Waddington watched Hudson run the midfield with all the practised blue chip hauteur he could muster, his languid style lighting up the stormy evening. If only he could integrate a player of his quality into the lacklustre Potteries set-up. The classic lineage of Stanley Matthews – Jimmy McIlroy – Peter Dobing badly needed updating. Hudson's personality interested him. He was obviously a complex character, spontaneous like his football. About that time the first signs were appearing that all was not well with him. Something seemed to be going on in his head.

One of The Las' songs on the eponymous 1990 album was called 'Son of a Gun'. It spoke eerily of:

'Boy of life, who lived upon a knife, he was burned by the twentieth century, now he's doing time in the back of his mind.'

Chapter Eleven: Here It Is, Come and Get It

The special quality which makes an artist . . . might also be defined, indeed, as an extraordinary capacity for irritation, a pathological sensitiveness to environmental pricks and stings. He differs from the rest of us mainly because he reacts sharply and in an uncommon manner to phenomena which leave the rest of us unmoved, or, at most, merely annoy us vaguely.
H. L. Mencken, The Artist *(1924)*

In the FA Cup final against our old enemies Chelsea, the playing surface was diabolical. It was the first time I had seen mud at Wembley, it was like a pudding.
Jack Charlton

A record that rode the Hit Parade of early 1970 was by a group called Badfinger. They were the new Beatles. Even the Beatles said so. But rich promise faded into bitter tragedy. They were best remembered for a record written by Sir Paul McCartney called 'Come and Get It', the theme song from a film called *The Magic Christian* starring Peter Sellers, which dealt with the subject of greed. The scene in which Badfinger's hit features consists of Londoners scrambling into human excrement to retrieve money scattered by a mad millionaire, who was anxious to make the point that people will do anything for money. The story of the band became as poignant as their smash hit 'Without You'. Beset by financial problems, the band's writers, Pete Ham and Tom Evans, both hanged themselves. I heard that song everywhere I went at that time. I always thought of the Cup. Here it is, come and get it.

Chelsea clung to third spot in the Football League after beating Manchester United 2–1 on 21 March 1970. Ian Hutchinson scored both Chelsea goals in the first half. A gigantic crowd of 61,479 packed into Stamford Bridge to watch Chelsea end United's unbeaten run of 18 games. United were involved in their three-match titanic FA Cup semi-final struggle against Leeds. They were to eventually lose 1–0 to a goal scored by the late Billy Bremner. Best was contained by the super-efficient Madely over the three matches and never again was the mercurial Irishman to be that close to appearing in a Wembley final. A

Chelsea v United final would have been by far the glamour choice of the fans. Best was at his zenith, before his career was flamed out on drink. In an earlier round he had scored six goals in a Cup-tie against Northampton. Best was just back from a long suspension but dazzled in an 8–2 victory. He admitted to playing out the last 20 minutes at left-back for United as he was 'bored' scoring goals. Years later United crushed Chelsea 4–0 in a Wembley final with Mark Hughes scoring one of the Red Devils goals. Had they met in 1970 the score-line would not have been so one-sided.

Chelsea were on the wrong side of a heavy defeat at Goodison Park which was to end their Championship aspirations. Before then they had beaten Sheffield Wednesday 3–1 at Stamford Bridge in a midweek match. The match had been brought forward from Good Friday by Chelsea to try to alleviate some of the fixture congestion at that time of year. Easter was considered to be the crucial time with three games in four days. It was always a traumatic time for Chelsea. Today the Premier players have those superb pitches, beautiful training grounds and an army of personal trainers, diet experts and gurus of all types. You would not catch them playing three games in four days, though.

Winger Jackie Sinclair gave Sheffield an early lead but Ian Hutchinson quickly levelled for Chelsea. The same player was brought down after 22 minutes when he chased a Peter Houseman pass. An amazing thing happened then, because Chelsea were awarded their first penalty of the season. This was incredible, considering the ferocity of the tackling that year and the fact that the Chelsea forward line was packed with players who liked nothing better than dribbling in the penalty area with the ball. Osgood still remembered where to place the ball for the kick and comprehensively beat the Wednesday keeper, Grummitt. (Around that time Sheffield Wednesday tried to buy the Scottish forward Willie Wallace but the deal crashed and the legendary Wallace and Grummitt partnership was never formed.)

Twelve minutes into the second half, and Alan Hudson sealed victory with a wonderful solo run from his own half. His run took him through the entire Sheffield defence and he finished perfectly with a low drive past Grumitt. Everyone in the ground rose to their feet to honour a wonderful piece of virtuosity. It was one of the greatest solo runs ever seen at Stamford Bridge. Even better than Ron Harris's run to Barclays on payday and on a par with the sheer genius of any of Greaves' greatest individual goals.

In the '80s John Neal's fine young Chelsea side butchered promotion rivals Newcastle 4–0 in a memorable, rainy (then Second Division) match at Stamford Bridge. The Newcastle side included the returning prodigal son Kevin Keegan, but the star of the match was Pat Nevin. I tried to sign Keegan for Chelsea later. It was Nevin's first winter down from Scotland and his star was rising. Pat had all the masculine elegance of the new French cinema idols. He mocked the Newcastle defence that afternoon in the same manner Hudson had mocked defenders all through that spring of 1970. Nevin ran 80 yards through the Newcastle team with an exuberance that his slender frame seemed to deny, to turn a shot just past the post. Not since 1970, when the likes of Cooke and Osgood were destroying defences for fun, had there been such a provocative use of talent.

ELEGANTLY WASTED

A young Matthew Harding was amongst the 29,590 crowd who saw Hudson score. Sitting in the old North Stand that cold March evening with his father Paul, he witnessed the wonder goal. It made a huge impression on the 12-year-old. Standing on the platform at Fulham Broadway station waiting for the District Line tube home, young Master Harding kept reading the official match programme with its royal blue cover; it cost one shilling, or five pence. Later on Harding was to eschew buying programmes as he stated, 'I was not interested in the opposition. I knew who was playing for Chelsea and that was good enough for me. If they did not wear a blue suit they weren't a member of my family.'

Matthew loved to look back at the great Chelsea players. He was a great fan of Tommy Docherty and was on record as stating, 'When this club was on its uppers, relegated, Ted Drake sacked and everything falling apart, along came Tommy Docherty. He took over and built a fantastic side. It was all English you know, not a lot of people realise this. We were the first to wear the all-one-colour strip. It was dashing football and great days.'

Shortly before his death in a helicopter crash returning from a Coca-Cola Cup-tie in October 1996, he wrote that Hudson's majestic goal against Sheffield was his own personal favourite all-time Chelsea goal. Coming from someone with his intensive knowledge of the minutiae of Chelsea folklore there can be no greater compliment. It is a compliment to both men, in fact. I can see him now as he spoke of the goal, smiling that old Matthew smile. I used to meet Matthew for a drink in his favourite watering hole, the Howard Hotel, and discuss Chelsea, old times and their future.

That was the crowning moment of Hudson's Chelsea career. Never again was he to play for Chelsea as well as he did then. Alan had played in fewer than 30 first-team games yet he was already a Chelsea legend. The quagmire of his relationship with Dave Sexton was to be measured in the trajectory of the scandalous decline in his Stamford Bridge career. For the last few seasons in the Chelsea side he was stranded out in a wide position, a criminal waste of talent.

In his head he was already pushing the buttons of his personal self-destruct mechanism. What did Oscar Wilde say about genius? 'The public is wonderfully tolerant. It forgives everything except genius.'

Everton had little respect for genius. The following Saturday they tore into Chelsea from the start. The West London team were hit by injury, especially in defence. Bonetti was absent with an ankle injury, Eddie McCreadie was also out with a knock, and Ron Harris had been carried off shortly after Hudson's goal in the Sheffield Wednesday game when he tore his left hamstring. In the absence of Harris, John Hollins captained the side. Hollins had just been named the Chelsea player of the year for 1970. Peter Osgood was named second in the Supporters' Club poll, with Alan Hudson third. The long-haired midfielder would have been named the most promising newcomer had there been such a section. Houseman did not figure in the poll, but had it been held a month later the final positions might have been a little different.

Howard Kendall and Alan Ball blitzed the new look Chelsea defence with two goals in the first four minutes. Nearly 60,000 Mickey Mouses (scouses) packed into the ground and the atmosphere was intimidating to the Londoners. Chelsea seemed highly strung that day. Joe Royle at his most deliberate weighed in with two more goals, out-jumping the Chelsea defence to glance home headers. The explosive winger Alan Whittle also scored to put Everton five up on the hour. The title was coming home to Merseyside. Tommy Hughes was on the receiving end of yet another five-goal thrashing. The Chelsea defence had no answer to the aerial threat of Royle, who was given a constant supply of crosses by his wingers Whittle and Morrissey. The swerving flight that they gave to the ball intimidated Chelsea as much as the Goodison fans. Hinton and Mulligan struggled to win anything in the air, whilst David Webb looked lost at right-back. Dempsey and Osgood scored late goals to give the score-line some air of respectability, but Chelsea had been blown away like so many dismembered dolls.

Leeds were beaten at home by a modest Southampton side, so Everton went five points clear at the top of the table with only four games left.

On Easter Monday, 30 March 1970, Chelsea visited the Hawthorns for a league match. The final was only eleven days away at Wembley and dominated everything. It was a very bad day for Chelsea, raining down continuously. Chelsea lost 3–1, their second successive defeat and something that had not happened since the first two matches of the season. You recall their away reverses at Liverpool and Upton Park. The Albion goals were scored by the ubiquitous dynamic duo of Astle and Brown, the latter scoring twice. Peter Bonetti was restored to the side after injury but in a roughhouse of a match he received two blows to the head, which zapped his reflexes. He was not the only Chelsea player to be injured.

After half an hour Alan Hudson, adrenaline washing through him, damaged an ankle in an innocuous incident. It was to cast a shadow across his whole career. I remember seeing him go down and knew then that it was bad. At that precise moment Hudson inhabited an isthmus of land between ingenious technical skill and the less conquerable territories of pure feeling. The ankle injury was to cause him to miss the final and a possible World Cup trip to Mexico. Both were theatres which would have raised his profile even higher. Had he made it into the England set-up who knows what might have happened. His injury was to leave an indelible mark on him. Stamford Bridge became like an alien planet to him. Planet of the Apes.

Osgood was never the same player after his dreadful injury at Blackpool, and Hudson was never the same player for Chelsea after his injury at West Bromwich. There were superb individual performances in the following seasons (notably against Bruges in the European Cup-Winners' Cup and Tottenham in the League Cup semi-final at White Hart Lane), but the consistency and fire were missing. The acutely angled passes, outrageous in their audacity, were still there but drive was no longer allied to genius. Tony Bennett, Alan's favourite singer, speaking once of the late comedian Lenny Bruce, lamented that he 'sinned against his talent'. Had he known Alan Hudson, the comment might also have been apt.

Bobby Tambling substituted for Hudson in what was to be his last-ever first-team game in a 13-seasons-long career. Tambling hit the bar on the hour and Hutchinson firmly headed in the rebound. Hutchinson hurt his ribs scoring in his usual courageous manner. In the closing minutes Tambling, singled out for a couple of tackles of considered nastiness, suffered a recurrence of the hamstring injury he had received a few weeks before. It ruled him out for the rest of the season and in the summer he joined Crystal Palace on a full-time basis.

Tambling spent three years at Selhurst Park before moving to Ireland. Bobby was very involved in his work for the Jehovah's Witnesses but he still found time to play, coach and manage Cork Celtic, Waterford and Shamrock Rovers. He returned to England in the mid-'80s. The curse of the frail identities of the Stamford Bridge stars fell on him. His marriage broke up and financial difficulties beset him. The same week that Eric Cantona drilled two penalties into the Chelsea net in another Wembley final, Robert Tambling was declared bankrupt. Terry Venables and George Graham had reaped big rewards in football but the record scorer in the club's history ended up working as a chippie for his brothers, Bill and Ray. Bobby was the youngest of eight. He would watch Cup finals from a showroom window, a whole lifetime away from the Prada-suited, Burberry-overcoated, Hilfiger-scented millionaires who play now in a blue kit which is a replica of Tambling's.

He still has a connection with football, teaching in holiday camps. Today Bobby lives in a terraced house just off the seafront near Portsmouth. It is a return to his roots; his father was a farm labourer and he grew up on Hayling Island. He is pleased he still has the record. Humbly and philosophically, he remarked:

> Kerry Dixon came close to breaking it, but I was so glad he didn't because I am very proud of that record. People don't want to know about guys who played years ago holding records. Naturally the kids want new blood, want their current hero to be the one that's breaking the records.
>
> I cannot see anyone breaking it now. Goals were possibly easier, a bit easier, to come by in my day as teams didn't concentrate on defending like they do now.
>
> Let's face it. There have always been great goalscorers at Chelsea, before me and after me. Greavsie was the greatest of them all in my view.
>
> The secret is you've got to want to score goals more than anything else. That may sound obvious, but it's something you can't coach into a player. It is either there or it isn't. Dixon struck me like that.
>
> Once I went 13 games in one season without scoring and the pressure was tremendous. So was the high when I finally scored.
>
> Some players, George Best for example, made their own goals. I depended on belonging to a good side and finishing off what they created.

Tambling rated the 1965 League Cup-Winning 'Catch Us If You Can' team as the best he ever played in. That League Cup memento was the only winner's medal he was to receive. Bobby's biggest disappointment was the 2–1 defeat by Spurs in the 1967 Cockney Cup final.

'We had reached the semi-finals for the previous two years and lost, so getting to Wembley only to lose was a real sickener.'

Terry Venables rated Tambling as one of the greatest strikers in post-war football.

Hudson had his ankle X-rayed the day after the West Bromich match. It showed no bone injury. The midfielder's face flooded with pain as his leg was put in plaster in the hope that the swelling would subside. Trainer Harry Medhurst and his assistant, son Norman, were now dealing with a casualty list of Stalingrad proportions. Ron Harris had resumed light training but was still very doubtful for the final.

Chelsea's last match before Wembley was a home game against Tottenham. Missing from the Spurs team was Jimmy Greaves who a few weeks before had joined West Ham. This was part of the transfer package that saw World Cup hero Martin Peters link up at White Hart Lane and become the first British player to be valued at £200,000. Greaves was the makeweight in the transfer, being valued at £54,000 in the trade-off.

It was the beginning of the end for the greatest marksman in the history of the game. Jimmy scored twice on his début for the Hammers at Maine Road. He notched up two more goals before the end of the season and finished sixth out of 96 starters in the 1970 World Cup rally that started in Wembley Stadium and finished in Mexico City. I recall that when Jimmy arrived there he heard that his old pal Bobby Moore was seeking sanctuary in the British Embassy after being falsely accused by a jeweller in Bogota of stealing a bracelet. Bobby was not allowed visitors, but guess who breached the defences? Jimmy Greaves.

He returned to West Ham and scored nine goals in his last season. Greaves retired at the age of 31. What a waste. I do not know which was the bigger loss to the game, him or Hudson.

Spurs could have done with Jimmy that April afternoon as they struggled in a lacklustre London derby. Tommy Baldwin scored the only goal early on with a crisp shot. Alan Birchenall and Peter Osgood set up the chance with a couple of nifty headers, while Peter Houseman played in midfield in Hudson's role.

Sexton gave Charlie Cooke the number eleven shirt and Baldwin came in at seven. He was resigned to losing Hudson for the final and his logic demanded that Houseman, with his tremendous workrate, pace and passing ability, would be the best replacement. The impact of the loss of Hudson from the team was never really appreciated at the time. His real inventiveness as an improviser would have been probed and exploited by the ferocious competitiveness of the Leeds pair, Giles and Bremner. They were excited rather than exhausted by the challenge of their bitterest rivals. Houseman later confessed to me that of all the midfield players capable of unnerving him Bremner was the most formidable. Unlike Hudson, Houseman's power did not come from a visionary genius but from an omnipotent ability to do what most other players did, but far better.

Leeds had played Celtic a few days before in the first leg of the European Cup semi-final. It was a game that was billed as the 'Championship of Britain'. The strain was starting to tell on Leeds, the pressure needles were quivering over red. Their brilliant full-back, Paul Reaney, had broken his leg in a bad incident at West Ham.

Don Revie was anxious to spare his players for a twin assault on the cups. He had fielded a reserve team at Derby on Easter Monday and took a heavy beating and a large fine. Today it would be rotation. Their bad spell continued. In the home leg Paul Madely made an early mistake and Celtic's midfield ace, George Connelly, toed home off a post. That was the only goal of the game. The Scots won 1–0 in a disciplined performance in front of 45,505 fans. The Leeds crowd were developing a reputation for being critical and not committed enough to their cause.

WEMBLEY

The team that lined up at Wembley on 11 April 1970 in front of 100,000 who paid £128,000 altogether (which would equate to the cost of 2000 Chelsea's Jody Morris's Porsche 911 Carrera, Gianluca Vialli's chauffeur-driven Lexus, and a varied selection of Frank Le Bouef's suits from Armani and Commes des Garcons) for the honour was: Bonetti; Webb; McCreadie; Hollins; Dempsey; Harris; Baldwin; Houseman; Osgood; Hutchinson; Cooke. Sub: Hinton.

Rather like Eric Morecambe's attempt to play Grieg's Piano Concerto, Sexton had selected the right names but not necessarily in the right order.

The day of the final was cold as had been all of that spring. Early in the morning a salmon-coloured sky hung over London. Hudson left the prefab early to go to Wembley, his heart breaking. Despite everything he had done he was not fit for the match. He was marking time; he felt he had reached a hurdle in his playing. His reputation as a wastrel was about to begin. Some seeds of dissatisfaction deep inside him were putting out shoots that were almost to strangle his career later. Sporting his pre-Raphaelite mane, Alan was wearing his best Kings Road threads; a checked Village Gate jacket, pistachio-coloured shirt and tie, black Cecil Gee trousers and the legendary suede topcoat, a garment which was to gain the mythical status of the suede coat worn by one Robert Zimmerman on the cover of the classic CBS album *The Freewheeling Bob Dylan*. Chelsea were the first players to dress like pop stars. Now the pop stars dress like footballers.

The clowning and bonhomie in the dressing-room was replaced by a quiet tension. The players were worried about the problem that had haunted them throughout the Cup run, the playing surface. From Burnley to White Hart Lane via Selhurst and Loftus Road, the dodgy playing surfaces had hampered their virtuoso performances. Each pitch they had played on seemed worse than the one before, if such a thing were possible. After the trials and tribulations of the Tottenham pitch the Chelsea players were horrified to see Wembley. A hundred tons of sand had been added to the surface which had recently hosted the

Horse of the Year show. 'First time I have played on a building site,' our own Mr Softee, David Webb, mumbled as he was about to be introduced to the HRH Princess Margaret. All the Great Houses were at Wembley that day, even the one in Windsor.

Shortly before Wembley the princess had visited the legendary jazz club of Ronnie Scott, occasioning what was regarded as a highly risqué gag about her friendship with the comic actor Peter Sellers. The comedian Spike Milligan had persuaded Scott to read the gag out to the audience, which had caused a storm in the tabloids. I sat next to her in the second half of the game, but I kept schtum. I was given the job of lighting her cigarettes throughout the proceedings.

Academics who study the subculture of CFC are split amongst themselves as to which was the greatest of the two finals.

Leeds were determined to win the Cup in style and remove the charge that they were highly efficient but compellingly dull. Fair play to all concerned, they did try. Leeds got the dream start they wanted, scoring first with a joke goal. It was the biggest cliché of the Leeds lexicon. Big Jack Charlton had a tactic of standing at the near post in front of the goalie for corner or free kicks. This caused consternation and was a staple tactic of their game. In his long career, Charlton scored over 50 goals from this move. Charlton put Leeds in front when he headed home from close range from a corner kick. Eddie McCreadie, patrolling on the goal-line, tried to clear but, expecting the ball to bounce, he kicked over it and it rolled under his foot. Ron Harris, standing next to the Scotsman, tried to hack clear but the ball eluded him and trickled over the line for one of the softest goals ever scored in a Wembley final. Such mistakes were handed down from one batch of Chelsea defenders to the others over the years, almost as if it were a genetic defect.

Chelsea were stunned by Leeds going ahead so quickly. Sexton lowered his head in disgust. Their only response was a shot by Peter Osgood which was blocked on the line by Charlton who spun to scoop the ball away. Osgood was desperate to maintain his cup-scoring record but found himself chasing his own tail as he tried in vain to outwit Charlton and Hunter.

The Chelsea defence toiled to contain Eddie Gray, who glided over the clinging pitch like Roberto Rivelino on a Brazilian beach. I always thought that Gray was tall for a winger but he was beautifully balanced. Like Cooke and Hudson, only his temperament had stopped him from being one of the biggest names ever. Don Revie had total faith in him. In the pre-match team talk he was simply instructed to tear Chelsea apart. He very nearly did.

Houseman started sprightly and confident, but as the match developed into a war of attrition he was increasingly drawn back to give defensive cover. His was a no-frills, direct role of tackling, spreading short passes and always being available. He spent all of the game mopping up. Close-quarter combat was the name of the game. No prisoners were taken by either side and punishment was dished out, then onto the next contest.

Four minutes from half-time Chelsea were getting increasingly restless; they dreaded going in at the break trailing. Leeds had dominated the game so far and the Londoners were worried that as the game wore on they would be slowly choked to death. They stared gloomily at each other.

Twenty-five yards out at the far end of the ground, Houseman picked up a loose pass as the Leeds defence opened up like a Chinese menu. Peter drove a low shot of ruthless accuracy towards the left-hand side of Gary Sprake's goal. It was a fierce shot but from that range should have lacked the pace to beat an international goalkeeper of Sprake's experience. He made a gorilla's salad of the save though and it spilled from his hands and across the line. Jack Charlton was always of the opinion that Sprake had dived over the ball. Tommy Baldwin raced in but the ball was resting snugly against the back of the net. Chelsea were level – against all the odds they were back in the game.

Perhaps scoring that vital goal in a Wembley Cup final was Houseman's greatest moment. As a player he was consummate, his performances that season were up there with the best. He scored six goals in Chelsea's epic charge at the Cup; the doubles against Burnley and Watford were match winners. The equaliser at Wembley gave Chelsea a lifeline, though, and must rank as possibly the most undervalued goal in the history of the club, scored by the most undervalued player in its history. Peter Houseman's name went up in lights on the giant Wembley scoreboard. Later periods in his Chelsea career were to see him suffer a vicious campaign of personal abuse from certain sections of the crowd. Nothing could alter that moment for him though. The goal, like his career, was understated. The fatal Englishman.

In the second half Leeds put Chelsea under tremendous bombardment. The Chelsea defenders huddled around their six-yard box as if in an air-raid shelter. They waited in vain for an all-clear that never came. Leeds struck the post and crossbar three times and only the superb Bonetti kept them in the game. Revie pushed Eddie Gray up on Webb and the tricky Scot came close to destroying the Desperate Dan of Stamford Bridge. The conditions suited Gray ideally and at times the Chelsea rearguard looked like the remains of a Vietnamese banquet. Time after time Webb would plunge into the Leeds winger, who would over-commit the right-back. Webb spent much of the game floundering on his backside. Gray drenched the Chelsea penalty box with crosses which the strikers should have made far better use of, though the then England coach Kevin Keegan, in the 1999 Euro championship qualifiers once, chided the press, 'You must not get obsessed that goals only come from crosses.'

Seven minutes from time Leeds scored. It was a goal made inevitable by the pressure. The Yorkshiremen had pounded Chelsea like surf crashing against the shore. Ron Harris had shackled Clarke all afternoon. If this Alan Clarke had kept a diary he would not have had much to enter in it for that April day. Ron Harris was tiring, still feeling the effects of his injury on that awful pitch. Finally escaping the clutches of the Chelsea skipper, Clarke twisted and thumped in a header that hit the post. Mick Jones instantly drove the rebound past Bonetti from a sharp angle.

The game looked over for Chelsea – the fans feared a late goal for Leeds, as it would not give Chelsea the time to equalise. They fell silent. Leeds were celebrating and it was said that somewhere in the stadium a steward was already tying white ribbons on the handles of the Cup.

Ian Hutchinson had battled like a prizefighter throughout the game.

Verbal exchanges were a standard ploy of the Leeds game, as much as Jack Charlton's antics on the goal-line. 'Hutchinson, you could not trap a ball if you dug a hole in the ground and covered it with sticks.' That was a common quip, it came with the terrority. There were in particular two Leeds players who singled out Ian for abuse. One of them, Norman Hunter, chided him shortly after they had taken the lead again, making the comment that the only reason he was in the team was for his long throwing expertise. Norman Hunter was the '70s David Batty. Yorkshire born and bred, very cussed, tough and extra mean, Ian Hutchinson was probably mentally much stronger than any other player in the squad. He shared Osgood's gunfighter mentality. Lesser mortals would have been undermined.

Chelsea won a free kick out on the right. Houseman ran to take it but was waved back by John Hollins. On the terraces, Mick Greenaway was wondering, in the words of the Clash song, 'Should I Stay or Should I Go?'. He did not want to see Leeds collect the Cup, yet he never deserted his heroes. He raised one more' Zigger Zagger'.

Osgood ran into the box. Baldwin was up there too; both could have engaged in the rough stuff but they avoided it, smiling instead of snarling. Leeds were exhausted, they were stretched like a rubber band. Eight games in a 15-day spell, three titanic battles in the semi-final with Manchester United. The team was haemorrhaging massively, due to the ingestion of too much pressure. Already they had played nearly 60 games, with rotation only a word that farmers used about their crops. Thirty-one years later they purchased a central defender for £18 million, yet Charlton always maintained that central defenders did not have to be good players, only effective.

Leeds made the strange error of not sending two men out to stand ten yards from Ron Harris as he prepared to take the free kick. Only Lorimer was available, about halfway. At that precise moment Princess Margaret asked me for a light . . .

Ron turned the ball to Hollins, who played it in. Charlton rose to clear but Hutchinson stole into the penalty area in front of him. There were 100,000 witnesses. Some say that the Leeds giraffe tried to nut Hutch, while theorists state that Sprake should have claimed it. The unfortunate Gary Sprake was looking for a cross though, not a flick to the near post. Hutchinson scored with a courageous header. The score was 2–2.

Chelsea were level, they had taken so much punishment it seemed inconceivable that they were still in the game. The terrrace, covered in blue, throbbed in rapture. I did not see the ball hit the net as I was giving the princess a light. Being in the royal box, I could not even celebrate the most vital goal Chelsea were to score at Wembley, even greater than Bobby di Matteo's Cup winners.

The game went into extra time. Ron Harris limped off to be replaced by Marvin Hinton, and Houseman dropped back to shield Webb. The pace dropped, though only marginally.

Dave Webb was not composed but such was his alertness that he restored some of his lost pride when he thumped a shot off the line with Bonetti beaten. Both sides might have won it. Osgood, his sideburns like scimitars, flashed a header past the post with Sprake and Terry Cooper stranded on the line.

Eventually the whistle blew, leaving a sense of unreality and tension. Nobody knew quite what to say or do, for the last time the final had ended in a draw was in 1912. The *Titanic* had set sail, but the iceberg was forming.

Ron Harris shook hands with the princess, though she had no Cup to hand over. Perhaps we could both have kept it for a week till the replay. Both teams joined in the lap of honour together; an exhausted Eddie McCreadie had suggested the idea and Billy Bremner was quick to agree. Halfway round McCreadie went down with cramp. Perhaps it was not one of his better ideas. Sexton sipped tea from a plastic cup.

It was like those Christmas Day matches played between the Germans and the British Army in the First World War. My father had told me how the East Surrey Regiment had downed their arms and climbed out of the trenches and joined the Germans for a kick-about in no man's land. Chelsea's very own Tommy (Baldwin) and Terry Cooper had been kicking lumps out of one another a few minutes earlier, now they ran around Wembley together. Hutchinson and Hunter who had been in a head-to-head like two sumo wrestlers, swapped wisecracks.

Hudson still hoped he could make the replay. As he walked across the mud heap he resolved to try and play in the game scheduled for Old Trafford. Eddie Gray was named as Man of the Match – no surprise in that one. Bonetti was voted by the Chelsea fans as their saviour. Jack Charlton said of him, 'He was brilliant. He got to shots he was never entitled to see. He caught balls he was only entitled to touch. If it had not been for him Leeds would have had six goals, and it could have been over by half-time.'

I was in post-apocalyptic mood at the club banquet and was quoted as saying, 'Today we made history . . . to draw the Cup final at Wembley. History will be made again, we'll be the first team to go on from there and win the replay.'

Peter Houseman sat quietly at the buffet. Some of his team-mates were drinking a honey-coloured punch. The band was playing the Jackson Fives' 'I Want You Back'. Peter was looking at his reflection in the window, squinting past his image, wondering what the next few weeks would bring.

HERE IT IS

> To retire when the task is accomplished is the way of heaven.
> *Tao to Ching, Lao Tzu, 551–479 BC*

Two days after the Wembley epic, Chelsea travelled north to fulfil a league fixture at Stoke City. Of the 12 who had played in the final only the injured McCreadie, Harris and Bonetti were absent. It would seem inconceivable today that such a fixture would go ahead. Chelsea ran out 2–1 winners, giving a spirited performance and showing no side effects from the marathon.

Cooke set up the win, Hutchinson drilling in his pass after a quarter of an hour for the first goal. Stoke defender Eric Skeels deflected Charlie Cooke's swerving cross into his own net for the second, Willie Stevenson, who had scored from the penalty spot for Liverpool in the 1965 semi-final defeat, pulled one back but Chelsea hung on to win the points.

Two nights later Chelsea, still on the treadmill, returned to Turf Moor for a league match at Burnley. The home side exacted their revenge for the Cup exit in a 3–1 victory. John Hollins scored Chelsea's goal. Along with Houseman he was the only ever-present in the league that season. Houseman played in all 42 league matches. His last league goal had been at Selhurst Park in the 5–1 thrashing of Palace at Christmas.

Leeds had the little matter of the second semi-final against Celtic to take care of in Glasgow. An amazing, fanatical crowd of 136,505 roared Celtic on to an enthralling victory. Leeds encountered a very hostile atmosphere that night.

They took the lead in their first attack, but had barely crossed the halfway line when Norman Hunter put in Bremner for a shot. The little Scot struck the airborne ball like Garrincha at his best. A wickedly spinning 25-yard banana shot went in off the far post.

Celtic came back with a vengeance and both Madeley and Cooper kicked shots off the line. At half-time they still clung to Bremner's goal. The score was 1–1 on aggregate. John 'Yogi Bear' Hughes, with great nonchalance, equalised early in the second half for Celtic. The same player collided with Sprake and the luckless Welshman was carried off. Sprake had seemed to be particularly affected by the atmosphere, still traumatised by the goals he had conceded against Chelsea and the vortex of noise.

Celtic scored again through Bobby Murdoch before the Leeds substitute keeper David Harvey could have a touch of the ball. Dave Sexton was studying the game and noted how the Celtic winger Jimmy Johnstone had turned Terry Cooper inside out that night, in a similar fashion to Gray's treatment of David Webb at Wembley. The Celtic midfielder David Hay had a great game.

Years later David Hay was to join Chelsea. He was a world-class player who would have been one of the few adequate replacements for the departed superstars. Hay's Chelsea career was dogged by a series of horrific injuries and the Stamford Bridge faithful were to see only a few brief flashes of his unique talent. Chelsea were to have more than their fair share of superstar players whose careers were terminated; Ken Shellito in the '60s, Hutchinson and Hay in the '70s and Paul Eliott in the '90s.

The 1970 European Cup semi-final was more like a civil war. The Scots on the Elland Road side were continually intercepted and impeded. Sexton was also noticing that both of the Leeds Scottish wingers, Gray and Lorimer, appeared to freeze on the night and performed nowhere near what they were capable of.

On 29 April Leeds and Chelsea met again. Old Trafford was the scene of the first of Chelsea's FA Cup final appearances in 1915. They lost 3–0 to Sheffield United (this was even before Alan Birchenall's time). Chelsea fans preferred to think of the string of results they had put together there in more recent times.

The game was played on a Wednesday night, but an army of Chelsea fans, in excess of 20,000 (including three chaps dressed up as the Banana Splits, forerunners of the Teletubbies) travelled north to see the final chapter of the drama unfold. The game was shown live on BBC televison. It was the third-highest viewed programme for that channel of all time, only beaten by the Moon Walk and the Royal Wedding. It was perhaps the first soap opera of the new football age, with goodies and baddies, heroes and villains, and the vaudeville talent of Cooke and Osgood. *EastEnders* wasn't in it. One of the things most people recall about that extraordinary night was the tequila sunset that bathed Old Trafford. That Wednesday had been a sultry day, cloudy in London. The whole day had had a grainy quality, like the opening shots of *Butch Cassidy and the Sundance Kid*.

Dave Sexton made one tactical change but it won him the match and the Cup. The Chelsea boss switched Ron Harris to right-back and Webb back to the heart of the defence alongside Dempsey. Otherwise it was the same side as played at Wembley. The alteration meant that Harris was detailed to mark Gray.

Again Hudson was to miss out on playing in a Cup final for Chelsea. His desperate measures to try and make the team had included a visit to a spiritual healer. This was in the days before Ellen Drewery made it fashionable. Drewery healed through the power of touch and faith. She was to have a great influence on the former Chelsea and England boss, Glenn Hoddle. Glenn made his full début for Spurs against Stoke as part of a side which contained a rejuvenated Alan Hudson. Hoddle scored the winning goal and was warmly congratulated by the ex-Chelsea star who was one of Hoddle's boyhood heroes. So began a mutual admiration of each other's skill.

Within a few minutes of the game starting at Old Trafford, Harris, in the words of Jack Charlton, 'gave Eddie a beauty. He was virtually a spectator after that.' I saw the tackle again on TV years later on one of those 'hardmen' shows. I can honestly say that it was the most bone-jarring I had ever seen. A train could not have made more impact.

That set the tone for the game, which continued with no quarter asked for or given. The tackling was ferocious in the extreme. Did Chelsea have the wherewithal to beat Leeds at their own game? The Leeds banners proclaimed that 'Norman Hunter bites your legs'. No fangs were sunk into Hutchinson's legs but soon he was reeling from a crunching tackle almost in Ronnie's class.

Leeds set their stall out for Bonetti. Mick Jones crashed into him and he received treatment on his knee. He still carried his ankle injury and it was clear that his movement was impaired. Alan Clarke, free from the attentions of Harris, set up Mick Jones spectacularly for the opening goal. He skipped through a couple of challenges and passed to the supercharged Jones who thundered a shot high into the Chelsea net. It was a superb goal, fit to grace a Cup final. Bonetti strained to reach it but even if he had been 100 per cent fit it is arguable whether he would have succeeded. But with his knee jarred, his ankle throbbing and his body aching from the buffeting he had taken, it was impossible. The Leeds fans were confident that Chelsea could not possibly come back from this.

That was how it stayed at half-time. In the second half, though, Chelsea enjoyed more possession than at any time in the whole contest.

The midfield finally made up for the loss of Hudson. Cooke was starting to play wide, Hollins was breaking forward with powerful runs. Houseman was spraying passes to Osgood and Hutchinson. The latter was still continuing his vendetta with the Leeds back four, but he was starting to wear them down and mimicked Bremner's protests after one of his challenges.

There was less than quarter of an hour to go when Charlton went up for a Leeds corner. It was always the same. The intention was to hinder the crippled Bonetti enough so that Leeds could scramble a goal. Charlton claimed that a 'nameless' Chelsea player deadlegged him (a deadleg was a knee in the thigh).

Chelsea broke quickly, Charlton chasing the 'nameless' Chelsea player over to the right. In the meantime a wonderful interchange between Hutchinson and Osgood fed Cooke, who chipped in a glorious ball for Osgood to equalise with a full-length diving header. Charlton claimed that he was still hobbling from the knock he had received and could not get back in time.

That was probably the greatest goal scored in the history of CFC. It contained everything, skill, power, passion. It was *Star Wars*, Geoff Hurst's extra-time goal in 1966 and Lennon grinning at McCartney all rolled into one. Osgood had his record. No one has come close since. There was not the slightest doubt now amongst anyone there who would win,

The game went to extra time. It was now all Chelsea. Houseman was full of industry, tearing down the line furiously to force himself back into a move he had initiated with a long ball. Leeds could see it all slipping away. Chelsea scored the winner with their cliché goal. An enormous throw from Hutchinson, Dempsey flicked on, the ball skimmed off the head of Charlton and Webb, wearing number six on his back, bundled the ball over the line. Some say it hit his shoulder, others claimed that it was ricocheted off his face. Whatever happened, it was enough to beat Harvey and take the Cup to Stamford Bridge.

Chapter Twelve: The Euro Star

That is how we play, flat out. And then we suddenly play harder still. It's hunger for goals that does it.
Dave Sexton

Chelsea celebrated their famous and remarkable victory with their usual panache. So much so that when they invited their jubilant fans to join them on the train back to London they literally drank it dry. Beer, spirits and cashew nuts were everywhere.

Chelsea had won the Cup in style. The 25 goals scored by them was the best by any FA Cup-winning club since the Second World War, beating a Jimmy Greaves-inspired Spurs total of 24 in 1961–62. Derby County had accumulated a total of 37 goals when they lifted the Cup in 1945–46, but that year's ties were played on a home and away system up to the semi-final.

Five days after winning the FA Cup, Dave Sexton splashed out £100,000 on the Millwall striker Keith Weller. Dapper, fast and aggressive, Weller was a shrewd addition to the squad. Keith became the third £100k signing in the club's history, joining Tony Hateley and the shoe salesman Birchenall. Weller was another Cockney rebel, a lifelong Arsenal fan who was born in Islington, before it was the most hardcore fashionable place in London. Weller's first job was as a £3-per-week floor tiler. Keith was briefly on Arsenal's books as an amateur before joining deadly rivals Tottenham. He made his début for Spurs in a 7–4 thrashing of Wolves and played 21 games for them before joining Millwall for £18,000. Weller really exploded at the Den, which was at a different location in those times. They boasted a stand that appeared to have been constructed from old orange boxes and the hordes of recalcitrant yobs that supported them. Dave Sexton was well pleased with his new acquisition because it gave him more options up front. Weller was equally at home on the flanks or playing through the middle. The Chelsea manager was planning a major assault on Europe and needed more strike power.

England enjoyed a mixed summer of heat and rain. Somebody daubed 'Osgood is God' on walls in the Kings Road. Norman Greenbaum had the top-selling record in the charts with 'Spirit in the Sky', a song that sounded like a wounded washing machine. If you wanted to sup a pint of bitter whilst you listened to it it would cost you just under two shillings, or ten pence.

Dave Sexton spent the summer watching Brazil win the World Cup. No team in the previous nine tournaments, played over 40 years, had won so convincingly or classically. At some point Sexton began to rethink entirely his tactics for the coming season. The Chelsea manager knew that his side would have to keep pace with the enormous changes that were happening in the game. Dave had been a great advocate of the man-to-man marking system, but he had seen the future and it was organic. Zonal marking was the buzz word. In his abbreviated playing career Sexton had experienced the effects of man marking and in his captain, Ron Harris, he had perhaps the finest man marker of the era. The Chelsea defence was packed with experienced, aggressive, highly motivated players used to containing the cream of attackers. With the game going through a tactical renaissance and the challenges of Europe looming, something revolutionary was required.

In the future two of the biggest names in European football, Ruud Gullit and Gianluca Vialli, were to manage the club and bring in their own revolutionary ideas, but at that time departures from the normal British tactics seemed mere flights of fancy. Even Bonetti's continental goalkeeping strip was regarded as a bit suspect.

England lost their grip on the World Cup, crashing out to West Germany 3–2 in the quarter-finals. In some sections of the media it was considered that the England team that started the 1970 World Cup was the best they had ever produced. Gordon Banks missed the game with a bad case of Mexican tummy and Bonetti was called up to deputise. England had led 2–0 at one stage, and it was the only time they were to surrender a two-goal lead in the reign of Ramsey.

The German side that day included the legendary winger Reinhard Libuda. Libuda was a winger in the Houseman–Jesper Gronkjaer mould and won 26 caps for the star-studded German side. He was tiring in the blistering Mexican heat of Leon after giving a fine performance. Helmut Schon, the wily German manager, replaced Libuda with Jurgen Grabowski, whose surging runs destroyed the English defence in extra time. The third goal was a direct result of Grabowski sprinting past Cooper. You recall what damage Cooper had inflicted on Chelsea at Stamford Bridge in the 5–2 thrashing. The German team of that era relied heavily on their pacy wingers. Grabowski was very quick and Libuda could also be fast, but he enjoyed drawing defenders towards him in a more languid fashion. He would then pick up speed and produce one of his slide rule centres.

Libuda's career went into freefall shortly afterwards, when he was banned for life for bribery. The ban was later lifted but he failed to re-establish himself in the glitterball of top-class football. He drifted into a life of heavy drinking and died of throat cancer.

YEAR OF THE CAT

For some inexplicable reason, Bonetti was made the scapegoat for the defeat and was heavily criticised for the three German goals. Bonetti's reputation as an England player never really recovered from that match, though he was to excel with Chelsea for many seasons more. His part in the débâcle was pardonable; Germany's first goal had been scored by Beckenbauer, who broke from deep to beat Bonetti with a deceptive shot that carried beneath the Chelsea goalkeeper. It was very similar to Houseman's shot at Wembley in its complete lack of distinction.

Gerd Muller's decisive third goal seemed to be a direct result of exhaustion on behalf of the England defenders, which led to inept marking. Perhaps the feline had used all of his luck up at Wembley and Old Trafford. What was more important – Bonetti winning the Cup for Chelsea or losing the World Cup for England? The game hinged not on Bonetti's form but on the fact that Bobby Charlton was a spent force in midfield. The Manchester United player was completely nuked by the heat and altitude. The most vivid image of the World Cup was of the subsituted Charlton as he trundled off, plastering the sweat-drenched strands of his remaining hair across his scalp. It was his 106th game for England and it looked like he had played them all consecutively. That was enough to give anyone nightmares. Had Alan Hudson, in the form displayed at Loftus Road, been available one can only speculate on the possibilities. The wingers had wreaked their revenge. The hot breath of irony was felt on the England manager's neck.

Brazil won the World Cup with perhaps the greatest assembly of talent ever seen on a pitch. The year 1970 was the golden age of football. The Chelsea side that lifted the FA Cup can be mentioned in the same breath as the Pelé-inspired impeccable Brazil side.

The new season of 1970–71 started in a 'Look what I got on my shoes' mood for Chelsea. The champions Everton beat them in the Charity Shield match by two goals to one. It was a game played in temperatures of Mexican proportions at Stamford Bridge. Once again, the jet-heeled wingers of the Merseyside club proved too much of a handful for the dysfunctional Chelsea defence. Alan Whittle fired them ahead and Howard Kendall made it two before Ian Hutchinson pulled one back by heading in a Weller centre. The militant Weller had taken Tommy Baldwin's place in the forward line. Alan Hudson was playing again, but he looked overweight and sheepish. Peter Houseman was wearing the number 11 shirt and enjoying life at the Bridge. He always looked immaculate. The Shed thought that he even ironed his bootlaces!

Everton were back at the Bridge a few weeks later for a league fixture which ended in a 2–2 draw. Houseman had his best game of the season so far, having a hand in both goals. He set up Dempsey for an equaliser, cleverly beating two tackles to send in a fine centre for the centre-back to head home. Later his corner was misheaded by the late ex-England back Keith Newton, and Keith Weller scored his first home goal. Weller won the crowd over in just a few games. For some players it was easy, while others never achieved no matter what.

Everton had evolved into worthy champions. The crux of their power was the midfield trio of Ball, Harvey and Kendall. They were nicknamed the 'Panzer Division' because they were like three tanks swarming all over other sides. All three were mobile, quick and highly committed. Both the attacking and defensive duties were equally shared. The one-dimensional theory of 'one man to win the ball, one man to pass it' etc was made obsolete. It was a perfect combination. Between them they had scored 17 goals in their push for the title. What was more significant, though, was that away from home they conceded 15 only. Sexton was concerned about his midfield which, despite its enterprise, lacked solidity. Houseman then missed two matches because of bursitis of the elbow. The first was a 2–2 home draw with Wolves and the second was the first leg of the European Cup-Winners' Cup-tie with Aris Salonika of Greece.

Charlie Cooke took Houseman's shirt over in what was a stormy match. After the mud and bullets of Wembley, the Blues were confronted by a dust bowl of a pitch. The penalty area looked like the contents of a skip had been upturned onto it. Osgood missed a penalty and Dempsey was sent off for a tear-up after 35 minutes of a rowdy first half. The Greeks went ahead early in the second half but Hutchinson hit a screamer home for a deserved equaliser. Osgood had set the chance up and battled throughout, despite some weak refereeing and scything tackles. The Greek backs were like alligators snapping away.

Mick Greenaway led a group of 70 Chelsea fans to Greece for the match. I saw them at the airport. The cost for a two-day trip was £34 plus a match ticket in the stand, which was £1.50. The only trouble was on the pitch.

Before the match Chelsea had won a portion of the crowd over with a spontaneous gesture by Peter Osgood. Whilst inspecting the pitch, the Os had taken the players over to shake hands with the disabled spectators in wheelchairs.

The programme for the match included a reference in Greek to Chelsea as the 'Pensioners'. It was a puzzle to the Chelsea party how the Greeks had obtained the old nickname, long since discarded by Ted Drake. I suppose you could say it was all Greek to them!

Chelsea took revenge in the return leg, crushing the Greeks 5–1. Proving that he was far from a geriatric pensioner, John Hollins was in superb form and scored with raking drives hit from both feet. Chelsea fans began to think he had entered into some Faustian pact with the devil. He never looked a day older and only seemed to get faster. Ian Hutchinson also hit two goals and even Marvin Hinton managed to get on the score sheet with a Hutchinson-created goal.

A few weeks earlier Hollins had hammered in what was regarded at the time as the greatest goal ever scored at Stamford Bridge in a 2–1 victory over Arsenal. Hollins' high level of fitness and boundless enthusiasm was never better exemplified. The goal was described as follows by Alan Hoby in the *Sunday Express*.

> Hollins scored the golden goal of the '70s, for, whatever happens in the future, none of us, I am sure, will ever see a goal quite like it. Rocketing through the middle like a blue streak, Hollins simultaneously 'killed' Ron Harris's fine through pass and held off the hulking Roberts. Then, as goalkeeper Bob Wilson came off his line, Hollins swerved breathtakingly to his left and, in full stride, chipped the ball over the horrified Wilson's head. Arsenal fans in the sweltering 53,722 crowd tensed in torment as a racketing roar rose from their Chelsea foes. But it was cut off abruptly as the ball rebounded from the bar. But Hollins, as if seized by a fever, sprinted on in a half circle, outpaced the astounded Arsenal defence and, with his back to the goal, pounced on the ball again. Then, swivelling, he cracked it with his right foot into the back of the net. Wonderful.

Chelsea fans were spoilt then, with the saccharine Alan Hudson goal against Sheffield Wednesday and Peter Osgood's header in the Cup final replay. Hollins' goal was even more remarkable because it was scored against the meanest defence of all time. Arsenal went on to win the league and Cup double that season, only the second team in the twentieth century at that time to have achieved it. Arsenal lost only four more games that entire season. They certainly never conceded a goal as remarkable as Hollins'. Arsenal built their double triumph on the zonal marking system. Don Howe took over as chief coach at Highbury when Sexton rejoined Chelsea following Docherty's departure. I liked Howe, his eyes took your inventory, openly. In those days he saw everyone as a possible adversary. I should have taken lessons.

Houseman's fine form continued, class oozing from every pore. He was setting up goals throughout the autumn and early winter of 1970–71. In a Football League Cup-tie against a spunky Sheffield Wednesday he played a particularly outstanding game, creating Osgood's winning goal with another of his trademark centres. Houseman was concentrating on getting the ball into the air with the outside of his left foot whilst running fast. Peter had noticed this particular skill whilst watching the World Cup. The drier climate of South America made it easier for him than the dampness of England. In the tradition of wingers like Stanley Matthews, Peter Houseman found greater percentage in swerving in crosses with the inside of the foot and he caused immense problems to the goalkeepers he encountered with this technique. If the keeper came out he was stranded, yet if there was an Osgood, Webb or Hutchinson hanging wide then a goal was likely. Should I stay or should I go? It could have been Chelsea's theme tune.

THE TALENTED MR BEST

Chelsea's challenge for the League Cup ended in a rare defeat at Old Trafford, when Chelsea went down to an amazing solo goal scored by George Best. It was as brilliant as Hollins' effort against Arsenal. When he set out on his devastating run I felt dread and excitement at the same time. At the end of the match I went over to congratulate Best in the players' bar. He sat at a wooden table; any table he sat down at instantly became his. His hair was the colour of smoke. I shook his hand; his palm was cold, shiny with moisture, his nails trimmed close to the cuticle.

I recently saw Jude Law's portrayal of playboy Dickie Greenleaf in the film of Patricia Highsmith's story *The Talented Mr Ripley*. That was George Best three decades ago. Nobody at the time could have known the cost of carrying such a burden of expectation, of such collective investment. Later that evening he would go to a club to find a surrogate for the enemy inside his own head, whom he could not deal with. Around that time he must have started running hard to distance himself from the myth of George Best.

BACK TO BLACKPOOL

The most bizzare match of that cardiac-arresting season was the 4–3 win at Blackpool. Picture the scene – with 20 minutes of the game left Chelsea were trailing by three goals. A young prospect called John Phillips was making his début in the Chelsea goal. Fred Pickering, the executioner of Chelsea at St Andrews in that bitter Cup defeat by Birmingham, had scored twice for the tangerine-shirted home side. Sexton was so angry that he had thick purple cords of blood coursing through his neck. I suppose he had something to be angry about. He gambled by putting Cooke on for Baldwin. Next he fine-tuned the configuration by pitching Webb up front, bringing Weller inside and switching Mulligan to the centre of defence. Houseman dropped back to slot into Mulligan's role. Sexton had great faith in Houseman's defensive abilities and the move worked even better than he had hoped. Commitment, see? Weller hit two frenzied goals and Webb, at his best when the chips were down, powered in another. The crowd were having their brains curdled. In the last minute of one of Chelsea's strangest ever games, Weller's centre was turned into his own net by Blackpool's Dave Hatton. It was marvellous fun. Me, worry? I always knew we would do it. That was about the only time we came away from Blackpool with a smile on our faces.

CSKA Sofia were Chelsea's next opponents in Europe. The Blues won both matches 1–0, Baldwin scoring in the away leg and David Webb sealing victory in London. Chelsea learnt a lot from those games. The long through ball had lost a lot of its value against sides like Sofia because it was almost impossible to get Osgood in on such a move. For long periods in both games Chelsea were compressed into midfield, unable to advance. Perhaps that was a warning of things to come.

The third round of the Cup saw the holders drawn away to Crystal Palace yet again. Chelsea seemed unable to avoid clashes with the Selhurst side. The match was played on an icy pitch and the only playable surfaces were in the corners, visible only from a light aeroplane. The Cup-holders opted to wear yellow shirts on the grounds that they would show up better in the hazy winter light.

Chelsea took an early lead when Houseman whipped over a centre and Osgood headed home. Palace protested bitterly about the goal, claiming that Baldwin had fouled their goalkeeper Jackson. Osgood turned and blasted the ball away upfield after scoring. The previous season he had scored six goals against them in three games and this looked like their epitaph.

But the home side came at a smug Chelsea like a melting avalanche. Palace equalised from a corner, McCormack scoring with an overhead kick as Hinton and Webb got into a tangle. The extravagant finish boosted Palace. Bobby Tambling missed the clash against his former club through injury. Another ex-Chelsea star, Alan Birchenall, was made captain for the day, though, and shot Palace ahead shortly afterwards. Thanks, Birch!

I supressed an overwhelming urge to down a large Scotch at half-time. Panic started to seep through the Chelsea defence. It is one of the hardest things in football to defend a trophy, as the opponents always raise their game. Eddie

McCreadie had not played in the first team since the Cup final and his career was in the embers. Dempsey was not included that day, nor was Hudson, whose form and fitness were giving cause for concern to Sexton. The extreme self-loathing that eventually destroyed his career started around then.

Cooke, who had been struggling to rediscover his form all season, suddenly found his familiar road to Damascus. Charlie saved the match for Chelsea with a stunning performance. He had the moon on a stick as he took the game to Palace and unhinged their confidence with a series of dazzling runs. He set up a number of chances, which Baldwin, teetering on the edge of mediocrity throughout the game, proceeded to squander. Eventually Tommy (standing in for the injured Hutchinson) equalised for Chelsea, stabbing home Cooke's pass. The Scot deserved to have won it with a shot near the end that almost split the crossbar in half, but the game ended 2–2. Cooke's genius was ablaze that afternoon.

The replay was on a freezing January night a few days later. Baldwin scored again in the first ten minutes, from a peach of a ball from the hard-hitting Weller. Keith had settled in quickly and was Chelsea's most consistent and productive forward at that period. He had scored a dozen goals already and was hungry for more. Houseman, having been Chelsea's most significant player for so long, had an air of solemnity about him at that time.

Weller had a hand in Chelsea's second goal, scored by Houseman. The luckless Jackson punched out Weller's swerving centre as Osgood raced in to convert it. The ball ran loose and Peter was on hand to smash home past Jackson and between fellow defenders Sewell and McCormick. It was a fine goal, Houseman's first since Wembley last April.

Houseman's goal was enough to kill off Palace's challenge. Steve Kember drove Palace on from midfield throughout the game. Croydon-born Kember had just been selected by Ramsey for the Under-23 squad and was regarded by many as the up-and-coming talent. Sexton was a big fan. He could see him as a dominant force and was impressed by his performance. Kember was to become Hudson's doppelgänger. The symbolic meanings of the doppelganger are myriad, but for Sexton the main significance of such a mirroring lay in the chance to oppose Hudson's growing influence on his side with a player that he believed to possess identical powers. Sexton was keen to sign him, I know that for a fact. He wanted to forsake iconoclasm and experimentation for restraint and simplicity. With the greatest respect to Kember, I never saw him as a player that was the equal of Hudson. How could he be? An unmistakable individuality was stamped on everything Alan did.

INNER-CITY BLUES

Manchester City put Chelsea out of the Cup in the fourth round. Since the opening game of the season Sexton had changed the system of marking in defence. Instead of each defender being responsible for marking one particular opponent throughout the game, the man-to-man system, Chelsea adopted the recognised alternative marking system. In this role each defender marked particular areas of the pitch, picking up in turn any forward who entered his zone. Zonal marking was utterly dependent on communication, or at least some type of mutual understanding, amongst the Chelsea players. Forwards were picked up by one defender after another as they ran all over the field.

Dempsey was a typical marker, great in one-to-ones but far more vulnerable when asked to co-ordinate his play with the other defenders. Consquently the former Craven Cottager lost his place for a while. Dempsey found it very hard to break the habit of trailing his chosen attacker all over the pitch. Marking an empty space and waiting for a forward to go in it was a distraction. Hinton won his place back in the defence and gave it more wit. For a while, Marvin flourished. Nobody at Chelsea read the game better and he got to the point of attack very quickly. Hinton would be there when you most needed him, he was always that extra man in defence when the team was under pressure. The problems came when forwards pushed up on him, or when, as in the 1967 Cup final, he was faced with an aerial bombardment. Frank Le Boeuf in the '90s Chelsea Cup-winning side is an interesting comparison. Frank said 'au revoir' in 2001.

Colin Bell destroyed Hinton at Stamford Bridge as the Cup was wrenched from their grasp. It was to be nearly three decades before it returned to them. Bell was a superb player. Imagine if you dare a mixture of Hudson's skill, Alan Ball's running, Richard Branson's workrate and the finishing of Robbie Fowler. He was the complete midfield player, but a dreadful knee injury wrecked his brilliant if slightly unfulfilled career.

At Stamford Bridge, Chelsea trailed to a Bowyer goal but were pressing hard for an equaliser. Bell took a pass in midfield and swept it out to Neil Young on the left. Bell moved forward as though to make a run, only to turn away looking almost exhausted. Young made a run then checked, as if in disappointment that his midfielder had not continued with support. Instead he centred, skimming over a low cross which flew in front of a line of Chelsea defenders. John Boyle, Webb and Harris stormed back to protect Bonetti's goal. Marvin Hinton was the last in the chorus line. Hinton had time to collect the cross, hack it clear for a throw-in, pass it back to Bonetti (this was not outlawed then), or even concede a corner. He did none of these four things, instead letting the ball run. Too late,

Colin Bell had come in behind him and instantly scored with a whiplash drive that flew past Bonetti. The Cup was gone.

The Shed screamed at Hinton; why hadn't he f****** looked?

The truth was that Hinton *had* looked. He told me, 'I had looked a second or so before the ball reached me. I had glanced over my shoulder to make sure no one was coming in from the right. The pitch was clear behind me, so I knew I could let the ball run, and then turn and collect it away from danger. At least I thought I could.'

Hinton had fallen for Bell's incredible vision. Such was his vista of the game that as soon as he had passed to Neil Young, Colin had made a diagonal run across the pitch, a run so subtle it did not raise the suspicion of any of the retreating Chelsea rearguard. Bell had spotted the space developing on the right of Hinton. Like a superhero with X-ray vision, Bell had accelerated to get around the flank of the Chelsea defence. I wondered how it would show up on Venables' 'prozane' TV thing. Like Osgood's run at Old Trafford, the timing of the movement was exquisite. The finish in both cases was immaculate. It was ironic that Chelsea were to lose the Cup to a goal as cunning as the one that had won it.

WHEN WE WAS FAB

Canals and waterways lace under humpbacked bridges through winding streets of gabled houses in the delightful city of Bruges. Today the Eurostar runs sightseeing and shopping trips to the Belgian town. The works of the Flemish masters Rubens and Van Dyck are on display in the many churches and galleries. Tourists can browse through the weekend markets or the chic boutiques. The Bruges side that Chelsea played in March 1971 contained its own Flemish masters in Lambert and Rensenbrink. Maybe they had a lick of emulsion in their team also. A bruised hip caused Peter Houseman to miss the game, but his wife had just given birth to a baby boy called Daniel and I had never seen him so happy. Peter Bonetti also missed the game. His last game had been the friendly against Santos in Jamaica, in which Pelé had played. I recall his satisfied face at the end of the match.

Bonetti had a bout of pneumonia and was convalescing in Portugal. John Phillips deputised. Phillips was not great on crosses, which is bad for a goalkeeper. The word on the street was that Bonetti was faltering. After the débâcle in Leon, Bonetti had left the England camp to holiday in Acapulco, and some said he was suffering a nervous breakdown. The emotional distress was weighing heavily on him. Today he would have had Max Clifford on hand to manufacture spin and a pizza advert. With Tommy Hughes having broken his right leg earlier in the season and dropping out of contention, it was down to John boy.

Only Phillips prevented Chelsea from being routed in the first game. Chelsea lost 2–0, both the goals coming from corners in the first half. The odds were stacked against Sexton's team; the ground was cramped and the pitch narrow, and the cold night air was filled with the sound of klaxons and horns. and what appeared to be dustbin lids banged with monkey-wrenches.

The Belgians had a tradition of playing in packs, building dangerous attacks from a system providing a variety of short passing possibilities. The Chelsea midfield struggled in a spectacularly cack-handed fashion to match them.

Missing Osgood (through a lengthy suspension) and the crippled Hutchinson (his knee was injured) Chelsea made few chances and on the night were 24-carat rubbish. Chelsea fans caused trouble after the game by kicking nine bells out of some locals. The whole evening prompted a dull ache in the spleen.

OH WHAT A NIGHT

Two weeks later Bruges came to Stamford Bridge, defending their two-goal lead. At home Bruges were virtually unbeatable, but away from their home, the 'Klokke', they were not so strong. Osgood was back from a two-month suspension. He felt that he had been harshly treated, as his only crime was obtaining three bookings. I defended him, which earned him the long ban. The Os had been training like Rocky for his comeback, losing three pounds in the process. His preparations were hindered by the fact that he had moved house on the day of the match. Flaubert once remarked that 'domesticity was the enemy of the artist'.

Houseman pulled a goal back for an overwrought Chelsea in the first half. It was his first and only Euro-goal that season and was a vital strike; what a player he was. The goal came at a time when it looked as if the Belgians had weathered the early storm of Chelsea attacks. Their two-goal lead was looking unassailable. Houseman's goal was as much of a lifesaver as his Cup equalisers at Burnley and Wembley.

Since the Bruges defeat, Chelsea had had a deluge of criticial opprobrium heaped on them. People love it when Chelsea win, but if you lose – well, that's headline news. The crowd were loyal though and, lifted by Houseman's goal, they roared Chelsea on in an astonishing manner. However, with only a few minutes left, Chelsea still trailed 2–1 on aggregate. Then Osgood scored from a mammoth goalmouth scrimmage to level the tie. The ground erupted as Osgood led the celebrations. The volume was pumped up even higher.

Greenaway was 'Zigger Zaggering' in that last desperate 20 minutes of normal time.

In extra time Chelsea, free from the tension of chasing the game, played their best football of that season, and possibly any season. Hudson, who had been self-absorbed and erratic for months, threw off his niggling injury worries and dominated. Following some truly innovative play, he set Osgood up for the third goal with a perfect sidefoot pass. At last Chelsea were in front. It became just shooting practice as they poured forward. Balding men still stop me and talk about that third goal. Chelsea played so well; it was timeless, moving and beautiful.

Hudson and Houseman later combined to conjure an audacious fourth goal for Tommy Baldwin. It was a night of sheer joy for Chelsea fans. Their side had won in style, playing a brand of football that had enabled them to achieve a seemingly impossible task. Bruges were to change their name to Club Bruges and went from strength to strength to become a formidable team in domestic and European competition. It was a night that was to live on in the memories of all who were lucky enough to witness it.

JACK'S RETURN HOME

The following Saturday Leeds were the visitors in a vital league game. They were six points clear of second-placed Arsenal, who had two games (then worth four points) in hand. Chelsea, despite their edge over Leeds in Cup matches, had not beaten them for five seasons in the league. Leeds were starting to feel the pressure again as Arsenal stalked them.

The blistering form that Chelsea had finished the Bruges match in continued. They simply overwhelmed Leeds and ran out easy winners by 3–1. Osgood scored another wonder goal and Peter Houseman recorded his first league goals of the season. The records show it was his only deuce in a league match.

Houseman was superb that day. At times he played the ball almost indifferently across the front of the Leeds defence, Hudson to Houseman on the left, infield to Hollins. Back it flowed to Osgood, a tap to Hudson on to Cooke . . . delightful stuff.

Leeds' defeat set up Arsenal for the double. Once again cracks were appearing in the Elland Road façade. Leeds on the rocks, ain't no big surprise. In their hearts Leeds must have known that despite their efforts to reinvent themselves they were still the London fall guys.

Chelsea travelled to Highbury the following week. They received a rare standing ovation from the North Bank for their performance in beating Leeds.

The crowd of 62,087 was the biggest for a league game that season. It beat the 61,277 who had packed into Stamford Bridge in November to see Spurs steal a breathtaking match with two injury-time goals.

Chelsea failed to recapture the form they had shown against Bruges and Leeds. Ray Kennedy battered us and plundered two goals to give the Gooners victory and Chelsea seemed preoccupied with their semi-final draw. It was against Manchester City, the holders of the European Cup-Winners' Cup and was a chance for Chelsea to avenge their FA Cup defeat.

Both sides were hit badly by injuries for these matches. Mickey Droy made his European début for the Blues in the first leg at Stamford Bridge. Droy looked as though he had stepped from the pages of a comic book. Standing at 6 ft 4 in and weighing nearly 16 st, he liked massacring strikers. Like Weller, Mick was born in North London. As a schoolboy he had played for the Islington District team with Charlie George. After being overlooked by Arsenal he played non-league with Slough before being snapped up by Chelsea.

Derek Smethurst, also making his European début, scored the only goal of a disappointing game. Smethurst was born in South Africa and was discovered by Dave Sexton. Whereas Droy went on to become a Chelsea legend, Smethurst was a hero 'just for one day', as Bowie sang. He never really made it and went down the path of no return like so many.

City played very defensively and went out to smother Chelsea from the start, far from the freewheeling side that had beaten them by three goals. Smethurst angled a low drive past Joe Corrigan at the far post after a scramble. John Boyle was pulled down in the box chasing a Houseman pass, but no penalty was given. The rest was appalling.

Chelsea returned to the city of Manchester almost a year to the night that they had won the Cup on the other side of town. City, shorn of their star forward Bell, pressed Chelsea from the start but the beleaguered Londoners' defence held firm. Just on half-time the City goalkeeper punched Keith Weller's swerving cross into his own net. David Webb was challenging in the box and it was just enough of a distraction to give Chelsea a two-goal lead.

In the closing minutes Chelsea finished strongly. They could smell the victory and opened up at City. Houseman started to attack Tony Book, the veteran full-back. Peter threw himself full length at Hudson's cross and saw his header crash against the post. Book, using some sleight-of-hand, scrambled the ball clear. Maybe a third goal would have flattered Chelsea but it was declaration of intent from the intrepid Londoners. They were out to lift a Cup again. Just as City had vanquished Chelsea on their own ground, Chelsea's victory at Maine Road wrenched the Cup away from the holders. As the final whistle blew the 10,000 Chelsea fans who had made the midweek trip north saluted their heroes. City had played Chelsea five times that season in three different competitions. Both league games finished 1–1. City and Chelsea were two great English sides who played attacking football and never gave an inch. I always regarded Maine Road as a lucky ground, till one season I was introduced to someone . . .

GAMES IN MAY

The final was held in Athens on 19 May. The Chelsea team that started the game was: Bonetti, Boyle, Harris, Hollins, Dempsey, Webb, Weller, Hudson, Osgood, Cooke, Houseman. Subs: Baldwin and Mulligan.

Crowd: 45,000.

Chelsea's opponents were Real Madrid, probably the greatest club side of the twentieth century. At the time of writing they are current holders of the European Cup and include a winger who cost £43 million in their team. When they met Chelsea in the early summer of 1971 those glory days were past. They still had delusions of grandeur, like a '60s pop star appearing on talk shows today, subverting expectations.

There was a time in the late '50s when it seemed that Real Madrid would continue to win the European Cup forever. Their superb attacking play had dominated the early years of the competition (when Chelsea had declined to enter) and they won it for the first five years. Their peak performance had been the 7–3 destruction of Eintracht Frankfurt before a massed crowd of 135,000 at Hampden Park, a crowd that had included George Graham.

Chelsea found themselves almost embarrassed by the high level of skill displayed by Real. However, they lacked the aggressive purpose which the earlier great teams had shown in winning the record amount of European Cups. Madrid could easily open up the Blues defence in the same masterly manner, but there was no longer a Puskas or Di Stefano to take the chances. Only Gento remained from the 'golden years', his murderous shooting had declined along with his pace but his crossfield passing was as immaculate as ever. At that time the great light of Madrid seemed to have almost flickered out. Midfield genius Amancio continually laid the ball off in the penalty area, but no forward had the bravery to contest with the likes of Webb or Harris.

Houseman found it equally hard against the tough tackling Madrid defence. He was shuttled into cul-de-sacs where defenders would eventually dispossess him.

Osgood had no respect for the Madrid side. I always thought he was at his most dangerous when defenders seemed to have him contained. He had the confidence to settle for only two touches of the ball when the going was at its toughest and space was at a premium. Osgood had a low centre of gravity despite his height, and his ability to control the most awkward of passes instantly before striking for goal was his most priceless asset. After 55 minutes he struck again for Chelsea in a Cup final, firing the Londoners ahead. That seemed to be it, but in the last minute Madrid equalised. An error from Dempsey let in Zoco to score a soft goal.

The match went to extra time but as was the case at Wembley neither side could score. The Spanish side finished on top, looking to grab the winner that would have restored their prestige. Bonetti made some fine saves, leaving the mental debris behind. However, it must be said that he had an easier time than he did against Leeds. He was never challenged once as he collected the ball. The Cat told me what an unusual experience it had been. Madrid were more concerned about getting their players back in midfield. Mick Jones, Clarke and Jack eat your heart out.

It is ironic that Chelsea, who had stolen the Cup from Leeds in their previous final, were now robbed themselves by a last-gasp equaliser. Had the final been played today, the result would have been decided then and there. Extra time would have been followed by penalties or a golden goal. Amazingly, the two sides met again 48 hours later. There were no sponsors to appease or TV schedules to accommodate.

Houseman rested as much as he could in the short space of time between the games, while Osgood and his cohorts sat by the pool partying. I went for a long walk through the town. The city was still packed with totally medicined Chelsea fans who had stayed over for the duration. Many had come on special one-day charters and had returned to London, but some missed the flight home to see Chelsea in the replay. What would you have done? Mick Greenaway obtained a loan from his friends in the Chelsea team to fund his additional stay.

Further injuries hit the Blues. Osgood was shattered by his exertions in the first game – the last two seasons were catching up with him quickly. Great emphasis is placed on the pressure on players today and the lack of rest they have. Osgood had played in the previous summer's World Cup and even when suspended he was training on the Epsom Downs, pounding his way to full fitness. His ankles had been wrecked by two savage tackles on Wednesday evening. Whenever he moved into attack he walked into a minefield of pushes, shoves and bodychecks. In the penalty area he was jostled and baulked but gave only a dignified response. Sexton knew that his main striker would not be able to play another full 90 minutes. The Wizard would have to weave his magic early.

John Hollins missed the game, a knee injury preventing him from being ever present for both of Chelsea's greatest seasons. He commentated on the match instead for the BBC, coming over like a young Des Lynam, a lot better than some of the commentators we have today.

Faced with these selection problems Sexton was always willing to gamble, as he had at Old Trafford. His decision to detail Harris to tackle Gray had worked perfectly as the Chelsea captain tackled the potential match winner into anonymity. Now he switched Cooke to Hollins' role in the core of midfield and brought Baldwin into the attack. He chanced his arm and Osgood's leg by starting with him.

Cooke was Chelsea's star man in the replay. Throughout the match kingpin Charlie danced past tackle after tackle, through a forest of flailing legs. The Real defence thrashed about aimlessly trying to catch him, as if playing blind man's bluff in the fog. Early in the game he treated the Chelsea fans to his famous version of the 'Ali shuffle'. He waved his left foot over the ball whilst running at speed at defenders Luis and Benito. Cooke did not make contact, but it confused the Madrid players as he accelerated away in one fluid movement. It was a crusher.

Dempsey appeared to bring down Amancio, and Real appealed vociferously for a penalty. The referee indicated to play on. Miguel Munoz, the Real coach, claimed that it cost them the game. Soon afterwards Cooke's sudden backheel took his opponents by surprise and changed the direction of the Londoners' attack. Cooke used that backheel as a psychological weapon; he sensed that the Madrid side would be unnerved. The Scot wanted to emphasise his control of the situation. After such a game Cooke had nowhere else to go, nothing to prove.

After half an hour Tommy Baldwin fired in an angled drive that the Madrid goalkeeper Borja just managed to finger away. Cooke curled the ball over deliberately and Dempsey, on the run, thrust his head at it. The Madrid goalkeeper punched it out but Dempsey met the rebound first time to smash Chelsea in front. 'It could have gone anywhere,' John admitted later. 'But it went in for the best goal I've ever scored.'

Chelsea went for the kill. This is the end, my friend, the end. Eight minutes later Baldwin made a great run into forward space. The whole move had *Mission Impossible*-style timing. Osgood went with him, and Houseman ran wide to open up a channel on the left. Too late, the Madrid central defenders saw the danger. Baldwin squared the ball to Osgood, who scored with a tremendous rising shot from 20 yards. A truly gorgeous move and a classic Os finish.

In the second half Madrid arose from their slumbers and went at Chelsea. Heritage, pride, whatever it was that drove them, stung them into action. Dempsey, reverting to his defensive duties, was oustanding. Ron Harris resolutely stood alongside Webb as they kept Chelsea's goal intact. Osgood limped off, no longer able to bear the pain in his ankles. Derek Smethurst replaced him, Houseman dropping deeper to support the midfield.

Fifteen minutes from time Webb was lured out of position. Fleitas robbed him of the ball before running on to slam past Peter Bonetti, bringing the score to 2–1. Could Madrid salvage the game again? Bonetti answered with a string of crisp saves to thwart Amancio and Zocco. Sexton's decision to restore Bonetti to the Chelsea side was totally vindicated. His experience was invaluable; no one could deny his excellence. There was a school of thought amongst some Chelsea fans that Bonetti had been traumatised by the World Cup and would never again be the same force. Under pressure from Phillips, worn down by injury, Bonetti reached the heights he had attained in the FA Cup finals.

The disappointing Velazquez was replaced by Gento, who desperately tried to lift his side. It was a belated attempt. The Real Madrid captain was still upset about the first-half penalty incident.

Chelsea had a great opportunity to clinch it through Smethurst, but he squandered an easy chance. Hudson was poor in both games. Chelsea held out to take the European Cup-Winners' Cup and Ron Harris collected their second major honour. All praise to them for that.

Chapter Thirteen: After the Goldrush

It was the best of times, it was the worst of times, it was the age of wisdom, it was the age of foolishness, it was the epoch of belief, it was the epoch of incredulity.
Charles Dickens, A Tale of Two Cities

In 1970 Neil Young brought out his seminal work *After the Goldrush*. This was the Canadian Neil Young, not to be confused with the Man City striker who laid on the goal for Colin Bell at Stamford Bridge that took the Cup from us. On this album, recorded before he joined Crosby, Stills and Nash, Young perfected a solo style which won him a cult following that is still with him today.

Chelsea were probably the first club to have planned their own extinction, even though they had no indication that their winning streak would come to an end so soon. The players' personalities started to change around then. Dreams, like the club, were soon to be all but bankrupted.

A weather vane was the symbol of our fall from grace. It was steeped in the history of CFC. The vane was originally fixed to the apex of the old main stand gable. Beneath it was the Doc's crow's nest, from which he would gaze down with wonder at his beloved diamonds. One side of the vane depicted a ball, the other sported the silhouette of a player. This was modelled on a Chelsea legend of the 1900s, a certain George 'Gattling Gun' Hilsdon. Remember his six goals against Worksop in the Cup on 11 January 1908? I must get the video out some time. Poor old George was mustard gassed in the First World War. Perhaps it had something to do with that Christmas Day match between the East Surrey Tommies and the German machine-gunners. Had the figure remained on the roof in the '80s it would have been CS gassed in the great hooligan wars. I remember a time when those friendly chaps at Everton fired a navigational flare into the Chelsea end. And you thought the only flares around were the mustard-coloured pair Osgood used to wear! It was said that if ever the vane came down so would Chelsea. This was highly prophetic.

HUTCH

Pathetic was the word really. The season started badly for Chelsea and got worse. In the first match we returned to Highbury to meet the double holders. Arsenal were in no mood to reciprocate the largesse shown to them by Chelsea the previous season and blasted us 3–0. A few of the team looked as though they would rather still be celebrating in Athens. They were spinning from the fame and the drink. Chelsea had added two stars to their shirts, next to the badge in honour of their win. It was an idea copied from the Italian sides who wore them in recognition of the honours they won. Next time you are watching Juve on Channel Four check it out.

On Tuesday, 17 August 1971, Ian Hutchinson was playing in the Football Combination team at Swindon Town. He was testing out his right knee, from which he'd had his cartilage removed in the spring. The injury caused him to miss the Cup-Winners' Cup triumph. Poor Ian had been through more rehab than Robert Downey Jnr. Sexton was desperate for Hutchinson to be restored to the side alongside Osgood, who had badly missed the support of his pal. Nobody except the Chelsea boss realised then what an important part of the puzzle Hutchinson was. He was like a small incendiary device waiting to explode. Chelsea had burned through their strike force, then Keith Weller, Smethurst, Garland and Baldwin – all cannon fodder. The club's resources were not without limit, as was soon to become apparent.

The game at Swindon started brightly for Hutch. He opened the scoring for Chelsea with indecent haste and was looking fitter than Caprice, first to the ball and full of running. If we could get him back in the first team, fully fit, everything else would fall into place. Then tragedy struck; he broke his left leg in a collision. The break was bad and an early prognosis ruled the soldier of fortune out for the rest of the season. The circle got smaller.

The next evening the George Best Roadshow hit town. A massive crowd of 54,763 shoehorned into the Bridge for the visit of United. Best was sent off after 40 minutes for a remark made to the ref after Baldwin had scored a disputed goal to put Chelsea in front. Best must have seen some sort of red mist that night, his whole performance was an extended tantrum. Whenever he played against Chelsea something sensational happened. His life now was all tightly choreographed tension. Houseman was substituted at half-time following a bruised knee sustained after a crunching tackle from the United hard boy Fitzpatrick.

A goal up against ten men, Chelsea should have made it count, but in the last quarter of the game United flattened Chelsea with a three-goal burst. It was a sharp reminder of their lost dignity and almost depleted vigour. John Phillips deputised for the Athens hero Bonetti, who had been injured at Highbury. John was given a painful lesson in life at the cutting edge of big-time football. It was similar to the introduction to life in the Premier for the Italian Massimo Taibi, the Italian who kept goal for United in the 5–0 drubbing administered by Chelsea to end the Treble winners' ten-month, 29-game unbeaten run.

Brian Kidd headed home United's equaliser. Shortly after Phillips conceded a penalty for a reckless foul on the same player, Willie Morgan, who bore a remarkable likeness to the departed Irishman, fired home. Then Charlton right-footed the coup de grâce with a slaughterhouse goal straight from his vintage scrapbook. Charlton still had to prove to the taunting London crowds that he had not sweated all his talent away in Leon. It transcended age. Near the end his heir (not hair) apparent Osgood scrambled a goal back, which set up a grandstand finish, but United took the points.

After the game Sexton placed Osgood on the transfer list for 'lack of effort'. Something had snapped deep inside Sexton that night – perhaps the loss of his most honest and courageous player the night before weighed heavily on his mind. His manic perfectionism was disgusted by the sight of the high-profile Osgood posturing on the field and Hudson, technically his (and England's) greatest midfield player, merely going through the motions. The two were about to be consumed by their own ego problems, drink and management troubles. The transfer listing of Osgood underlined the widening gulf between Sexton and his key players. Pandora's box had been momentarily opened. Looking back, I should have done something about it in those troubled times but it was all happening so fast. So very fast.

For the next few games Osgood galloped around like a man possessed. The Shed were vastly amused. It was fantastic fun to see him dashing around as if his shorts were on fire. Osgood was taken off the list on the following Tuesday and an uneasy peace returned. It was a question of the cracks being papered over with tissues, though.

Chelsea were now the hardest-drinking team in football. It was often remarked that the lack of discipline of certain players led to substandard performances on the pitch. It gave the impression that only players like Houseman and Hollins were the real professionals among a crowd of irresponsible drunkards. This begs the question of why Chelsea's greatest performances always featured the players most likely to be in the pub.

The Shed loved Osgood because he retained their favourite, typically 'Chelsea', qualities of slipshod, good-natured man-of-the-people, combined with a huge amount of star quality. Hudson they were less sure of because of his moody, surly, introverted style. Houseman was in complete contrast to the pair of them and the fans were always sceptical of him. He had honed his skills in his long apprenticeship in the Docherty era. Not just his choice of clothes (office worker suits), but everything about Houseman seemed at odds with the glamour of Osgood and the hip Hud. If Houseman's humour was of a resigned, self-deprecating manner, then Osgood's was cocksure and Hudson's peevish. Houseman's ambition before he became a footballer was to be a draughtsman, a job which is now part of an older culture, almost like the position of left-winger. Houseman bridged the gap between the working-class culture of the Shed and the essentially middle-class world that professional footballers inevitably moved into. There were no glitterati with picture-book houses and racing cars then. Jordan wasn't even born.

Houseman loved playing chess. I had a few games with him when travelling away. Chess is all about pattern recognition, and there was no one better in football than Houseman for building up knowledge of key moves. At the height of his career the Spassky v Fischer contests were raging and the winger followed the series closely. His real hero was Paul Morphy (1837–84) who had a meteoric chess career. He exploded upon the international scene and defeated all comers in scintillating fashion. Paul's descent from the top was as abrupt as his rise. At the height of his powers he abandoned the game and grew increasingly withdrawn. It was said that he suffered from a persecution complex and died a lonely death. Sounds familiar.

Peter scored his first goal of the season for Chelsea against Plymouth Argyle in the second round of the Football League Cup. It was a rare header from the winger, he bent low to head in from a John Boyle cross from the byline. Alan Harris, Ron's brother, captained the Devon side which went down 2–0.

The following week Houseman scored twice as Chelsea returned to Europe. Their opponents were the Cup winners of Luxembourg, Jeunesse Hautcharge, an amateur side. Chelsea beat them 8–0, their highest-ever away score. Osgood scored a hat-trick and Hollins, Webb and Baldwin the others. Houseman just kept the crosses flying in like bats when the sun was going down. His placid exterior concealed a burning ambition to play for England.

Chelsea were 6–0 up at half-time. Osgood, keen to show he was still in 'rehab', hit the post twice. He had become only the second player in the history of the club to score a hat-trick in a European match, Venables being the first in the home tie against Roma. The return game with Jeunesse was a goal riot.

The only thing that Luxembourg had been known for was its radio station, which had livened up the radio scene by bringing rock 'n' roll to British youngsters in the '50s. Houseman had grown up listening to the crackling programmes on Fab 208. Years later he was playing football against their cup winners.

IN OFF THE POST

I attended the Chelsea match and was delighted with the new goal record, but not with the attitude of some 'supporters' towards Peter Houseman. Barracking in this way can do nothing but gradually undermine a man's confidence. (I remember Eric Parsons suffering in the same way until the crowd were forced to eat humble pie when we won the Championship.)

But for Pete Houseman they would not have been here the other Wednesday. Cast your minds back to the Cup-tie at Burnley (27 January 1970). We were 1–0 down and who equalised? Peter Houseman. Who laid on the pass for Baldwin to score number two? Pete Houseman. And who scored number three? Need I say? Cup final day – who beat, yes beat Sprake with a long low drive? Pete Houseman!

Please try to publish this letter, as I hope it may do some good and make a few of the lame brains think.

Dennis Ottrey
Hastings

* This is one of many letters we have received expressing condemnation of those who barracked Peter Houseman against Jeunesse and marred our night. Our left-winger answered in the best possible way – with a foot in several of the goals.

These letters were extracted from the Chelsea programme v Nottingham Forest on 11 October 1971, a match in which Houseman was replaced by Eddie McCreadie after falling on his left shoulder and damaging a ligament.

EURO THRASH

Chelsea 13, Jeunesse Hautcharge 0
(Chelsea win 21–0 on aggregate)
Scorers: Osgood 5, Baldwin 3, Hudson, Hollins (penalty), Webb, Harris, and Houseman
Referee: Mr R. Navarra (Malta)
Attendance: 27,623
Receipts: £10,449

To this day the return game against Jeunesse Hautcharge remains the biggest-ever Chelsea win, smashing all previous aggregates in European history. For me, though, it was also one of the blackest days in the history of Chelsea because of the abuse given by the crowd to one of its own players. The lowest-ever moment in the club's history was to follow in the next decade when Paul Canonville became the first black player to play for the club. The match was a Bank Holiday fixture against Palace in what was then known as the Second Divison. Chelsea had fallen through the trapdoor and were close to relegation to the Third Divison. It was like some kind of parallel existence. In an era when at best Chelsea can field a handful of Londoners in their line-up, it would seem unthinkable that Canonville, born in one of the black ghettoes of London, was abused for the crime of having a different colour of skin. Four summers before Houseman played in the European Cup-Winners' Cup, the Black Power salutes of the American runners Tommie Smith and John Carlos in Mexico City were making worldwide headlines.

Canonville's treatment prompted the famous 'you lot make me sick' outburst from Pat Nevin. The 'Wee Man' was the only Chelsea player at the time with the courage to make a stand for his friend who was a product and victim of a racist system. What balls! I am not talking about those pinpoint crosses he used to sweep over for Dixon and Speedie.

Houseman's treatment by the fans was not racist, but it was still morally indefensible. Chelsea were 4–0 up in the first 13 minutes of their home tie against Jeunesse, six up at half-time (the same as they had been in Luxembourg). Chelsea scored the last four in the final 13 minutes. For long periods Houseman was picked on by the crowd for his apparent inability to go around his full-back, one of four people with the name of Welscher in the Hautcharge side. Eventually he cut inside Welscher to run towards the penalty area and score with a firm, low shot. There was not a lot of applause, for the crowd were jaded and they had done it a dozen times before.

Something was wrong though. I sensed that it was a weird time. The curve of success was taking some Chelsea players to places they did not want to go. The scene was set for nihilism and attitude problems. Sexton had gone into the transfer market to bolster his squad. Mick Greenaway once said to me as we travelled back from an away game, 'He [Sexton] should have been taking more care of the players he had. Hudson was just a kid, there was a lot of drink around. Osgood had some control but some of the boys did not care.'

Within a few days of Hutchinson breaking his leg Sexton purchased Chris Garland from Bristol City for £100,000. Chris was this year's blond. He had a great heart and was hard running but how could you replace a legend? Steve Kember was his next purchase, Sexton finally getting his man after almost a year of trailing him. Dave had this grandiose idea to play Kember alongside Hudson, but they never gelled together. Hudson never rediscovered his sparkle at Stamford Bridge. How successful these buys were is questionable. Both had long spells in the first team, but neither enabled Chelsea to build on their recent success. The gods came out sometimes when Osgood, Cooke and Hudson were on song, the later buys that came along were not in the same class. Kember at times groped around blindly in midfield and looked out of his depth in the really big games.

The books had to be balanced and surprisingly Weller was sold to Leicester. It was not my idea. Weller had missed the start of the new season with a stomach complaint. The circumstances of his departure had more intrigue than an episode of *EastEnders*. Rumours of a fist fight with Harris in the car park during a training session swept around Fulham Broadway. It was said that when feelings ran high an ugly scene developed following a Harris slide tackle. I heard rumours of a fracas in the canteen. Neither player could be described as timid. It was all clouded. The real truth was that Weller was the first of many star players to go because of financial concerns.

Derek Smethurst was also transferred to Millwall after just 17 first-team games. Strangely enough, both Weller and Smethurst are now resident in America. Derek is a youth soccer coach in Florida. In 1978 he experienced a 'vision' and is a born-again Christian. Like ex-Liverpool star Craig Johnston and the former President Bill Clinton, he named his daughter 'Chelsea'.

Weller was a big hit at Leicester and went on to play for England.

Chelsea's next tie was against Atvidaberg of Sweden who, like Smethurst, were to be famous for 15 minutes. More like 180 minutes, the time it took them to eliminate Chelsea from the competition. Since then they have returned to obscurity.

THE DUSTBIN OF EUROPE

Chelsea drew 0–0 in the first leg in Sweden which was seen as a creditable result. The problem was, as Chelsea were to find out to their cost, that it was vital to score an away goal. Sweden was a wild place for some of the carousers in the Chelsea team.

Houseman missed the game with his shoulder injury and Garland was not eligible to play, so Hollins was drafted into a striker's role. John was on a roll, he had already scored nine goals in the opening two months of the season. This was a phenomenal record for a midfield player and included a burst of scoring in five consecutive games.

With Chelsea a goal up in the return leg, Chelsea were awarded a penalty. Hudson was keen to take it but Hollins strode up and smacked the ball goalwards. The ball beat the keeper's dive but hit the foot of the left-hand post and bounced out. Fate, kismet, bad luck, call it whatever. A few minutes later, in the confusion, Atvidaberg equalised in one of their few attacks. Like a tennis player hugging the baseline, the Swedes returned everything and awaited an error. Chelsea went out on the away-goal rule despite a massive bombardment in the closing minutes. Dempsey, whose marvellous goal in Athens helped to win the Cup, almost saved it. In the closing minutes he powered in a header which crashed against the bar with the goalkeeper again powerless. The Swedes went through, though.

It was the biggest sensation to come out of Sweden till three years later when Abba won the 1974 Eurovison Song Contest with 'Waterloo'. The odds on Abba were 20–1 that night, legend has it that Benny (not the one that was married to the blonde) had a tenner on them. Money, money, money. Mama mia. The Blues had met their own Waterloo, though, and were exiled from Europe for longer than Napoleon.

It was the end of my little jaunts abroad. Can you hear the drums?

WASN'T TOMORROW WONDERFUL?

Chelsea's only salvation that season were the domestic cups. In November they stood ninth in the league, nine points behind leaders Manchester United. Some things never change. Arsenal came to Chelsea and inflicted a double on them. It was a comfortable win for them and Kennedy scored a deuce. Present at the game was Zagallo, Brazil's manager, who witnessed his first English league match. He made the interesting comment that 'Pelé and our other great players would not survive in such games week after week. It is not so much they would be injured as they would lose all pleasure from playing – and without pleasure you cannot have great play'. This was an astute comment which passed without much comment at the time. George Graham must have taken it on board though. He was in the Arsenal side alongside Charlie George.

Hudson, Osgood, Cooke and record signing Kember played in that match for Chelsea. They were some of the finest footballers of their generation, each one known in the buzz word of the time as 'flair players', yet to the Brazil chief the match was a joyless affair. Possibly the fact that the team sheets also included the names of Harris, Webb, Roberts and McLintock had a negative influence. The heavens opened all afternoon, and the poor weather must have added to the oppression and the diminished vision that the Brazil boss experienced.

BOLTON AWAY IN THE LEAGUE CUP

Second Division Bolton had come to Chelsea and forced a draw in the League Cup. The replay was held on the Monday after the débâcle against Atvidaberg and the knives were out for Chelsea in the red tops. There was the inevitable bad press and speculation about star players leaving the club. Pass me the 'Chelsea Crisis' headline number 7,853. Derby were keen to usurp Chelsea's reputation as the best footballing side around. Another Cup exit to a mediocre team would spell big trouble. Moderation, like mediocrity, had only a small part to play in that Chelsea team's life. They thrashed Bolton 6–0 with almost effortless ease in front of their own fans. Baldwin, under severe pressure from the new signings, plundered a hat-trick. He had been guilty of some bad misses against Atvidaberg in Sweden but made up for it that night. Hollins, still numb with the disappointment of his costly penalty miss, scored twice at Bolton, one of them a spot kick which he lashed home with his face fixed in a scowl. A midweek League Cup-tie at Bolton ended with a coach ride home. In those days nobody took helicopters. I remember thinking we could get a Cup double as I left the Burnden Park directors' box. Twenty-five years later, Matthew Harding left the Burnden Park directors' box after Chelsea had been beaten by Bolton in the League Cup. His last words were 'we must win the FA Cup now'. Harding was in such a hurry to return to London that he had a two-engined Squirrel helicopter standing by. I heard the news of the crash as I lay in bed recovering from a heart attack. It was not a surprise to me. I feared for his safety.

HUDSON'S WAY

> I had made the classic error of taking something for granted when Alan Hudson tried a hopeful shot from an acute angle.
> *Pat Jennings, on the Chelsea goal that stopped Spurs from winning a hat-trick of League Cup finals.*

Norwich were next on the Chelsea agenda in the Football League Cup. Bonetti showed glimpses of his outstanding form by denying the Norwich forwards with a string of quality stops. Osgood scored the only goal of a cracking match with a powerful header from a Houseman corner. It was another move that other teams found so hard to counter. Such was the accuracy of Houseman's crosses that Osgood could time his runs to perfection. He could even delay his run by that vital split second that deceived defenders.

Three days before Christmas 1971 Chelsea played Tottenham in the first leg of the semi-final of the Football League Cup. Spurs were keen to regain some of the glory that their West London rivals had stolen. Coates had joined Tottenham in a big-money transfer from Burnley. The little midfielder had a score to settle after the epic Cup game and wanted revenge.

In a dramatic match Chelsea edged ahead in the tie 3–2. Osgood fired Chelsea in front after 38 minutes with an angled drive that deceived Jennings. There was little venom in Tottenham's first-half performance but after the break they surged forward. Two goals in two minutes from Naylor and Chivers put them in command. Garland was Chelsea's main threat with his sporadic raids. He smacked the bar in the first half then almost equalised when Knowles stumbled to let him in. Jennings narrowed the angle and Garland flicked the ball into the side netting when it looked easier to score. But score he did a few minutes later when he climbed to head Houseman's corner past Jennings. It was his first-ever goal for Chelsea. Near the end Hollins scored from the penalty spot after Naylor had handled. Funny, the only penalty Hollins missed, to my knowledge, was the one that plunged us out of Europe.

If that game was a Christmas show-stopper then the return at White Hart Lane on 5 January 1972 was simply out of this world. Chelsea fans called those years of 1972 and '73 the 'Wonder Years', because they wondered what happened to their side in that period. Chivers was making the art of dynamic centre-forward play seem easy for Tottenham. On the stroke of the interval he volleyed home a cross from Coates to level the scores. It also gave the 'Lilywhites' a psychological edge at half-time.

Garland, rapidly becoming the 'golden boy', put Chelsea in front again after a tremendous run by Cooke had mesmerised the Spurs defence. After his superb display in the European Cup-Winners' Cup final he appeared to lose concentration. Perhaps he had grown tired of Chelsea or simply bored with his achievements. I found him edgy, coiled and always keyed up that season.

Chelsea were under severe pressure when Cooke ran at the Spur's left-back, Knowles. Cyril was already occupied marking Garland but switched his attention to Cooke. Charlie had started going past players as if they were shadows on the White Hart Lane grass. He just had that skill at cranking up the pace by a few notches. Garland took the ball from Cooke and cut inside. He ran across the penalty area and beat Jennings with a thunderbolt of a drive. It was a superb, confident goal, the best in his Chelsea career. The goal was executed with his left foot, though he was naturally right-footed.

Peters equalised for Spurs with a penalty seven minutes from time after Hudson had handled. It looked like extra time but Chelsea lucked out when Hudson's last-minute free kick ended up in the Spurs net. Chelsea were back at Wembley again!

I fancied ourselves for a cup double. The third-round draw took us back to

Blackpool. No traumas this visit, though. Nobody was sent home for being blotto and Osgood was unharmed. Dempsey scored with a looping back header at the near post after 30 minutes from an immaculate right-wing corner from Houseman. The winger had returned to the team after missing Chelsea's victory at Manchester United the previous week due to a stomach disorder.

Houseman scored again when Chelsea beat Bolton again in the other cup competition. The Lancashire side cursed their luck in once more drawing the Londoners. Peter volleyed Chelsea's second goal from a great cross from Cooke. Hollins had opened the scoring with yet another penalty and Cooke himself scored the third as Chelsea strolled to an easy victory. There was something about Houseman in the Cup competitions. In a total of 25 FA Cup games for Chelsea he scored ten goals, but in the league that season his only goal had been in a home game against Wolves.

The win over Bolton put Chelsea into the fifth round against dirt-poor Orient at Brisbane Road in the last week of February. The following week Chelsea had their big date with Stoke at Wembley. It was a monster week but the hopes were high in the Chelsea camp. Always the self-mythologiser, I wanted us to be true winners.

PAYBACK

With almost 45 minutes gone in the Orient Cup-tie things were looking bright for Chelsea. Clad in the lucky yellow and blue, they were 2–0 up and cruising towards the quarter-finals. Webb, the old Cup warrior, headed Chelsea in front. It followed yet another Houseman corner that was partially cleared. Peter immediately slammed back a centre for Webb to score. Still reeling from the burly defender's strike Orient fell further behind when Osgood headed in from a Cooke centre. The Os looked incapable of a comeback. Perhaps that was the moment it all started to go wrong. With virtually the last kick of the half ex-Palace full-back Hoadley shelled a tremendous shot past Bonetti. A few Chelsea players seemed unconcerned, but five minutes into the second half Orient were level. A terrible tangle in the defence allowed a chap called Bulloch to run the ball into an unguarded net for an equaliser. The Orient fans were delirious. 'Bulloch!' I heard Harris say, or something like that.

Chelsea were shaken but seemed unable or unwilling to raise the tempo of their game. The Chelsea forwards wasted chance after chance. Barely two minutes from time and disaster stuck again. An even worse mix-up in the Chelsea back four allowed Orient's Barrie Fairbrother to run amid the buffoonish defenders and tap home. It was an even softer goal than their equaliser. Harris was particularly at fault, losing control of the ball and then failing to clear his lines. Sexton could not believe the lacunae at the heart of the Chelsea rearguard.

In the last ten seconds Cooke pranced and pirouetted in the six-yard box to set up Webb for what appeared to be a certain equaliser but he missed, scooping over the bar whilst almost standing in the back of the net. It was one of the most atrocious misses in the history of the game, at any level. Whatever grief Gray had given him at Wembley, this was far, far worse. It was unpleasant to behold. Osgood looked over at his lieutenant Webb and shook his head. Unbelievably Chelsea had crashed out of the Cup to Orient.

Sexton appeared in the tunnel as Chelsea trooped off. It was early spring and the evening was light, the sun just breaking through, but broken-hearted Blues fans said you could almost see the rage dripping off him.

At Wembley the nightmare continued. Chelsea fans had more than a whiff of Joseph Conrad's *Heart of Darkness*. It was a journey to the dark side of the club's psyche.

The Chelsea line-up for their second Wembley final in two years was: Bonetti, Mulligan, Harris, Hollins, Dempsey, Webb, Cooke, Garland, Osgood, Hudson, Houseman. Sub: Baldwin.

Stoke took an early lead with a goal as bad as any of those Chelsea had conceded to Orient. Dobing took a long throw (trust Chelsea to be hoisted by their own petard) which caused great anxiety in the Chelsea penalty area. They failed to clear, the ball bobbed around for an eternity and eventually Conroy, their Irish striker, headed past Bonetti. Like the Orient game, the Chelsea fans felt as though they were watching events in slow motion. The goals conceded took so long to be scored, like a bad dream rewound.

It could not have been a worse start for Chelsea. I was shocked that it could deteriorate so much. Virtually the whole town of Stoke had descended on Wembley to support their team. It was like an incitement to riot. The Potteries had waited 109 years for their side to win a major honour. Stoke were an old side supposedly lacking a match winner and relying on the camaraderie of the highly motivated veterans. They had only a little talent but a lot of magic and some days that is enough.

Garland was easily Chelsea's best player that day. His pace and aggression worried the Stoke defence throughout the game. Twice in the first half he broke through a mêlée and roared down onto the Stoke goal, but each time he was cut down by the crude defenders Bloor and Pejic. They were both booked for their cruel fouls, but in today's paranoid climate neither would have stayed on the pitch.

Right on half-time Osgood equalised to maintain his record of scoring in every Cup final he appeared in for Chelsea. Cooke played the ball in and

Osgood appeared to stumble. The ball bobbled but on one knee, still on the floor, he drove instantly past Banks. It was a fabulous piece of timing and ingenuity and caused total mayhem at the Chelsea end as the raucous Shed boys celebrated. Four finals and Chelsea were yet to score first. It was an incredible goal by the 'King of Stamford Bridge' and it appeared to put Chelsea in the driving seat. Stoke looked to be there for the taking; they were so much older and slower, and surely their triple bypasses and wooden legs would not last the second half . . .

Paddy Mulligan had bruised his ankle in a clash with the abrasive Pejic and did not appear for the second half. Tommy Baldwin substituted and Houseman was switched to left-back. Sexton was keen to experiment with him and Houseman responded with a fine display of economy and care, the prototype of a wing-back! Some sections of the press thought that the match hinged on Mulligan's injury, as with Houseman deployed so deep Chelsea had no supply from the left.

Chelsea ran the second half with their midfield of Hollins, Cooke and Hudson in almost complete control. The Stoke midfield palpably lacking stamina, Hudson started to dominate. Baldwin missed a couple of easy chances but with less than 20 minutes to go Stoke went into the lead again, every one of their forwards was involved in the build-up. Dobing began the move by finding Conroy who crossed for the big centre-forward Richie to nod down for Jimmy Greenhof to stab in a shot. The exposed Bonetti made a great save but the ball spilled to George Eastham, who scored from a yard. Eastham was immune to the ageing process. Players younger than him were consigned to the knackers yard as burnouts but he won the Cup for Stoke. Once again the defence had frozen like Eskimos when the pressure was on.

Chelsea were in a frenzy. They poured down on the Stoke goal, but with Banks commanding as ever, they could not equalise. The keeper made a string of great saves. Baldwin suffered the most as his attempts were blocked. It was to be Banks' swan song; in a few months his illustrious career was in ruins. In October of that year he was seriously injured in a car crash. He had set out by car one fateful Sunday afternoon to watch highlights of a game he had played on the previous day at Liverpool. A controversial decision against him had cost him a goal and he was anxious to see the replay. He never made it. His car was in collision with a van and his right eye was hit by shards of glass.

One flying save from Garland at Wembley was better than the legendary save from Pelé's downward header in Mexico. It was just bad luck for Chelsea that they came up against the greatest goalkeeper the world has ever seen. The killjoy stopped everything, he was just a green blur of muscle and effort as he threw himself at Baldwin's feet.

Houseman, revelling in his new role as full-back, saved a certain third goal for Stoke by heading Ritchie's effort off the line. The whistle went, Stoke collected the Cup and Chelsea's Cup dreams died. That week was under enough bad stars but Banks put the hex on it. Nothing on land or sea, in the air or in the bowels of the earth could have possibly sounded quite as wretched to the Chelsea lads as the tumultuous noise of the celebrating Stoke fans. Robbie Williams grew up in the Potteries and Alan Hudson was one of his boyhood idols. He recorded a song a lifetime later called 'No Regrets'. If Chelsea players of that era have any regrets they must be about losing at Wembley to the dog soldiers of Stoke.

Houseman played at full-back against Liverpool immediately following the Cup defeats. Harris was dropped and relieved of the captaincy. A splinter group in the dressing-room were concerned about the errors in defence that had cost them so dearly. Sexton was delighted with his performance and commented, 'Don't be surprised if I give Peter a long run in the position. He is strong enough to win the ball and he knows exactly when to go into forward positions.' Shortly afterwards Peter was injured in a reserve game and played only a few more games in that miserable season.

It was the beginning of the end for the great Cup-winning side. They had lost to three minnows in the Cup competitions, all games that they should have won easily but threw away through bad defensive mistakes and spurned chances.

Plans were unveiled to give the ground a £5 million facelift. This would have made it the most luxurious soccer ground in Britain. The project was to have been completed by 1979 and would have accommodated 60,000 spectators, all under cover. The 'Space Age' plans included 156 private drive-in boxes, an electronic scoreboard, a huge indoor practice area, a new admin. block, warm air heating, and 33 bars and public restaurants.

John Parsons wrote in the *Daily Mail*, 'Both in concept and cost, the scheme is the most ambitious ever undertaken in Britain . . . and Chelsea add the pledge to their fans that Sexton will still have all the money he needs to buy new players.'

It was noticeable that in the summer no new additions were made to the squad despite the shortcomings. Imagine if the Euro transfer market had been entered and Chelsea had secured the services of a young Cruyff. Ajax had just won their league again and the golden age of Dutch football was just dawning. The press in their early season predictions were administering the last rites to Chelsea as a dominant force. The admission charges on the terraces had risen from 30p to 40p. That's right, 40p. The first stage of the reconstruction of Stamford Bridge involved the construction of a new two-tier cantilever East Stand which would provide 12,000 seats. The old structure was torn down in the summer and when Chelsea kicked off their first match of the season against guess who, Leeds United, the ground literally looked as if a bomb had hit it.

It started brightly as Chelsea crushed Leeds 4–0, the Blues' biggest first-day win for 22 years. The score flattered Chelsea because Dave Harvey (who had been beaten by Osgood and Webb's goals in the Cup final replay) was taken off with concussion early in the game. Lorimer took over in goal and was beaten by Osgood, Cooke and twice by Garland. The ex-Bristol City man had started the season with tremendous energy. Houseman was only sub at the start of the season, Cooke playing in the number 11 shirt with Garland on the right.

Peter came on as sub against Liverpool when the genetically modified Mickey Droy went off injured. The Blues were trailing 2–1 at the time. A youngster called Kevin Keegan had just joined the Merseyside club and was already making a name for himself. Keegan was operating as a lone wolf up front and hit the bar from 25 yards. Phillips was just another spectator. Garland scored for Chelsea in that match to record his fourth goal of the season. Chris had the eyes of an assassin, around then he was like a harnessed supernova. Comparisons were being made in the press between Keegan and Garland, though at that time there was little to choose between them. Both were tremendous workers, with great courage and an eye for the goal. Keegan went on to become European Footballer of the Year twice and to play for and manage his country. Garland now has MS. The difference between great success and bad luck is wafer thin. There were always plenty of people around to confer loserdom on a player. I tried to sign Keegan for Chelsea in my last seasons there. I found him an honest and warm person.

Chelsea appeared to have lost the magic formula; perhaps Harris had left it on the bus or Osgood had lost it in the pub. A lot of what was happening around Chelsea was 24-carat rubbish. The ground looked like a giant skip. Tactically they were stunted by Sexton's inward thinking.

Houseman was sub for the next game against Manchester City. Sexton sent him on 20 minutes from time with the game locked at 1–1. Osgood had put Chelsea ahead in first-half injury time but City had equalised soon after the restart through someone with the unfortunate name of Mellor. With his first kick Houseman almost put Chelsea in front when he shot across an open goal. It was a relatively easy chance but he made amends ten minutes later. Hudson centred, Osgood headed on and Houseman ran onto the ball to score with a left-foot cross shot. Houseman received a kick on his instep and missed the next game at home to Ipswich.

That was Cooke's last game for Chelsea in his first spell of 277 first-team matches with the club. Charlie and Paddy Mulligan made the short trip to Crystal Palace to join the other Chelsea ex-pats. Cooke's departure was a shock to the Shed, as he was the first of the established superstars to leave. Charlie had scored at Highbury, from Houseman's clever pass, a few weeks beforehand in a 1–1 draw. For periods in that game Chelsea showed glimpses of their old form. Harris was involved in a kicking match with Charlie George. Ronnie was coughing up blood for days afterwards. Only a Webb own goal (deflecting a George Graham header) near the end denied Chelsea a morale-boosting win. Cooke's place looked assured despite rumours about him being schwacked on drink.

Cooke, like Hudson and Osgood, was a racehorse. Thoroughbreds are highly strung, they need to be taken proper care of and run great races when they are looked after. The problem with Cooke was that he had no cut-off point. The sceptics in the Shed could see it was coming apart at the seams. Without Cooke, Chelsea lost a major personality. He always came on with charisma and polish, those nuances which contributed so much. Chelsea were being killed from within.

Mulligan's transfer paved the way for Gary Locke to make the right-back spot his own over the next few seasons. Locke was a product of the youth system, agile and cultured, almost a Shellito. Almost.

Houseman scored again at Coventry as Chelsea won 3–1. Near the end he clinched the game by slipping the ball past the Coventry keeper from Hollins' long pass. Bill Garner had recently joined the club from Southend and scored his first goal in that game. Hutchinson had now been out of the game for almost two years with injuries. Garner was a huge guy of bewitching power, well over 6ft with a big round head and long hair. Sexton saw him as a minder for Osgood. He looked like he was designed solely for the purpose of kicking lumps out of opposing defences. Later in his career he had the record of being sent off in successive games, a feat yet to be equalled by a Chelsea player. He had a persistent glare that I found disturbing.

Houseman was booked at Coventry, as he had been the season Chelsea won the Cup. He was also booked in the 0–0 draw at champions Derby in the League Cup. Houseman was by no means a dirty or even a physical player but he was no angel either, which made a mockery of his rather fey image. The records show that the last time he had been booked was the previous autumn for a foul on the Liverpool keeper Clemence. This was another no-score draw that had infuriated Shankly.

The replay against Clough's team was at Stamford Bridge the following Monday and 26,395 were present to see Osgood score perhaps his greatest-ever goal. Houseman, naturally enough, played a pivotal role in it. Osgood had three stitches in a gashed ankle he picked up whilst scoring at Birmingham the previous Saturday, Ramsey had not included the Maverick in the England squad to play Yugoslavia at Wembley two days later. By a quirk of fate Ramsey was present at Chelsea that night with the England entourage. They witnessed an amazing game. Kember shot Chelsea in front after five minutes. It was one of Kember's finest games and he was really reved up.

Hudson was out of the side with ankle injuries. The alter ego thing was strange – both played their best games when the other was absent. So often when they played together the work was duplicated. Hudson's best form last season had been reserved for the League Cup matches, a competition that Kember had been excluded from.

Derby hit back to equalise quickly with a solo goal from their winger Alan Hinton and started to play like champions. Webb put Chelsea back in front with a flying header from Boyle's corner. It was against the run of play and Derby then proceeded to overwhelm Chelsea. That is how it stayed till seven minutes into the second half when Hollins surged down the left. He fed Houseman, who nimbly picked his way to the byline before looking up. He seemingly aimed the cross for Webb lurking at the far post. Osgood was behind him though and shouted for David to leave it. Webb froze on the spot. It was the perfect Trojan horse as he let the ball run on. Osgood, coming in behind him, met the ball first time. The ball flew into the net – very few people actually saw it in flight. It was the hardest shot ever seen at that time. Gary Stanley, then just breaking into the Football Combination side, once scored for Chelsea against Charlton with an even harder free kick from further out. Ruud's first goal for Chelsea against Southampton was equally as vicious but in over three decades they are the only goals that are remotely near it for sheer power.

Osgood being Osgood ran over towards Ramsey to remind him of what in his heart of hearts the World Cup winner knew. Peter was the best footballing centre-forward this country had ever produced. The world picked on Osgood sometimes. He always had to pay the fiddler for being this insane creation but he loved it. He lived in the house on top of the hill and he had the best view. In moments like that it was worth it all.

Derby's captain, McGovern, headed a second goal for Derby. Ramsey had left the building though, as they say in *Frasier*. Clough's team dominated the rest of the game but Chelsea put them out 3–2. Typical Chelsea, only they could have won the game with a goal reminiscent of the cross-cutting technique of a French art movie.

Chelsea should have gone on and won the trophy. In the next rounds they edged out Bury then struggled past Notts County, eventually winning 3–1. A bizarre own goal from Osgood was the only worthwhile feature of the game. The semi-finals saw Chelsea drawn against Norwich City. The first of the games was at Stamford Bridge. Chelsea had played Norwich on the Saturday before and had run out 3–1 winners. The game marked the comeback of Ian

Hutchinson after 22 months and in a storybook return he scored twice in the second half, Only the post stopped him completing a hat-trick. The Shed gave it up for him like never before. The gladiator was back and Chelsea had high hopes of crushing the hicks and returning to Wembley.

Norwich played their own version of Mohammed Ali's rope-a-dope trick, though. They caught Chelsea on the break and in the first 13 minutes scored twice. The match was postponed from the previous week due to torrential rain and the pitch was heavy. Chelsea never recovered from the poor start. Houseman swerved a free kick into the net but the goal was disallowed.

The second semi-final at Norwich was an anti-climax. The game was abandoned through thick fog with just a few minutes left. Chelsea trailed 3–2 on the night, 5–2 on aggregate. They had another chance but there was to be no fairytale comeback. They had nearly all of the play but could not make it count and lost 1–0 in a dreary match. Hutchinson was in the wars again. His twice-broken left leg stood up well to the comeback but his right knee puffed up like a balloon after each game. On New Year's Day 1973 he went into hospital for yet another cartilage operation,

The only thing left to go for was the FA Cup.

An appalling decision cost us the game in a sixth-round Cup replay at Arsenal. We were like a poorly wrapped bomb parcel about to go off. Something had to give. After a training ground bust-up in January 1974, Osgood and Hudson were sold. Alan was the first to go, surprisingly signing for Stoke. Osgood's departure dragged on but he eventually joined Southampton. It broke my heart to sell them but the board felt obliged to support Sexton. I could not have acceded to player power; Vialli was unseated because of this.

The price was terribly high. The following season Sexton was sacked and Chelsea were relegated.

Chapter Fourteen: Left and Gone Away

WHAT THE PAPERS SAY

Not a Sunday goes by when some ball-kicking scumbag isn't revealed in the tabloids as having beaten up his wife–girlfriend–a woman in a bar between bouts of sex with girl-children, that is.

Football is all about emotional incontinence and blind devotion, it is as camp and overblown as a Bette Davis film and hardly the best thing to dangle in front of young men who are already punch-drunk with hormones and hysteria. What does it feel like waking up on a freezing morning to go to your minimum wage job, and seeing those golden boys on the front of the tabloids earning £1,000 per hour and sleeping with beautiful young household faces?

Julie Burchill, The Guardian, Autumn 1999

How Celestine Babayaro, the Chelsea left-back, managed to stamp on Fredrik Ljungberg, kick out at Dennis Bergkamp, and then take a swing at Lauren without the officials spotting him is beyond belief. After the players had calmed down, Barber's booking of Wise, Jimmy Floyd Hasselbaink and Arsenal's Thierry Henry was akin to pinching someone for dropping litter during the Gordon riots.

The Guardian, March 2001
(Covering Chelsea's Cup exit at the hands of Arsenal)

Soccer legend George Best was yesterday said to be 'very, very poorly' as he battled with a bout of pneumonia in hospital. His manager, Phil Hughes, said the condition of the 54-year-old former Manchester United and Northern Ireland player was not life threatening. He is being treated with antibiotics. Mr Hughes said, 'He is now able to sit up and he is smiling and cheerful but I expect him to be in for another week.'

The hard-drinking star's London physician says his underlying liver is improving and he has been abstaining from alcohol.

Best was admitted to Belfast City Hospital after developing a chest infection at his home near the fishing village of Portavogie, Co. Down.

He and his wife Alex, 27, bought the £200,000 house six months ago and have been dividing their time between there and London where Best works as a soccer analyst for Sky Sport.

Last March, Best spent nearly five weeks in a London hospital with liver problems and was warned to stay off alcohol forever.

His doctors appealed to barmen not to serve him if he entered their pubs.

Metro, February 2001

After the death of baseball legend Joe Di Maggio the *New York Times* asked Paul Simon to pen a tribute to the man who famously featured in the 1968 hit 'Mrs Robinson'.

A few years after 'Mrs Robinson' rose to number one on the pop charts I found myself dining at an Italian restaurant where Di Maggio was seated with a party of friends. I'd heard a rumour that he was upset with the song and had considered a lawsuit, so it was with some trepidation that I walked over and introduced myself as its composer. I needn't have worried. He was perfectly cordial and invited me to sit down, whereupon we immediately fell into conversation. 'What I don't understand,' he said, 'is why you ask where I have gone. I just did a Mr Coffee commercial. I'm a spokesman for the Bowery Savings Bank and I haven't gone anywhere.'

I said that I didn't mean the lines literally, that I thought of him as an American hero and that genuine heroes were in short supply. He accepted the explanation and thanked me. We shook hands and said goodnight.

Paul Simon, *New York Times*, March 1999

I READ THE NEWS TODAY, OH BOY

Soccer Star Peter Houseman was killed in a car crash yesterday, victim of the jinx that struck members of the Chelsea team who typified the trendy Sixties.

The jinx has brought tragedy to several big names from those days –

among them Tommy Baldwin, Charlie Cooke and Ian Hutchinson.

Houseman and his wife Sally died in a three-car crash at 1am while on their way home from a dance. Two other people in the same car also died in the accident on the main A40 trunk road a mile outside Oxford.

One of the crashed cars, a Maserati sports coupé, was sliced in half. Its back wheels and rear engine were found 30 yards from the spot.

ABOUT A LUCKY MAN WHO MADE THE GRADE

Houseman, a 31-year-old midfield player, has been with Oxford United since 1975. He and his wife were returning from a fund-raising social which had been attended by other members of the Oxford team.

The Housemans were travelling in a Hillman Avenger car in which Mr Alan Gillham of Witney and the woman driver also died.

Two men were released from the Maserati and a husband and wife from the third car, a Singer Salon. All were taken to the Radcliffe Infirmary, Oxford, where their conditions were said to be 'satisfactory'.

HE BLEW HIS MIND OUT IN A CAR

A fire brigade spokesman said, 'It was a shocking accident – one of the worst we have experienced. All the cars were extensively damaged and it took us half an hour to free some of the injured.'

The Houseman's three young children have been told of the tragedy and are being looked after by relatives at their home in Witney, Oxfordshire.

Oxford Football Club's manager Mick Brown said:

'Everyone is totally devastated by the accident. We have lost a tremendous player and a wonderfully good-natured person. I was with him at the dance and both he and Sally were laughing and joking as usual. Nothing was too much trouble for either of them and they would always help anyone out of a jam. Our biggest concern now is for their three children and Mr Gilham's three youngsters.

Houseman, who joined for a fee of £30,000, had previously played with Chelsea for 13 years since leaving school. He made more than 250 first-team appearances with them, and among his trophies from his Chelsea days were Cup final and European Cup-Winners' Cup medals.

Chelsea chairman Brian Mears commented:

'It is all so sad and tragic. Rest assured that if there is anything the club can do to help, then people only have to ask and we will be pleased to assist.'

Houseman was a hero to Chelsea supporters in the 1970 Cup final when he scored against Leeds at Wembley.

The Chelsea forward line for the replay was Tommy Baldwin, Houseman, Peter Osgood, Ian Hutchinson and Charlie Cooke. The Chelsea jinx touched them all.

Daily Mail, 10 March 1977

DAYS IN A LIFE

Houseman played a total of 72 games for Oxford. In his first season he played 40 games (37 league, 1 FA Cup and 2 League Cup). He did not score in any of those games as Oxford were relegated from the old Second Division.

In the last season of his life he played in 32 matches, 28 league games and two apiece in the FA and League Cups. He notched two league goals. Houseman was always popular with the Oxford fans; they had a famous 'name' in their side and a player honed by domestic and European Cup competitions. Oxford used him in a role deep on the left side of midfield but sometimes he would go off on guerrilla runs upfield. The most remarkable match he played in for Oxford was a league game at Blackpool in which he was one of three Oxford players sent off. It caused a sensation at the time, being only the second time in the history of the league when a side had three men dismissed in one game. It was the only time Peter Houseman had been sent off in his career. His last-ever match was a 1–0 home defeat to Crystal Palace in the Third Division on the day of the crash.

Houseman died a hero, perhaps the greatest that Chelsea ever had. He never declined. He never grew old, he always looked the same. Like Cary Grant used to say of himself, 'Wouldn't it be great to be like Cary Grant'. It would be great to be Peter Houseman today. Not an effigy. At the time of his death the posthumous epithet of 'greatest' was bandied around, too late to do him any good. His death signalled an extraordinary outpouring of grief across the sporting press. Perhaps they were worried that with his passing the last bridge to the great Chelsea side of the '70s was lost. His reputation was never besmirched.

Graham Le Saux, the '90s reincarnation of Houseman, was described as 'cerebral' in the *Hello* magazine feature on him 'proudly showing off new baby Georgina with wife Mariana at home in South London'. Houseman was never cerebral . . .

The following letter was published in the Chelsea programme's 'In off the post' feature, shortly before he departed to Oxford.

ON BEHALF OF THE OAKLEY LADS

I would like to dedicate this letter to Peter Houseman. Being just a young lad living in the village, I was a keen soccer fan and Peter set up a lads' team to play in the local league at Basingstoke.

He also brought me to the Bridge for about the third time in my life and has transformed my life into being a true Chelsea fan. Thank you once again, Peter – not only from me but I am sure from all the Oakley lads.

David Smith
Basingstoke
(Chelsea Pools Agent 4100)

Oakley won the Cup and League in the last full season of Houseman's life.

Houseman was the last true left-winger the club had on the left. He was truly the 'fatal Englishman' of Stamford Bridge.

In the same week that Chelsea defeated a mediocre side from Berlin to top their Champions League group, an 'Enchanted Garden' launch party for Cartier's Haute Joaillere collection was held. The event was a resounding success, despite initial concerns. The turfed carpet survived the attack of the Manolo heels. The guest list included novelist Frederick Forsyth, hotel owner Anouska Hempel, fashion designer Ben de Lisi and his muse Debbie Lovejoy, K bar owner Piers Adam and model Tania Strecker, socialites Tara Palmer-Tomkinson and Madeline Farley and footballer Frank Leboeuf and wife Beatrice.

ES Magazine, *Evening Standard*

ELEGY

The rest of the Chelsea team assembled for the funeral of their colleague and to mark the beginning of his *Big Sleep*. It was a wake as much for Peter as for themselves, for their dreams, for the best years of their lives They all looked dour, smart, straight-backed and almost stoical in their outwardly calm demeanour in the face of this terrible event. How could a day that started with a defeat by Crystal Palace and an evening that started with the straightening of a tie end in this manner? Like survivors of some moon launch that had ended in tragedy, the Chelsea boys were together again. A real family, sometimes proud and sometimes embarrassed by each other, but always supportive with their armour-plated humour.

They assembled in the little pub across the road. No one felt like pinting it. Too tired to speak, they gazed through the windows at the first signs of spring, a troubled distillation of buried yellows and greens. For the first time some of the team began to realise they no longer had a grip on their lives. The barmaid studied the once-famous faces. Peter Osgood was like John Travolta, beefy, slightly faded, waiting for the *Pulp Fiction* that never happened. It was Osgood who broke the Kleenex-drenching ice, asking for a half of lager and raising it for a toast to their former colleague.

EULOGY

Chelsea Football Club. People of a certain age have such strong feelings for the Houseman-era team. What is it that keeps fans loyal from Houseman's début in 1963 to the twenty-first century? They associated the ups and downs of the club with those of their own lives over 30 years. Brian Clough, possibly the greatest manager of all time, a man whom players would kill to work with, spoke from his retirement of the socio-economic state of modern football. 'TV is a killer, it has taken away the working man's pinnacle of the week, a Saturday or a midweek match. Now he just sits in his armchair watching TV matches with hundreds of seats vacant in the stadiums.'

Chelsea are just a brand name now. Many fans who would once have stood in the Shed now do nothing more strenuous than sitting around drinking Bud and watching Sky Sports.

It was a lovely Sunday afternoon in late February 2001 and I went to my local to watch on Sky Chelsea crash out of the Cup 3–1 to Arsenal. It had been a bad-tempered match and in the end Chelsea were well beaten (seven days later Manchester United slaughtered Arsenal 6–1 to emphasise the yawning gap between the two teams still further).

It reminded me of a premier game when Chelsea had led Arsenal 2–0 with only a few minutes remaining, but were sunk by a Kanu hat-trick, the last breathtaking goal bearing the signature of Osgood. A team of 11 internationals, three World Cup winners and an average age nearer 30 than 20 should have been more than capable of protecting a lead, but we're talking Chelsea here. They are never going to win the league, no matter who they buy, and now they lost the Cup. As I left the pub the jukebox started playing. A man's voice sang that he was stuck in a moment and he could not got out of it. Chelsea Football Club, stuck in the same moment for 46 years . . .

A crisp packet blew down the gutter. On it was a badly drawn cartoon of Michael Owen, the latest wonder-kid of English football, looking like Nik Kershaw circa 1984. Already there were vague rumblings of the discontent with

Vialli's successor Ranieri. The chances of Chelsea winning the Premier League that year looked unlikely. Like film negatives dissolving on a hot coal, another Chelsea season was over.

Same old Chelsea, wasted opportunities in which personal neuroses have prevailed over remarkable talents. Even their most ardent fans were perplexed. I was quiet as I waited for the bus to take me home. The mist started to close in, just like at Turf Moor a lifetime earlier. A young man in a yellow shirt with blue cuffs picked up a loose ball in midfield and started to run towards the Burnley penalty box . . .

A survey of a typical family of Chelsea fans in 1999 indicated that they had spent £3,077 so far that season on supporting the club. This sum was divided up as follows:

Tickets: £1,686, including two season tickets at £595 each, one junior season ticket at £210, two club memberships at £28 each, away tickets totalling £230.

Travel: £545 including £150 to Skonto Riga and £120 to Berlin, each time using air miles, plus rail trips to Bradford, Leicester, Wimbledon, Watford and Middlesbrough.

Food and drink: £540 including meals out abroad.

Programmes: £35.

Merchandise: £271.91, including home shirts £42,99, two champions league polo shirts at £24.99 each, one striped leisure shirt at £26.99, one rugby-style shirt at £29.99, one Ben Sherman–Chelsea men's shirt £24.99, one sweatshirt £26.99, plus one V-necked T-shirt at £24.99 and a Desailly hooded sweatshirt at £44.99.

Chapter Fifteen: Tango and Cash

TANGO AND CASH: THE RAY WILKINS STORY

Carter: 'Football?'

Regan : 'Yeah, you know football. Little round thing, people kick it.
It's all the rage.'

The Sweeney, *Euston Films, 1975*

Of the second generation of Chelsea players Ray Wilkins was always one of my special favourites. A midfield passer of the Hudson type, he gave a dimension that the modern Chelsea lack. Perhaps Frank Lampard, he of the Calvin Klein poster-boy looks, will supply it. Of all the huge names that I worked with, he had the most successful career, one that was also without a major injury. You look at Ray now and he looks increasingly like Frasier's younger brother Niles Crane. Almost as well dressed. When he played for me he was right up there with Starsky and Hutch as a teen dream.

Like Osgood and Hudson, the class of '76 spent time in the pubs on the sunny side of the Kings Road. I recall once the *Express* phoned my office wanting to do a photo special on him and the other resident matinee idol and heart-throb in the club, Garry Stanley. I liked Garry a lot, he was ambitious and proud as a panther, though injuries stopped him being overwhelmingly huge. The *Express* called it 'Stanley and Butch' and for the piece they had that red-and-white Mustang and a couple of sexy models. There was no sign of Antonio Fargas, alias 'Huggy Bear'.

Wilkins was more canny than most. This moth did not choose to live inside the flame. His looks were always presented as a form of weirdness. He knew he could never rely on looks alone. Hair loss is harsh on pretty boys. Wilkins was too short to be an action hero, but he was one of the cleverest midfield players ever to grace Stamford Bridge.

He was part of a footballing dynasty – his father George had played for Brentford. But his older brother Graham was, in the words of Ann Robinson, often the weakest link. The Shed gave him a hard time and he endured prolonged spells of public humiliation. It is true that he was guilty of some terrible howlers. I remember him being given a police escort from the ground after his errors had cost us a fifth-round replay Cup-tie against Orient (why was it always Orient?). His other brother Steven was also on the books around the time that Butch made his big breakthrough from wannabe to starring in the first team. It was the only time that Chelsea ever had three brothers as professionals at the same time. Steven, two years younger than Ray, was another midfield prospect and the talk was that he was the most talented of the brood. With dark, smouldering eyes and cheekbones you could cut cheese on, he was set for stardom. Sadly he never made the first team, as weight problems and a tendency to lose concentration for periods in a match curtailed a promising career. Almost like the brothers Hudson, Ray went on to become a legend whilst his brothers drifted out of the game.

Only lack of pace stopped Ray from being the complete midfield player of the late '70s and '80s. Wilkins had an overwhelming sense of presence and was both a maker and taker of goals. Today they would give you all that terminology about playing in the 'hole', whatever that is. Wilkins, like Hudson before him, was an inside-forward. For the benefit of younger readers, the role required him to provide chances and appear regularly on the score sheet. Around the time Wilkins (R) made his début, coaches like Don Revie were devising systems and methods of play that were to seriously interfere with the initiative of the truly gifted and few were more gifted than Wilkins.

He won 84 senior caps between 1976 and 1987. He was a remarkably consistent player. In 1975–76 and 1976–77 he made maximum appearances for us. Considering how young he was it was amazing. Venables achieved it in 1962 but Hudson never did it.

I recall his début as sub in a Friday night match against Norwich. His full début was against Spurs at White Hart Lane, the vital match where Harris shot the winner and kept Chelsea up that season.

Al Pacino says he owes the 'method school' of acting to his guru Lee Strasberg, and in the same way Wilkins owed Venables and Hudson for being his role models. Butch was like a sponge, soaking up everything he could about the game. He was always driven by a fierce ambition. Unlike Hudson, he enjoyed his success and sustained his working relationships.

The person he owed most to in the early days was McCreadie. Eddie had a Svengali-type relationship with the youngster. After the departure of Sexton, Ron Stuart had stepped into the breach but he could not stop Chelsea from sliding down. The legs had fallen off the pantomime horse in blue and white. Eddie approached me towards the end of season 1974–75 and asked me if he could be manager. With three matches left I decided to give him the job. McCreadie was transformed almost overnight; his hair was beautifully groomed and he wore a finely waisted grey flannel suit together with tinted aviator glasses like Elvis Presley wore on stage at the International Hotel, Las Vegas.

Not many people knew that Eddie started his working life in his native Glasgow as a window dresser. There were no frills or fudging PR speak about him. He was a product of the renegade Docherty school of management (Docherty had brought him to the Bridge), placing great emphasis on fitness and running power. A great disciple of attacking football, he ensured that Chelsea never went looking for a draw. Eddie made Butch, at 18, captain as he gambled everything on the gilded youth in those last few games. Despite his rare maturity I think Butch was the youngest skipper in league history. It wasn't enough to avoid the drop, though.

Wilkins took the captaincy from John Hollins. Like Kirk in *Star Trek* there was only ever one captain at the Bridge, one of my little rules. It was the death knell of Hollins' playing career at Chelsea at the time. He later rejoined the club after more glory at Arsenal. At that time John had been with us, literally man and boy, for 13 years and nearly 450 games. Consider yourself part of the furniture. John ended up going to QPR. That's the funny thing about football, you never know how it's going to pan out or where you are going to end up.

It was hard for Eddie to axe players who had been friends and team-mates. He told me once, 'I am not afraid of making decisions. I have always been a positive person. But I am not impulsive. I do not act till I have done my homework. It was not easy telling old friends they were on their way. But it had to be done.'

The game that sent us down was a 2–0 defeat at Tottenham, who were in a terrible position themselves. Teddy Maybank, another highly rated teenage striker, made his début that day. With the game locked at 0–0 Butch had a great chance to put us in front but fluffed an open goal. Spurs' in-house maverick, Alfie Conn, a throwback to the Gallacher era, put Spurs ahead soon afterwards and that, as they say, was just about that.

The last game that season was a 1–1 draw against Everton. A win would have kept us up. In the great maelstrom of Chelsea's history, that was a weird day. The astonishing scenes in the office afterwards stick in my memory. Champagne flowed, celebs abounded and there were flowers and tears, but despite the inevitable development of hubris the mood was very up. The king was dead, long live the king. Amongst the high level of corporate responsibility and anxiety McCreadie had stimulated interest. There was now a 'do or die' attitude that I sense is missing at the club now. The circumstances were different. Chelsea had this terrible financial problem. The new stand dominated everything; it was the original money pit, it would eat away at a cash mountain. The team was a mess of inadequacies, despite the huge potential of the youngsters. Our financial prospects were slim and it preoccupied me .

Butch was enjoying success though, leading the England youth team to victory in the Little World Cup in Switzerland. I recall the side was packed with famous names including Glenn Hoddle, Peter Barnes and Alan Curbishley. Chelsea were also well represented with Steve Wicks, Tommy Langley and John Sparrow. The confused rainbow of adolescence.

In season 1975–76 Eddie McCreadie used the time to develop his protégés. Chelsea finished an unremarkable eleventh as he carried out major surgery. They were the bookies' favourites to bounce straight back just as the ebullient Docherty's side had done in the '60s. Very few clubs managed to retrieve their status first time round though. Life was tough, especially away from home, where we were the team everyone wanted to beat – nothing changes. Marcel Desailly said on the eve of the 2001–02 season Chelsea had to be stronger anyway. Soon McCreadie built up a tremendous relationship with the fans. In my time he was certainly the most popular of all the managers I worked with. Eddie always acknowledged that the club had a cosmopolitan crowd but insisted that the 5,000–6,000 fans in the Shed were as partisan as anyone. Chelsea fans of that generation, 'My Generation' as The Who used to snarl, understand this. We are the last remaining compatriots of a long-vanished kingdom who have not entirely renounced the old ways.

They were in his view the heart of the club and vital in his plans to reshape a new, virile Chelsea and provide a team to match the grandeur of Europe's finest stand.

The match I recall most of all that season was a 3–2 home Cup defeat to Crystal Palace. For the first time in a long while the Bridge was packed for the clash. Malcolm Allison, the Palace manager baited the Shed before the game, but it was Peter Taylor who destroyed our dreams with his lethal left foot. Our defence looked about as secure as a dive-bomber.

Wilkins was learning all the time, McCreadie taught him to tuck in tight the moment the ball was lost and tie up the spaces attackers exploited. His short passes could pierce even the most metallic of defences. Modern midfield players are probably even fitter and about equal in class, but they seem to lack emphasis and clarity. Under McCreadie Chelsea would try and suck opponents into an attack. Wilkins' ability to win the ball and initiate quick-fire breaks would be the key to put the strike force of Steve Finnieston and Kenny Swain through on goal. Finnieston was seen as the new 'white hope' having scored over 150 goals in four seasons of youth and reserve football. He peaked ridiculously early, and for a brief while in the McCreadie side he could not put a foot wrong. Unfortunately, he was playing in the wrong decade to be as big a name as he should have been. Chelsea were always so stretched that the front runners could never play good football. Tactics were changing rapidly, the typical spearhead centre-forward was becoming more tightly marked and the quick breaks gave more scope for perceptive midfielders to get forward. Wilkins' penchant for getting beyond the main strikers to find the net was soon rewarded.

Butch won the first of his England caps in New York against a powerful Italian side, 2–0 down at the break they rallied to win 3–2.

The following season Butch stormed the battlements. The teenager led Chelsea to promotion, sandwiched between champions Wolves and third-placed Forest. It was a hard season on and off the field.

MONEY MONEY MONEY

Before that came about I had to save the club from extinction. Having missed out on promotion first time around the wolves were at the door, and they were not the ones who played in gold and black. The pressure exerted from the creditors was as severe as that of Leeds on our defence at Wembley in 1970. The massive borrowings at crippling rates of interest and the low Second Division gates had put us in a position of financial meltdown. In 1972 our total home attendance was 815,000. Four years later it was 399,000, down by 50 per cent. We were £3.4 million in debt and burning up money. Our position was so bad that I thought that we were contravening the Companies Act by trading insolvent. If they played hold music on the Stamford Bridge switchboard it would have been Dire Straits.

One morning the VAT man had come with a court order and a demand for nearly £20k. I had till 5 p.m. to come up with it or the club was out of business. I knew I could not argue. I was in a real spin. We were down, but before they started the count I recalled a long outstanding debt to Chelsea by a London club on a transfer and I called that in. With some other bits and pieces and money I hustled from friends and contacts I just scraped up the funds in time. They were really mad frantic deal-making days. The pop group KLF's scam of burning a million pounds always interested me, I could relate to it somehow. For weeks I had played telephone cat and mouse. I knew that we could not go on like this moneyed up, almost bottomed out. I was nearly burnt out, the financial juggling had exhausted me. The art of football never translates well into commerce. Read the headlines most mornings if you don't believe me.

We had a crisis meeting in the City with Barclays Bank, our biggest creditor. It was May '76 but I can recall Chelsea's finances being raked over the hot coals vividly. This crisis occurred ten years before the 1986 Insolvency Act and the opportunities for rescuing dangerously insolvent companies were somewhat limited. Nobody had invented Corporate Voluntary Arrangements and admin. orders. I thought that we were about to be thrown to the lions.

Barclays were brilliant; I expected them to be like Prussian generals but I was so wrong. A man called Colin Toole gave me expert advice and made some calls. He was a tremendous help. One of Barclays' calls was to the Bank of England informing them of our plight. The Old Lady of Threadneedle Street got the tip that a major company with a household name was likely to hit the wall. Somebody picked up the red phone and was on to Downing Street and Prime Minister Harold Wilson. I only found this out years later. If I had known then what I know now it would have saved me some sleepless nights. Wilson, as intimated before, was a great football fan and a friend of Chelsea Football Club. I recall he had disported himself on the balcony of the Royal Garden Hotel with Sir Alf and the boys the night that they were waving about that object Pickles the dog had found.

Those little chats we had after the matches when Huddersfield were at the Bridge about the merits of Frank Worthington and Osgood must have stuck in his mind. Harold asked to be personally informed of all developments. The word was out in the City and nobody was going to be the first to pull the trigger and alienate the PM. Real power is not having to demonstrate its possession. Wilson was a man of the people, and one of the first to recognise that football symbolises local grassroot tradition. I recall when the pipe-smoking PM met the Beatles at the Variety Club luncheon at the Savoy. This was when the mop-tops were just peaking and their reflected glory was valuable. England's World Cup win coincided with Harold's rise to power. He was a brilliant politician. He knew his voters, what they wanted, what they liked. And what in their eyes was fair and square. Bankrupting world-famous football clubs was not acceptable behaviour. Even if you hated a poncy team like Chelsea, your club could be next, then your firm . . .

A man called Martin Spencer was brought in from Stoy Hayward, the red-hot insolvency practitioners. Spencer had been involved in sorting out the tangled web of the group Pink Floyd's finances. I must admit that Spencer and I never quite saw eye to eye. A meeting was set up to arrange a moratorium – a freezing of debts. We were on shaky ground (and I am not talking about the West Stand either).There was no way of binding the dissenting creditors and there was no protection for our assets from them.

I gambled on bringing down Butch Wilkins, Ron Harris, David Hay and Garry Stanley to meet the creditors. The Chelsea captain with his pop star looks and Hugh Grant charm made a great success of the meeting. He was always exceedingly polite and had picked up that American way of learning your name and then dropping it into his chat as if to indicate that it was deeply significant. It was the Stamford Bridge Road Show, next stop Carey Street and the ghost of Hughie Gallagher. Butch was in top form, wearing a superlative navy suit with pointy lapels. The only person that could work a room better than him was the master Venables. His voice was very distinctive and years later he landed a series of adverts promoting the orange-flavoured soft drink Tango. They were brilliant and were aped on the terraces by fans who appeared in the middle of winter, stripped to the waist and painted orange.

With the tension at breaking point I self-consciously stepped up to give the speech that Chelsea's destiny literally depended on. It was the hardest thing I ever did. The point I tried to put across was that if anybody actually bankrupted Chelsea the repercussions would be tremendous. I was not a financial conniver but I had to save the club. The public would have hated to see us fold and the fall-out for the banks and government would be incalculable. The pound was falling and if Chelsea fell . . . Though I am sure that in certain parts of London (the East End for example) there would have been street parties and jellied-eel jollity. Only the motivation of wanting to beat all the people that wanted to do Chelsea down made me carry on. And still does.

I stood up and looked for the heart of the audience. Sometimes I noticed that at the start of a game Osgood would gaze across at the terraces as if searching for a certain face, something intangible. I made eye contact with some stern-faced individuals in the front row. We had no formal presentation as such, today it would be all overhead slides and flip charts. I began by saying we were an industry, we were something people cared about. Dreams, hopes, memories, a legacy were linked to it. (Matthew Harding never put it more eloquently than when he once spoke to me of the 'emotional investment' of the fans.) Now I was asking for six months' grace, during which time an investigation would be undertaken to analyse the causes of Chelsea's difficulties and attempts made to address them. People like a story. I gave them one. I talked of being bedevilled by the building problems. Of greed, jealousy and my overwhelming desire for Chelsea to survive. I concluded by reminding them of the need to avoid the final all-consuming stage of delusion and hysteria.

I sat down, judging the noise level (it was silent). All eyes were on me. Now I was waiting for the vote, waiting for the hammer to fall as Freddie once sang. I could not predict the firepower of the creditors' response though. It went better than I thought, the audience were sympathetic, they held their fire. I looked a little pensive. Butch leant his head on his hands. A moratorium was granted, not just for six months but for a year. We left to a ripple of applause.

Harris had sat silently at the table throughout the gathering, noting the details of the dissenters.

(Mick Greenaway was in constant contact with me with offers of cash collections and messages of support. He also offered his services as a counsellor to discuss our repayment proposals to any particularly zealous creditor. Yeah, right. I could not see it then but he was a Don. The Shed boys would have collected pictures of him on bubblegum cards if they had made them.)

The scheme worked. The breathing space created by the moratorium enabled us to regroup. After a year 20p to the pound was paid to the creditors in the form of a dividend. The moratorium was extended by a further 12 months and at the end of that a further 20p was paid in full and final settlement of the debt.

We won the first game of the season away to Orient. It was not a cup match so I knew we had a chance. It was a poor display on a hot afternoon but near the end, Steve Finneston popped up to shoot the only goal in front of 11,456 people. Despite our penury I thought McCreadie might just drag us up by our bootlaces. We started well, apart from an early setback against Millwall who hammered us 3–0. It was the first time we had played at the Old Den and I found the whole experience intimidating to say the least. Even the army of Chelsea fans who travelled everywhere with us (and literally terrorised the Second Division) seemed subdued. Every gangster, hardboy, ageing tough guy, bootboy and troubleman in South London came down the Old Kent Road for that one. It was colliding cultures.

On New Year's Day 1977 we were well on course for promotion and celebrated with a 5–1 thrashing of Hereford. Wilkins was outstanding and looked every inch an England player. Early in the match he pounced to score with a delightful finish. After that the result was in the bag. In the Cup we drew the holders, Southampton, away and a fine solo goal from Gary Locke almost gained us a shock victory. Near the end, though, Mick Channon, at the peak of his career, equalised with a brilliant shot. He had the sweetest first touch and I recall his famous windmill arm swing as he celebrated in his trademark manner. (I think he copied that arm thing from Pete Townshend of The Who.)

The Bridge was packed for the replay on a freezing January night. It was like old times. Channon turned on the magic again, every bit as good as he had been at the Dell. We took the Saints to extra time but in the last half-hour we cracked disturbingly and were routed 3–0. Eddie said it was because we had no lateral movement. It was men against boys – we were so young and totally inexperienced. I had a brief flash of the future.

When we arrived back in the big time we needed to beef up and strengthen in several positions. It was chaotic but we stumbled to promotion despite a dreadful Easter. On Good Friday Fulham beat us 3–1 at Craven Cottage. Guess who was playing in the cocaine white of Fulham? Our old pal George Best, scoring with a great strike and generally running the show. Best had a brief Indian summer at Fulham, where Rodney Marsh partnered him for a while. They played some vintage football together before it all fell apart again. Sweet dreams are made of this.

We scrambled a win over Luton the next day but on Easter Monday we travelled to Charlton and were butchered 4–0. We were, as Mick Channon would say, not at the races that night. It could have been really demeaning as Charlton should have had ten. Butch could only make a microscopic contribution to proceedings. The Chelsea fans who went to the Valley for the match took it very badly as it looked like we might blow our promotion chances. So much was at stake, we just could not afford not to go up. I remember the Shed boys built a huge bonfire on the terraces and later kicked the crumbling gates down at the south end of the ground. There were more smashed seats in the Main Stand than when the Stranglers had played at the Rainbow the same year. Outside they rioted, cars were overturned and windows smashed. The same thing had happened a few days after Christmas when Chelsea had lost by the same score at Luton. When Chelsea lost to a side considered by the fans to be their social inferior it fuelled a revolution. They always seemed to overreact. The worst incidents in my experience always happened at places like Watford and Luton.

That reminds me of the time I was summoned to Number 10 by the original Lady in Blue, Margaret Thatcher. It was in the '80s and hooliganism was the buzzword. 'Should I know you?' she barked at me when I arrived.

I shrugged. 'Brian Mears, chairman of Chelsea.'

'Chelsea?'

It must have registered with her – she used to live in Flood Street, around the corner from the Bird's Nest, Osgood's local.

'Can I have a word?' She beckoned me into the cabinet office and shut the door. 'Let's get away from those old duffers,' she said, referring to my colleagues in the working party on hooliganism. 'We have heard what the FA have to say on the subject. What do you think?'

'It's a big subject.'

'Do your best,' she said, leaning forward.

I was ready to say all these clever things about 'the enemy within' etc when she said, 'It's terribly hot in here.'

The next thing I knew she was standing on a chair, wrestling with the window catch. So there I was, alone in the cabinet office with the 'Iron Lady', talking about the Chelsea Headhunters. As you do.

Our next match on the second Saturday of April was at home to Notts Forest, managed by one Brian Clough and assisted by Peter Taylor (not the Palace one), perhaps the greatest managerial combination of all time. Forest were neck and neck with us and nobody could afford to lose with Wolves looking favourites.

NUMBER NINE DREAM

Chelsea won 2–1. Steve Finniston shot the winner near the end. Forest claimed he was offside, but it was pretty close either way. Clough rocked the casbah by attacking the facilities at the Bridge, saying that the conditions in the dressing-room were poor. When asked to comment about the winning goal he said that the dugout was the worst in the division. A few days later I received a letter from him in which he apologised for the remarks. He pointed out that his chairman also wanted to disassociate himself from any criticism of Stamford Bridge. At the foot of the letter he scrawled 'I still think they are a pighole', referring to the dressing-room. Typical Brian, endlessly inventive and unrepentantly scathing.

His outburst worked a treat. I replied stating that I thought he was being ironic. The fact that Forest had lost to Chelsea and all but blown their promotion chances was neatly deflected. The pressure was lifted from his side. He snowed me, but then he snowed everybody that he came in contact with.

A chunk of football history could have easily been rewritten that season but it will forever remain one of those 'what ifs'. Forest did sneak up in third place behind us. Bolton (always the fall guys) had been in the top three from the start of the season but on the last day Forest won 1–0 on their ground and edged them out. The next season they won the First Division title. (Such a thing would seem impossible today. The only other team to do so was Ipswich in 1961–62 managed by Sir Alf, the same season that Greaves joined runners up Spurs from Chelsea–Milan.)

Clough stunned the football world by going on to lift the European Cup for two successive seasons. Clough was a supreme triumph of ability over ego, whereas people like Keegan are the reverse, a triumph of ego over ability. Forest were a Banana Republic under Clough. Chelsea are forever on the cusp of the big time but Clough took them there. Two European Cups, think about it.

In the penultimate match of the season we went up to Wolves, needing a win to take the championship. Tommy Langley struck an early goal for us in a game that was played out in pouring rain. A second-half equaliser from Wolves gave them the title, but the great thing was we were up. I liked Tommy, he had scored his first senior goal for Chelsea on his seventeenth birthday coming on as sub for Gary Locke against Birmingham. It was also notable for being the game in which Butch Wilkins scored his first goal for Chelsea, the season we went down.

The last game of the season was at home to Hull. We coasted to a 4–0 win as we roared back to the big time. Over 40,000 fans packed the crumbling Bridge. It was a big day for me and Eddie. He imparted some of the swagger of his team by draping his shoulders with his Burberry raincoat. It crossed my mind that now was the time to bow out at Stamford Bridge, while we were still ahead of the game. We were back where we belonged, in the big time with an exciting young team and an exciting young manager. I had saved us from financial extinction and bought us time to regenerate income. If I had left then history would have been a lot kinder to me.

I should have listened to that little voice that told me to do so. It would have saved me a lot of trouble.

SHOULD I STAY OR SHOULD I GO?

I stuck around for the same reasons that I wanted to quit. Chelsea had a potential top-six team and I had great faith in McCreadie. We were very close, much closer than Sexton who was awesomely self-contained. Eddie and I had been through so much together. It was like the war, Pearl Harbor whatever, ships being sunk all around us. I wanted to see how it worked out, I was delighted to be sailing with him.

We went on tour to America. It was a great time. Chelsea found the way to San Jose, visited *Frasier*'s spiritual home of Seattle and ended up in Los Angeles. It was in the City of Angels that it all started to go wrong, horribly wrong. Eddie approached me in the foyer of our hotel and asked if he could see me. I knew by the look on his face that it was not going to be good news. We found a cool corner and I listened. I could scarcely believe what he told me. As unconventional in business as he was in football, he proceeded to make many demands that the club could not afford. They included a new contract and an expensive car. The car was the most contentious issue.

BABY YOU CAN DRIVE MY CAR

That car was always cited as being the main reason why Chelsea and Eddie got a divorce. I blame Bobby Campbell for winding Eddie up about the new motor. Campbell's spell in charge at Chelsea, some time after my departure, can hardly be described as a golden period. Bobby was in charge when Chelsea were relegated in the season John Hollins left, at the time Eddie left he was in charge at Fulham. He was always popping into the Bridge and one morning he came over to see Eddie, parking up near his office in a gleaming new piece of steel. At the end of the meeting Eddie happened to look out of the window of his office and spied the car. He asked Campbell to whom it belonged. 'We all get one at Fulham,' Bobby replied. Eddie could hardly believe it. Things were never really the same for him at the club after that revelation. In my opinion Campbell contributed to the departure of potentially one of its greatest managers.

After hours of haggling it became obvious to me that Eddie was not going to change his stance and Chelsea could simply not afford to accede to his demands. He then used the emotional blackmail of saying that he would quit if he did not get his own way. He hinted at all sorts of dire consequences: the star players would refuse to play for Chelsea (where had I heard that one before?) and the fans would kick up such a fuss that I would be ousted. Well, he was right about that, but it was still some time away and the road had a few more bends and twists in it. I made one last appeal to him. I told him to wait another year. He had done the hard bit getting us back to the big league. If further progress was made, the world, as it said on the side of the airship in *Scarface* (the Pacino version), was his. Eddie would not reason. He didn't hear me, he was too busy listening to something inside his own head. For a while I thought he had lost the plot. I had never seen him like that before, he seemed to have contempt for orthodox financial behaviour. The meeting broke up and there was nothing more to say. Just like I had rebuffed his former team-mates Hudson and Osgood years before, I had to make a stand for Chelsea's sake. At least that is how I saw it. To this day no individual has ever been bigger than the club in my view, from Gallacher to Wise, Docherty to Vialli, Mears to Harding.

The board convened an emergency meeting back home and Eddie's resignation was reluctantly accepted. That night I wrote him a sad little letter informing him of our decision and thanking him for all he had done for the club as a player and manager. I think he thought that the club would back down, but how could we? Had we learned nothing from the Osgood–Hudson–Sexton affair? We were still walking through a financial minefield. One wrong move and the whole thing would go up in smoke.

Three days later I was at home listening to a record I had brought home from the American trip, *The Pretender* by Jackson Browne. He was singing about being caught between the longing for love and the fight for legal tender. Eddie was on my mind. The phone rang and it was no surprise to me when I heard his voice. He wanted his old job back, he apologised. But it was too late. We had already offered the job to Shellito. By some strange twist of fate, Ken was a great friend and his full-back partner in the best club pairing of full-backs football ever saw.

'I am so sorry Eddie,' I said. We never spoke again for many years. Later I met up with him again in the USA and we made up.

THE PRETENDER

To this day I can never figure out what drove him to take that extraordinary course of action. I try and think about it sometimes but it is too deep and I only become more confused. Eddie was a very emotional person. Houseman's death around that time hit him hard. They were closer than people thought. Houseman even ended up wearing his beloved number three shirt when Eddie's injuries finally wore him down. One night, shortly after the funeral, some fans approached him in the bar at one of the social nights. They were old-time Chelsea boys and wanted to talk about the glory days. Houseman's name came up in conversation. Eddie became very upset and refused to talk about his old friend. I saw tears welling up behind the Elvis shades. Soon Elvis was to leave the building for good.

Eddie was worried about the financial constraints put upon him by our economic plight. Shortly before his departure we had analysed Spencer's cost-cutting White Paper together. He fought tooth and nail to overrule the decision to scrap the reserve side, he knew that the only chance Chelsea had was to keep the production line of young talent rolling. Every season he needed a Wilkins to break through. We could not compete in the transfer market anymore.

It was a combination of these things and something far deeper that prompted his departure. Like Hudson, he had been to the bottom of the ocean but getting back up to the surface. Osgood told me stories of Eddie's dark moods, of how his first wife would call the Wizard around to sit with him throughout the night when he had a fit of despair. The Chelsea supremo would sip brandy and milk and shake his head a lot.

Perhaps he just decided it was time to back out of the limelight. People still ask me what was the true story behind his departure, but the answer is there wasn't one. Conspiracy theories abounded about the anti-authoritarian punching out of a director after he dared to criticise Wilkins.

Our renaissance period was shortlived. Shellito was appointed manager. He lasted a little over a season. Shellito was the finest back that ever played for Chelsea, still is. He was also Jimmy Greaves' best pal at Chelsea. Imagine a defender with the pace of Le Saux at his peak, the polish of Le Boeuf and the toughness of Harris. His career was destroyed after a terrible knee injury.

If Shellito had not sustained that injury you would never have heard of

George Cohen, for Shellito would have partnered Ray Wilson in the World Cup final, he was that good. Let me add that Cohen was a distinguished player. The trouble was Ken was too nice a chap for the cut-throat world of big-time soccer. Unlike McCreadie, who perhaps took it too seriously, Shellito handled his appointment as if it were a rather embarrassing charade.

Ken Shellito was born in East Ham, the same part of London that was the birthplace of Venables and Greaves, in April 1940. He played for London and Essex Schoolboys and joined Chelsea in 1955. (We all know what happened then.) Two years later he signed professional and made his début in the first team in 1959. He grabbed a regular first-team spot in the 1961–62 season and within a year had burst onto the England scene. He first won an Under-23 cap to showcase his talent against what was then called Yugoslavia.

Ken won a full cap against the Czechs on the 1962 summer tour. A glittering future looked assured. Sir Alf had seen the future and modernist players like Ken were (to borrow from his description of Martin Peters) 'ten years ahead of his time'. Ramsey was already planning his assault for the 1966 competition. It was his dream of winning the trophy, named after the FIFA president at the time it was conceived, that drove him relentlessly.

Ken was best foraging for possession further down the pitch, operating as a staging post for the start of an attack by supplying both Venables and Bridges. He was able to do this without detriment to his own extensive playing range. Shellito's movement was superb. Docherty encouraged him to go one against one against players. Tommy reasoned that an additional attacking back would bring more defenders into the play and clutter the playing area. That is when mistakes were made. Shellito was a more thoughtful player than the reckless braveheart, McCreadie. Like Greaves he had ice water in his veins. When faced with a high-octane winger or a thuggish defender he always used his high-quality technical skill.

With McCreadie alongside him Docherty had the greatest pair of club backs ever. The only modern comparison could be with Lee Dixon and Winterburn at Arsenal and they had Tony Adams operating between them. The Chelsea duo's overlapping and marauding in the opponents' penalty box was seen by many as an replacement for the conventional winger but Docherty used it as an additional attacking ploy. His plan was to keep the field as small as possible – on a huge pitch like Stamford Bridge a great deal of running and covering back for Ken and Eddie was required.

Ken was good enough to play and flourish at World Cup level but he was fated not to reach it. A tragic, chronic knee injury suffered at home against Sheffield Wednesday led to the first of four operations. The injury was sustained in October 1963. A few weeks before Peter Houseman made his Chelsea début against the other team from Sheffield, Jackie Bouvier Kennedy's husband was killed in Dallas and the Beatles released their first album, *With the Beatles,* on the Parlophone label.

The injury was agonising; on a rainy autumn afternoon his studs stuck in the drenched turf, he spun away but the studs remained embedded in that famous, huge old pitch. There was always a sadness about Shellito, the sadness of a man who had greatness in him, but only attained it momentarily. The second operation was in November 1964, the third at Christmas 1965, each one was excruciating. There was no laser or keyhole surgery then. The last operation was in July 1966, Ken watched George Cohen collect a World Cup winners' medal on TV from a hospital bed. His mate Jimmy Greaves also watched from the sidelines. One can only wonder what was running through their minds.

By this time Shellito had no cartilage left in his knee. Among the after effects of such operations are the collection of injury fluid in the joint, and muscle-wastage above and below the joint due to disuse. Ken had these to a massive extent and it was necessary in the rehabilitation of a knee with these disabilities to remove the fluid and build up the muscles. The harrowing periods spent in hospital added up to only a fraction of the time occupied in rehabilitation. Only Ken's courage, determination and dedication kept him going through that time. I used to see him from out of my office window, running up and down the terraces hour after hour, his blond head dripping in sweat. In the end, though, the damage to his knee proved too severe and he was forced to quit. He played only 123 first-team games for Chelsea.

It could be said that most of the great Chelsea legends crashed and burnt. Most of their careers collapsed into poverty and destitution. They did it their own way, in their own time, each one fashioning the climax of their story with the degree of finesse accorded to their own special talent. Shellito's end was particularly bitter. Each generation seems to throw up its own heartbreaking injury story, Hutchinson's and Hay's were also in my time. Later the brilliant and underrated Paul Elliot had his career wrecked in an unpleasant incident. I thought he was a particular loss to Chelsea.

Shellito joined the backroom staff and was responsible for shaping the early career of Wilkins along with Stanley, Langley, Walker *et al.* It was a natural progression for him to take the step up. I wanted to emulate Liverpool in their halcyon days with the promotion from within – boot room policy.

Season 1977–78 was a schizoid one for Chelsea. It started badly with a 3–0 drubbing in the first match away to WBA. Welcome to the real world, Brian! Wilkins grew in stature with each game but I was very aware that we were far too brittle to survive for long in the big league. In our first Saturday home match Coventry came to the Bridge and roughed us up to win 2–1. We won at Old Trafford but took some bad beatings .

The best result of the season was an amazing 4–2 win over Liverpool in the third round of the FA Cup. Liverpool won the European Cup that season; Dalglish's chipped goal was enough to beat Bruges (remember them) at Wembley. That day, though, Chelsea overwhelmed the Reds. Walker had forced himself back in the team at Christmas and was not going to vacate his place. He beat Ray Clemence with 2 thunderball shots in the first 25 minutes to set the Bridge alight.The first was so savagely hit that Clemence never even moved. Walker had no respect for Liverpool, he just terrorised them. I suppose Clemence was not expecting anybody to shoot at him from such range. Chelsea never let Liverpool settle and quick second-half goals from Langley and Finniston put us an unbelievable 4–0 up. Dalglish and McDermott scored late consolations for Liverpool. They were so upset that a few days later they went out and bought Graham Souness from Middlesbrough, then managed by one John Neal.

To rub salt in the Reds' wounds and show that it was no fluke, we beat them again a few weeks later 3–1 in a league match. Finnieston had another fine game. That was typical of our season, we scored plenty of goals. At Birmingham 5–4, with Langley grabbing a hat-trick, 5–3 against Ipswich and then a 6–2 victory over Burnley in the next round of the Cup. We fancied a long Cup run but Orient put us out at the Bridge in a replay. We slumped badly at the end of the season and only just stayed up. The youngsters were showing signs of battle fatigue and it was obvious that the team needed strengthening. Ken had no money to spend though.

Season 1978–79 was a nightmare. Everton won 1–0 in the opening match at Stamford Bridge. It was a sweltering afternoon and an early lobbed goal from Andy King settled the match. We hardly created a chance and the manner in which we were beaten filled me with despair about the coming season.

Langley scored the only goal of the game up at Wolves and our next trip took us to White Hart Lane. We wore yellow with green trimmings, very much like Norwich. It was the home début of the Argentine pair Ardiles and Villa fresh from their World Cup triumph. They were greeted with a huge ticker-tape welcome and the blazing sunshine must have made them feel at home. For years foreigners had been excluded from the English game, but the small Argentinian opened the floodgates. Soon he became the greatest crowd-puller in the game. That was the season the influence of the foreign players was first noticeable. Ipswich had recruited the midfield duo of Muhren and Thijssen. I longed to bring players of their quality to Chelsea to help our youngsters. In an exciting derby Spurs led twice but Kenny Swain scored two quick equalisers. The midfield of Wilkins and Stanley were more than a match for the World Cup stars.

I felt briefly encouraged but as the autumn descended it was obvious that we were going straight back down. Leeds beat us 3–0 at the Bridge, then Man City came down and demolished us 4–1. I recall the previous season they had thrashed us 6–2 at Maine Road.

If I could not bring foreign players to the club then maybe I could bring in a top-flight continental coach to help Shellito. Now this was 20 years before it became vogue, 20 years before Gullit–Vialli–Ranieri, over 20 years before Sven. I approached Miljan Miljanic, then the top Yugoslavian coach, to work at Stamford Bridge. He had a huge reputation in world football with a great record. (Sounds familiar.) He seemed keen to work in London. I knew it was a long shot but something had to be done. I apprised Ken. 'I know goodbye when I hear it,' he said to me. Wilkins must have felt the same when he was on the coaching staff at Chelsea and then Ranieri and his entourage moved in.

I told Ken that I wanted Miljanic to work *with* him. We both flew out to Belgrade to fix up a deal, and he agreed to come to London and take a look around. I was sure that he would sign for Chelsea when he saw the vast potential there. He spent some time around the club assessing the situation. Miljanic was highly disappointed with our youth set-up. He warned that in a few years we would not be producing youngsters up to the standards of Wilkins. It was a chilling prophecy that was to come back to haunt me.

I pushed him for a start date, convinced that he was the man for the job, but Miljanic stalled. He claimed that he had a commitment to Yugoslavia and could not join till the end of the year. I was anxious to secure his signature immediately so that he could start moving us up the table. I became increasingly frustrated at the situation. I thought that maybe Miljanic did not intend to join us after all, and it felt as though he was playing us along.

Ken was becoming destabilised. Suddenly he changed his mind on the appointment of Miljanic. You must appreciate the enormous scepticism there was around at the time about appointing a foreign coach. Now we have a Swede in charge of England, but then there was a lot of resentment against Chelsea choosing the man from Yugoslavia. The magical mystery tour did not start just yet for Chelsea, there was a lot of peer pressure on Ken from other managers to stop the appointment. They were worried that it would usurp their position and start an influx of foreign talent that would dominate the game. They were not far wrong there.

Miljanic was my guest when Chelsea played host to Bolton in 1978, mid-October. Twenty minutes remained on the clock and we trailed 3–0. To say we had not had a kick would be pretty accurate. Shellito gambled and pulled Stanley off to a storm of booing. He had been our best player and was always a firm favourite with the crowd. The man replacing him was Walker, who by his high standards had a wretched season, troubled by injuries and an unfortunate court case that was to haunt his career. Sometimes, though, Clive looked the best player in the world. For 20 minutes that afternoon he was. He set goals up for Langley and Swain then plundered an equaliser with a truly magnificent goal. The crowd were hysterical. I thought back to the amazing comeback at Blackpool the season we won the Cup Winners' Cup.

In the dying seconds Walker hammered over a cross and Allardyce, now Bolton's manager, sliced in an own goal for the winner. It could only have happened at Chelsea. After the match, Miljanic told me that we did not need him because of the great spirit in the club. I would have liked to have agreed with him. I know goodbye when I hear it. A few weeks later Miljanic was appointed national coach of Yugoslavia. He had a successful spell there, taking them to the 1982 World Cup in Spain. I wonder how he would have worked out at Chelsea? A few weeks before Christmas Shellito resigned after a woeful home defeat by Villa.

Epilogue: London Fields

Where was I? At Stamford Bridge over 20 years ago, before I was so rudely interrupted. The clock on the wall says I have to wrap this up now.

Wilkins was sold to Manchester United. Danny Blanchflower was appointed as manager, legendary, venerable and entirely inappropriate. Chelsea went down in flames. Danny became a prisoner to Alzheimer's disease and died a virtual recluse. Geoff Hurst followed as Chelsea chief. In his autobiography he tells of how I interviewed him in a Chinese restaurant in Kew. I do not recall much about it, but I remember telling him I was looking for a manager of indefatigable style, audacity and flamboyance. If I gave him the job he could help me look . . .

Under Hurst Chelsea had the direst period (goalscoring-wise) in their history. Chelsea completed their last nine football league fixtures without scoring a goal. Incredible really, when you look at the endless reruns of Hurst's World Cup goals. I sacked him and appointed John Neal, who was later to take Chelsea back up with another fine young team. I wasn't around by then, though. That's another story. Maybe I can tell you it another day . . .